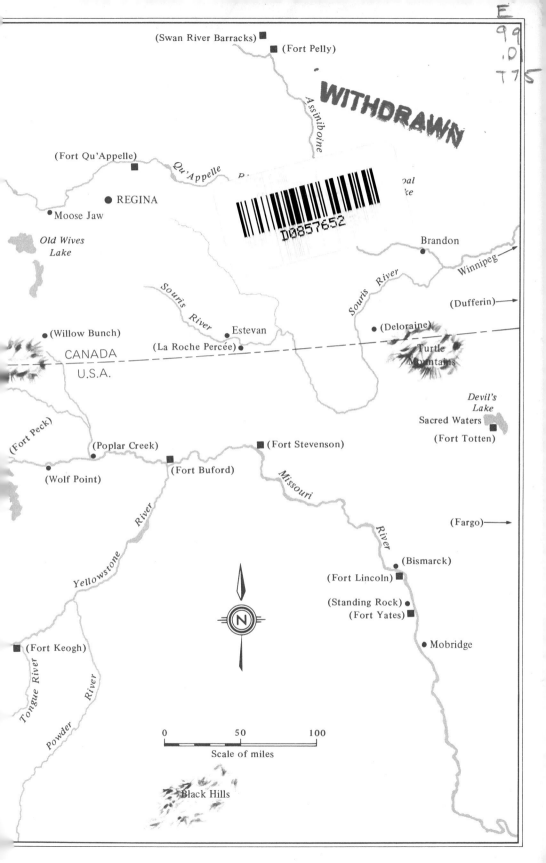

(Swan River Barracks) ■

■ (Fort Pelly)

*Assiniboine*

(Fort Qu'Appelle) ■

*Qu'Appelle R.*

● REGINA

● Moose Jaw

*Old Wives Lake*

D0857652

*oal ke*

● Brandon

*Winnipeg* →

*Souris River*

(Dufferin) →

● (Willow Bunch)

*Souris River*

● Estevan

(La Roche Percée) ●

● (Deloraine)

*Turtle Mountains*

CANADA

U.S.A.

*Devil's Lake*

Sacred Waters ▪

(Fort Totten)

(Fort Peck)

(Poplar Creek) ●

■ (Fort Stevenson)

*Missouri*

■ (Fort Buford)

● (Wolf Point)

*River*

*River*

*Yellowstone River*

*Missouri River*

(Fargo) →

● (Bismarck)

(Fort Lincoln) ■

(Standing Rock) ●

(Fort Yates) ■

● Mobridge

■ (Fort Keogh)

*Tongue River*

*Powder River*

N

0    50    100

Scale of miles

Black Hills

# Across the Medicine Line

## C. FRANK TURNER

McClelland and Stewart Limited

0-7710-8616-4

*The Canadian Publishers*
McClelland and Stewart Limited
25 Hollinger Road, Toronto

PRINTED AND BOUND IN CANADA

*To Doris and Susan*
*and to the family*
*wherever they might be.*

# ❖❖❖ Contents

# ❖❖❖ Foreword

❖❖❖ A century ago when the Indians were standing insecurely on the sacred hills of their ancestors, they were pleading with the Great Spirit to save their birthright – the land, the animals, and all the growing things.

The hills of southern Alberta and Saskatchewan, where the Mounted Police first confronted the holy men and the war chiefs, are a continent away from my old stamping grounds, and practically everything is different; the soil, the vegetation, the contours and the climate. There is, nonetheless, one clear affinity that affects me. It is the inner exultation for the spectacle of unspoiled nature, the abiding magnetism of country and sky. To stand in solitude at a pebbled high point along the Canadian border or on a fern-clad hill in mid-Wales is to grasp the truth of the world. In researching this book, following the paths and scanning the horizons of the Indians and the police, I have attempted to grasp their world.

There were other means for me to sample history: biographies, autobiographies, diaries and official reports. There were knowledgeable contemporaries and descendants of the principals. There were archives, museums and libraries, friends and advisers, also younger eyes to transcribe scrawls, academic brains to translate, and always a patient wife to sacrifice sea-air holidays for the dust of the trails.

I wish especially to thank Father G. Laviolette, OMI, of Winnipeg whose working life among the Indians has endowed him with a depth of perception that he so willingly applied to my working manuscript. S.W. Horrall, historian, Royal Canadian Mounted Police, assisted me several times with biographical information that enabled me to look beyond a name to discover a character.

Accuracy has been a prevailing objective in the writing. I mention firstly the excellent two volumes of J.P. Turner's *The North-West Mounted Police 1873-1893,* published in 1950 by the King's Printer. I am indebted to the legacy of Superintendent Edmund Dalrymple Clark of the NWMP who died while on duty at Fort Walsh in October of 1880. Clark, as adjutant of the force, was proficient at shorthand and recorded the dialogue at the crucial encounters between the Mounted Police and the American exiles headed by Chief Sitting Bull. His words are documented, officially, in 41 Victoria – Sessional Papers (No. 4) – A 1878.

Formal recognition would be incomplete without mentioning the scribbled reminiscences (mostly in letter form), memoranda and reports of James Morrow Walsh, who was the first Mounted Police officer to shake the hand of Sitting Bull.

In conclusion I wish to acknowledge the assistance I received from the following: the Toronto Public Libraries, the Metropolitan Library Board of Toronto, the National Historic Sites Service, the Alberta Government Travel Bureau, the Glenbow-Alberta Institute, the Office of the Chief of Military History United States Army, the Public Archives of Canada, the Public Archives of Manitoba, the Saskatchewan Archives Board, the Province of Saskatchewan Department of Natural Resources, Ontario Archives, the U.S. National Archives and Records Service, and the Smithsonian Institution National Anthropological Archives.

# ❖❖❖ The Sioux: An Explanation

❖❖❖ Sioux! The name conjures up images of hawk-nosed Mongolian-featured horsemen with tall, sinewy bodies and painted faces under flowing eagle-feathered war bonnets swarming shrilly into battle against the cavalry. This is the legendary portrayal, part fact and part fancy.

In their prime, Sioux warriors epitomized the white man's fear, his hatred, and his grudging respect of the Indians who attempted to block his path to a new destiny.

Two hundred years before the climactic Indian wars of the last century, the first white intruders, the French Canadians, were bumping into the Sioux west of the Mississippi. The coureurs des bois and the traders called this warlike people the *Nadowessioux* (derived from a contemptuous Ojibway epithet meaning snake-like) and in time the shorter word Sioux was commonly used in French and English.

There were several tribes and loose political and linguistic associations of Siouan stock, including Canadian Indians. The most prominent, the most powerful, were the Dakotas (the Allies) who were divided into three main groups:

–The Santees, who spoke the Dakota dialect. They lived mostly west of the Mississippi and closest to the Great Lakes.

–The Yanktons, who spoke the Nakota dialect. These people were west of the Santees, closer to the Missouri River.

–The Tetons, who spoke the Lakota dialect. They lived, fought and hunted west from the Missouri as far as the plains stretched to the mountains and north beyond the Medicine Line, the British border.

Some of the greatest names among the Teton Sioux, the hard and independent buffalo men who fought the whites to a standstill before being overwhelmed by technology and starvation, sought sanctuary in Canada in the late 1870's. The Tetons had their own tribal delineation, the sacred circle of seven council fires, the circle representing the Great Spirit in that like Him it was without beginning and without end. The seven tribes emerged into comparative recent history with a trilingual assortment of Indian, French and English titles as follows:

–Blackfoot (the people who walk the burnt prairie without moccasins. A different tribe to the Canadian Blackfoot).

–Brûlés (the Burnt-Thighs or Burnt-Backs).

–Hunkpapa (those who dwell at the entrance to a Teton camp).

–Minneconjou (the people who plant near the water).

–Oglalas (the dirt-throwers, those who express contempt).

–Sans-Arcs (the people who were once without bows, the No-Bows).

–Two-Kettles (the people who cook twice, people with plenty of food).

Of all the Dakota Sioux who turned to Canada in their plight, the Tetons caused the most profound anxiety. They tested the stamina of a new nation and a fledgling frontier security force.

# Across
## the
# Medicine
# Line

# ❖❖❖ How It All Began

❖❖❖ In the politically eruptive year of 1873, Canada was a nation of only six years, a British dominion embracing the Atlantic and the Pacific, an empty land that was culturally, spiritually and geographically insecure.

Confederation in 1867 had first joined together, in the east, Nova Scotia, New Brunswick, Quebec and Ontario. In 1870 the North-Western Territory was acquired along with Rupert's Land, which was surrendered by the Hudson's Bay Company. A portion was legislated as Manitoba, the first province of the west. This uneasy Canada was proclaimed a transcontinental union in 1871 by the addition of British Columbia.

The flanks of the boisterous nation were separated by close to a thousand miles of vulnerable, unprotected wilderness, all of it bordering on the United States. This in-between land was the core of Prime Minister Sir John A. Macdonald's big, wholesome Canadian future. Stretching westward from Lake Superior to the Rockies, the prairie seemed like an awesome, tempting infinity. Beyond the Red River settlements of Manitoba the unconquered emptiness rolled away, a sparsely trailed hinterland nurturing its few roving native and mixed-blood inhabitants; mostly a flat terrain dissected by great rivers and endowed with abundant grasslands; a beautifully deceptive utopia; a lonely paradise, in the eyes of Macdonald, beckoning for population and railway development; a land coveted by the U.S. expansionists, emotional and egoistic in their pledge to save it from royal institutions and economic backwardness.

The time for meaningful possession and law and order in the north-western wilderness was overdue. There were continuing, ghastly reports of wholesale murder, Indian fights, brigandism, of the native population being decimated by smallpox, and debauched, swindled, starved and inflamed by the whisky traders who were flying homemade American flags from their bastions in Canadian Blackfoot country. Hudson's Bay had, by and large, been able to protect its own territorial interests with roughshod justice; Canada, the new landlord, had opened the door to lawlessness.

The Canadian Government dispatched Colonel Patrick Robertson-Ross, Adjutant General and commander of the militia, on a thorough, definitive investigation of the western lands. He came back with alarming observations, and probably some exaggerated reports gleaned from biased Hudson's Bay factors and missionaries, of foreign anarchy in the new Canada, a huge area north of Montana incredibly under the control of American bandits or businessmen of questionable character and ethics – army deserters, Civil War outcasts, villainous adventurers, smugglers, freebooters, wolfers, gamblers, bilkers, bullwhackers, muleskinners, whisky-runners and trading-post bootleggers profitably peddling guns and booze (diluted would be a complimentary description of the varnished brew) to vision-seeking Indians with unquestioning palates, in return for horses, furs, pelts or buffalo robes.

The renegades operated out of Fort Benton, an upper Missouri River town that throbbed fitfully with enterprise, money, immigrants, the greed of illegal trade, bars, bordellos and hope. It had pretensions of being a Chicago of the northern plains, a gateway to the gold fields, a transportation terminus for the east to the west – the Canadian west included.

In summer the place could be a Sodom of sagebrush and shacks, over-ripe with the stench of dung and sweat from the hundreds of pack horses and oxen harnessed for the northern runs.

The biggest, most notorious whisky fortress in Canada was Whoop-Up, at the St. Mary and Oldman Rivers near present-day Lethbridge. The loopholed log stockade, over which the American flag fluttered, was twice the height of a man; two corner bastions of cottonwood trunks were deliberately sturdy enough to support a cannon or a howitzer, both of which had been used by the U.S. Army to defend their Missouri forts. Even the chimneys were iron-barred.

Trading hours were heralded by the clanging of a brass bell. Indian customers, who were usually kept outside, bundled their furs through a hatch and in return a trader pushed out a cupful of brownish or red-hued wallop that he kept handy in a tub at his side. When a brave was already drunk enough, or desperate enough, he could get a quart of firewater for his most valuable possession, a horse.

A proprietor at Whoop-Up was Johnny Jerome Healy. A six-footer from Ireland, a Fenian sympathizer, an unprincipled frontier emperor, Healy was affably tough. He had dozens of men on the payroll.

Other U.S.-owned whisky forts were strategically located. There was Standoff, aptly named to commemorate the "standing off" of a U.S. marshall who had unsuccessfully attempted to confiscate an illicit cargo. The Spitzee post was built by uncouth, grey-haired Dave "Don Quixote" Akers, who, it was said, had bought thirty or more Blood Indian wives for liquor. His partner was John "Liver Eating" Johnson who claimed he had scalped more than twenty Injuns and eaten their livers. At the Old Bow, Elbow River post (in present-day Calgary), H.A. Fred "Slippery" Kanouse worked for Healy. Kanouse, an incorrigible killer, a dispenser of medicinal wonders to combat the pox (venereal disease), was the son of a respected Benton "judge."

The Indians were slaughtering each other in drunken brawls or in horse-stealing raids. The law of the six-shooter, in the hand of the wiliest and the fastest, applied to whites and Indians alike. One halfbreed in a stupor severed the tendons of an Indian woman's arms and murdered his own wife within sight of Fort Edmonton. No one had any authority to arrest him, nor, apparently, the motivation. On the other hand, lynchings were frequent manifestations of justice (or injustice).

The accelerating inclination of Canadian Indians to violence was hardly surprising. The liquid doled out to them was often raw grain alcohol surreptitiously mixed with copious portions of water and perhaps a dash of Jamaica ginger and molasses. Cayenne (hot) pepper was added to give the concoction the necessary kick; chewing tobacco or red ink gave it the colour. A cheaper potion to produce consisted of low-grade wine, water, tobacco and tea leaves all stirred up.

Robertson-Ross recommended the immediate establishment of a chain of military posts from Manitoba to the Rockies and that a regiment of mounted riflemen, 550 disciplined men, be recruited and judiciously posted to bring sanity to the prairies and to protect "the surveyors, contractors and railway laborers about to undertake the great work of constructing the Dominion Pacific Railway."

On the third day of May, 1873, the Prime Minister, who was also Minister of Justice, informed the Commons of his intention to form a police force for the north-west. To cap his decision, the Government received word via the British ambassador in Washington, Sir Edward Thornton, of the massacre of possibly fifty Assiniboine Indians in the Canadian Cypress Hills by a group of revengeful whisky-soused frontiersmen from Montana whose horses had been stolen one night (probably by Crees) when they were journeying to Benton after wintering along the border. The gang also captured five women, one of whom was saved from outrage by trader Abe Farwell's wife, Big Mary, a fullblood Crow Indian who had the nerve to point a gun at the rampaging killers.

These white men were mostly wolfers, Canadian as well as American, hated by all Indians because they unscrupulously poisoned baited buffalo carcasses with strychnine to kill predator wolves for their skins without any regard to the obvious deadly danger to all other life, human and animal.

Two thousand miles away, in the dignified decorum of Parliament, on May 23, 1873, Royal Assent was given to the formation of the North-West Mounted Police. In his original statement, Macdonald had mentioned Mounted Rifles, but after some adverse reaction, mostly from alarmists south of the border who clamoured that Canada was displaying warlike intentions, Sir John crossed out the word Rifles and wrote in Police; actually a better definition because the duties of the civil force, although governed by military discipline, would be to preserve peace, prevent crimes, arrest offenders, and apply the letter of the law. The commissioner and the superintendents, yet to be appointed, were to be *ex officio* justices of the peace.

To perform all these duties in the vast, almost unknown and uncharted land, the commissioner was authorized to recruit, by degrees, not more than 300 men, each constable to be paid not more than one dollar a day (the country was in recession) and each sub-constable not more than 75 cents. At the end of three years of honourable service, they could apply for a grant of 160 acres of prairie land.

Macdonald wanted as little gold lace, fuss and feathers as possible; he did not envision an elite cavalry regiment but rather an efficient, mobile constabulary. He felt strongly the NWMP should stop the whisky trading, collect customs dues, gain the confidence and respect of the Indians, and pave the way for the white man's civilization: settlers, farms, towns, and a Pacific railway.

In this context it was decided the uniform of the force should convey British tradition, with which some of the Indians were acquainted, and British justice. Robertson-Ross, in his western reconnaissance, had observed that the Indians associated the scarlet jackets of the soldiers with the beneficence of the great mother, Queen Victoria. The Mounted would be the new Redcoats.

❖❖❖ The White and the Red

❖❖❖ James Morrow "Bub" Walsh, a cavalry officer, an incurable Ontario adventurer frustrated by a string of civilian jobs from clerking to firefighting, was among the first to volunteer for the newly formed North-West Mounted Police. In September of 1873, he was appointed superintendent and sub-inspector (a confusing dual rank paying $1,000 a year) with urgent instructions to recruit in Ontario "men of sound constitution, able to ride, active and able-bodied, of good character and between the age of 18 and 40, able to read and write English or French."

Major Walsh was energetically forceful (God help the slackers), fastidious with his uniform (when absolutely necessary) and erratically meticulous (abruptly so). Of medium height, and lithe, his responsive features were darkened by a moustache and a suggestion of a beard, a carefully scissored tuft tucked under the lower lip. He was still carefree enough at thirty-three to be flamboyantly unconventional and embarrassingly prone to anti-bureaucratic tendencies. Now he had a new career, and suited to his temperament and leadership, a new challenge.

He had recruited before, in the army; he could usually recognize the calibre he wanted. Service in the militia, which rewarded his zeal and catered to his ego with rapid promotions, had moulded Walsh for a senior responsibility in the experimental Mounted Police. The men he signed up soon knew how they stood. They found him to be constantly active, demanding the maximum from everyone. He could be stubborn, dominant, impatient and abusive in a most emphatic way. His choicest vocabulary, his impromptu references to the deity, curdled proper Victorian sensitivites.

Walsh startled even his most admiring subordinates with the vehemence of his tongue-lashing of a Department of Public Works engineer who had kept him and the men waiting for twenty minutes in an open barge during an October snow flurry on the notorious Dawson Route to Winnipeg. The first troops of the NWMP were being transported through a wilderness of rock and muskeg to Lower Fort Garry for training. The major was furious, accusing engineer George Dixon of maliciously impeding progress. He tried to get him fired. Dixon, in his own defence, claimed Walsh would not heed any explanation.

"He called me a murderer, a Goddamn blackhearted villain and told his men to kick me out and do as they like with me. He continued abusing me for a full half an hour in a very vile manner."

The Dawson Route, which was encountered after the steamer trip from Collingwood on Georgian Bay to Prince Arthur's Landing at the head of Lake Superior, was the first severe test for the 160 all-ranks burdened with their equipment and stores. The route was Canadian-all-the-way, more than 500 miles of forests, swamps, rivers, lakes and rapids, and a sporadic log road involving the unceasing loading and unloading of wagons, tugs and scows at the innumerable, back-breaking portages.

One contingent, the last, slogged through below-zero blizzards. They were without winter clothing or uniforms and actually walked with sacking or shirts wrapped around their feet after their boots froze in the snow. When they arrived at St. Boniface, opposite Winnipeg, winter had come to the plains with forty-below severity. Goods and equipment were loaded on cow hides and hauled across the Red River ice by local halfbreeds. The initial trek westwards was an ordeal not to be forgotten.

In early November, the assortment of recruits, among them former policemen, soldiers, sailors, students, teachers, hoteliers, tradesmen, farmers, telegraph operators, gardeners, lumbermen, surveyors, immigrants and one bartender, and inevitably a few undesirables and political appointees, lined up to take the enlistment oath. In fact, the NWMP actually came into being as an accredited force on a cold, miserable November 3, 1873, with the signing of the roll.

The men were now rested and ready for training. Walsh, a graduate of the Kingston Military School, and cavalry school where he had been complimented as the best-drilled and most adroit student, was the logical choice for developing a total mounted unit. Back in 1866, when the Irish-American Fenians were threatening in upper New York State to overpower Fort Wellington at Prescott for an assault on Ottawa, he had been commissioned in the local volunteer militia. This led to an assignment to recruit and command a troop of cavalry.

Police equipment and uniforms might still be snowed in on the Dawson Route but equitation could be started at once on unbroken broncos bought from the local Métis, the French-speaking mixedbloods. Men were thrown violently onto the frozen earth with relentless regularity, as orders were that riding and breaking would go on unless the temperatures dropped beyond thirty-six below. As acting adjutant (in charge of camp routine), Walsh, the riding master, drew up a daily schedule that accounted for almost every minute from Reveille at 6:30 to Lights Out at 10:15.

Early in '74, adverse reports of conditions on the primaeval plains were continuing to filter through to the Government (Macdonald's Conservatives were out; the new Prime Minister was Liberal Alexander Mackenzie). The Sioux who had escaped to Canada following the Minnesota massacres of 1862 were still not welcome to their Indian neighbours, the Crees and the Saulteaux, especially when they were being visited by their Teton cousins from the camps of Sitting Bull, who already had his eye on the buffalo ranges and trading posts north of the line. Farther west, the outlaws were committing their flourishing depredations at random.

By June the original three troops were ready to tackle the trek to the foothills of the Rockies. Without fanfare, but with regret, they marched from the Stone Fort en route to Dufferin, a collection of shacks, saloons, a store and a Boundary Commission depot on the west bank of the Red River closer to the international border. At the head of the column was the recently appointed assistant commissioner, Lieutenant-Colonel (Superintendent) James Farquharson Macleod of the militia. At Dufferin they would await the commissioner, Lieutenant-Colonel George Arthur French, and three additional troops whose journey west was in comparative luxury, by train via the United States as far as Fargo, Dakota Territory. Commissioner French, only thirty-two, a former member of the Royal Irish Constabulary, was a doctrinaire artillery officer. The preciseness of his moustache, waxed and twirled, was a symptom of his attitudes. A tall, dignified man, he was sharp-minded, ferociously keen, an ultra-disciplinarian.

At last, on July 8, 1874, despite defects in stores and armaments and a near disastrous stampede of the temperamental eastern horses, it was time to start the march of at least 800 miles. In late afternoon, the 275 officers and men formed up with a hint of parade-square finesse, their scarlet jackets soon faded by the inescapable dust. The excitement and expectancy of adventure spread down the line with the commissioner's orders to get the wheels rolling. Fifteen-year-old Frederick Bagley, astride Old Buck, the horse of his choice, put a bugle to his lips and the notes spluttered hesitatingly above the clatter of side arms and equipment, the thudding hooves of balky, restless horses, and the banter of spit-and-polish policemen and their sobered-up, buckskinned half-breed cart drivers. The entire conglomeration swayed into motion for a Hudson's Bay start, a trial run of up to twenty miles.

The orders, the cracking of whips, the neighing of horses and lowing of cattle and oxen, the teeth-gritting, agonizing creaking of wheels of new wagons, of greaseless Red River carts, of field-guns, carriages, an ambulance, mowers, portable forges, plows and harrows, and kitchens, the shouts and cursing, the rattling of accoutrements, and the yellowish dust, spiralling – all of it slowly receded as the astonishing column, two and a half miles long in proper order, was engulfed by the vastness of the realm. Behind them they left the stillness, their tracks, and somewhere, thirty-one constables, deserters all, chicken-hearted rascals to French, probably deterred by lousy cooking, sweltering living conditions and reports of very recent murders and scalpings by Sioux in the nearby Dakota village of St. Joe.

The ordeal of the march quickly substantiated the need for discipline; only the best of men could possibly see the task through. In the first days wagons and carts broke down continually, wheels and axles succumbing to the strain of incessant rocks and bumps. The cavalcade of men, animals and vehicles stretched to ten miles. The big eastern horses wilted in the 100-degree-in-the-shade temperatures, and at night, marble-size hailstones pommelled them.

Grasshoppers, carried by the south-west winds, their wings shining under the sun and their bodies almost blotting it out, descended upon the land and living things in the millions. They devoured all the grass, leaves and wild flowers. They batted against tents, got into blanket rolls, covered the wood of the wagons and swarmed on the food supplies. They eliminated the natural pastures for the horses; drinking holes were clogged with them. Water as black as ink could not be touched. The stifling, oppressive heat, winds that were oven-hot, mosquitoes that came in clouds, as did the dust, tormented the men as well as the beasts. Horses and oxen dropped in their tracks and had to be left behind. Sometimes men went hours without water and existed on half rations. To remind them of their plight there were bleached buffalo bones everywhere.

Such conditions, as the straggling column pushed on following the daily three A.M. reveille, brought about severe cases of depression and diarrhea. At one point, twenty or so men were down with dysentry. There were speculative reports in the U.S. press that the policemen-adventurers had been wiped out by the Sioux.

By July 24, the van of the column reached a prairie landmark, La Roche Percée, a formation of limestone rocks on the Souris River at Short Creek near today's Estevan, Saskatchewan. Humans and animals flopped down with exhaustion.

The distance covered in sixteen days was 270 miles. Much too slow for French. He inspected his bedraggled contingent from front to rear. All his forethought had been unable to assess the severity of the plains upon the inexperienced. It was obvious there were too many sick policemen, too many played-out horses and cattle, and too few carts for all the expedition to reach the foothills in one piece before winter.

French and the main force carried on from La Roche Percée July 29 on a northwesterly, Canadian course to avoid the border hills. Troop A, reduced and loaded with the weakest men and fifty-five sick horses, prepared to change direction for Fort Edmonton, a safer undertaking but a trek of more than 850 hardship miles that would take 88 days.

French, with his expert placement of stars, and his compass, and an odometer to measure distance, guided his five troops onward in the general direction of the Bow River. They skirted prairie fires and swamps, but they couldn't avoid the alkaline water, contaminated by buffalo droppings, that purged the already emaciated, exhausted horses. The dysenteric men were calling themselves the Unmounted Police while the halfbreeds began to sound lurid warnings of impending attacks by hundreds of organized outlaws hiding and waiting in the Cypress Hills.

24

The first Indians to confront the dust-covered cavalcade were Sisseton Sioux, destitute and dirty. They were anxious to see the white mother's pony soldier chief. On August 15, at Old Wives Creek, a small party of Métis buffalo hunters, people of mixed French and Indian ancestry, their two-wheeled carts laden with robes, came into sight and stopped out of sheer wonderment. They were searched for liquor – the cost of their curiosity – and allowed to proceed to Winnipeg.

By August 25, 600 miles from Dufferin, at Swift-Current Creek, in sight of the wooded Cypress Hills, the policemen were nearing the edge of Blackfoot country, 60,000 square miles. The Blackfoot, the self-styled Real People, and their confederate allies the Bloods, Peigans, and Sarcees, were violently possessive of their sovereignty and were reported by a new guide, Louis Léveillé, to be on the war-path. Only the shouts of the Métis bullwhippers and the unending creak of wheels and saddlery disrupted the silence. There had been plenty of dire warnings of trouble ahead. The Blackfoot, for sure, would be aware the police were approaching. Léveillé, a hard-bitten, wizened plainsman, knew his Indians.

French formed an elite squad of twenty men who rode with lances and pennants to impress any Blackfoot war party that might appear. He had also created a Cripple Camp of men and animals and had left them in "safe" territory away from any likely action against Indians or outlaws. One constable, Frank Norman, summed up the predicament by rewording the National Anthem, as is the custom of soldiers in times of stress:

> Confound their politics,
> Frustrate their knavish tricks,
> Get us out of this damned fix,
> God save all here.

Near the middle of September, after more than 700 miles, the plight of the travellers was alarming. Ice was already covering the prairie mud patches; pasturage was practically nil, eaten by buffalo. The men were using their own blankets to warm their starving horses to try to keep them alive. The trail behind was littered with dead or deserted horses and oxen.

The objective of the column was the forks of the Bow and Belly (South Saskatchewan) Rivers where French expected he would uncover the whisky traders' headquarters – an incorrect assumption – and find luxuriant grazing land for the stock. On September 10, Walsh, who had been promoted to superintendent and inspector, believed he had located the forks, although there was no sign of life, just three roofless shacks in a desert. French and the command had been misinformed and misdirected. Extremely alarmed for the safety of the force, the commissioner sent out scouts, whereas Walsh, in accordance with original plans, was ordered to Fort Edmonton on the North Saskatchewan with B Troop (to which he had been transferred) and a part of A Troop. The inspector, with seventy men and fifty-eight horses and stores, forded the South Saskatchewan and set up a camp on the north bank.

On September 14, French desperately turned the ragged main column southward, toward the Sweet Grass Hills where the half-breeds had promised there would be plenty of wood, clean water and pasture. Most importantly, the hills were on the borderland, only about 100 miles from supplies and the telegraph at Fort Benton, head of navigation on the Big Muddy.

Horses were now dying of cold, hunger and exhaustion at a rapid rate: nine in thirty-six hours. French was persuaded it would be too much of a risk to expect Walsh and his train ever to reach Edmonton. The major was instructed to turn around, follow the column to the west butte of the Sweet Grass Hills and collect any played-out horses or oxen in the wake of the main caravan.

Walsh, who wouldn't stand on rank when a helping hand was needed to pull carts and horses out of a river or the mud, who could cuss with a trooper's annoyance at conflicting orders, re-crossed the South Saskatchewan.

Near hopelessness set in along the tarnished red-coated line. Weak, gaunt, sometimes almost staggering, and drawn out for eight miles, the policemen pushed themselves on towards the hills in gales, sleet and snow. The majority were having to walk, blistered and bleeding.

On September 18, the vanguard reached west butte and discovered, thank God, enough of what had been promised – wood, water and grazing ground, and coal! After at least 850 miles of slogging from Dufferin (the scouts had covered a thousand), an ordeal of miscalculation and desperation, everybody put their feet up. The North-West Mounted Police was back in circulation.

26

Discipline had been maintained; esprit de corps established; the croakers of a critical press vanquished.

French had been ruthlessly tough with officers and men. He had been cursed, damned, openly questioned but rarely disobeyed. The men had complained about everything; the rations, the inferior quality of their uniforms, the misuse of constables and horses, French's abiding mismanagement (for instance, there had been no issue of water bottles) and his brutishness. The commissioner, for his part, withheld comment on the quality and stamina of some of his subordinates. He was more relieved than outspoken.

Two days later Walsh rejoined the encampment. He had lost six of his horses and one man, Elliott Thornton. The constable had left the troop to hunt, alone. The prairie swallowed him up. The following day, however, Thornton came in, exhausted. Five days without food, he had wandered about until his horse collapsed. Then he started to walk in the direction of the landmark butte.

Walsh and his men, well indoctrinated to hardship, recuperated in less than comfortable conditions. The west butte country – Dead Horse Coulee – was a favourite area of transient Indians. One large band had left a profusion of dormant lice which were revived by the warm bodies of the policemen. Oil of juniper, used to combat mosquitoes, routed the parasites. The original owners were not far away; they were keeping the Redcoats under steady surveillance.

French's main concern was the quickening approach of winter and the necessity for permanent quarters for the men who would be staying in the west. Having brought the nucleus of the NWMP to Whoop-Up land, he was preparing for his return trip with Troops D and E. The remainder, Troops B, C, F and a sprinkling of A, were to establish themselves farther north and west in the heart of whisky territory. The responsibility of fulfilling the role and objectives of the Redcoats in the foothills was handed over to Assistant Commissioner Macleod. Henceforth he would be master of his limited resources, isolated in an unmapped terrain, surrounded by unknown and unpredictable Indians and bandits, and without expectation of help or reinforcements.

Macleod, thirty-eight, a tall, lean, kindly and tactful officer with a background in law and the military, fully realized his priorities. The first was to build a fort secure from the elements and the marauders who, he had been led to believe, would attack in hordes. On October 13, 1874, with the aid of Jerry Potts, a skilled halfbreed guide who had strong ties with the Blackfoot, he chose a perfect island site (except when the water was high to overflowing) on the sheltered Oldman River, within sight of the snow-peaked Rockies, thirty miles northwest of Whoop-Up, which had been abandoned by the illegal traders, eighty miles north of the border, and about 240 indirect miles from Benton. Macleod hoisted the Union Jack. The Indians had a new owner.

Natural curiosity, abetted by information circulated on the widespread moccasin telegraph by native messengers (riders and runners) put the Indians on the trails to the fort. Presents were handed out with the assurances of equal protection and justice for Indians and whites.

Macleod stood by his pledge to crack down on illegal trading, Montana Redeye liquor in particular. Before the end of October, on the complaint of Three Bulls, a minor chief who had swapped two ponies for two gallons and considered himself cheated, five men were arrested. One was Harry "Kamoose" Taylor, a rough-and-tumble entrepreneur, a former leader in the Spitzee Cavalry of wolfers, a preacher, squawman and whisky trader who was to become, amazingly, a generous and respected proprietor of a res-taurant and the first hotel at Fort Macleod. The sobriquet Ka-moose, from an Indian word meaning "thief," recognized his talents for attracting other men's Indian wives.

The police seized two wagon-loads of booze, sixteen horses, five Henry rifles, five revolvers and 116 buffalo robes. The valuable robes were made into police winter clothes; the liquor was ordered dumped. Taylor was fined $200. He had been caught, arrested, charged, tried and sentenced – all by the same long arm of the new law.

Whether all the booze was poured into the dust is conjecture. The lawmakers, almost to a man, had a perpetual affinity for grog that was officially embarrassing. The most noteworthy of the imbi-bers was Macleod whose passion for whisky, and his ability to handle it, created a legend in every officers' mess he visited, Canadian or American.

Walsh's first assignment out of Fort Macleod took him into Montana. It had been decided that as many horses as could be spared should be herded south for winter grazing. Walsh, at the head of an escort for eighty of the weakest mounts, had as his guide Jerry Potts who had already become almost indispensable to the force since it reached its western periphery.

Potts, a tight-lipped mixedblood in his mid-thirties, had been hired in Benton as guide, advisor and interpreter at a salary of $90 monthly. Invariably attired in beaded buckskins and an eastern hat, he was a small man with piercing black eyes and sloping shoulders, a drooping moustache and bow legs. His body seemed to lean sideways even when he stood erect. He was a curious and astonishingly able mixture of two cultures. His mother, a Peigan, had died in his infancy. His father, a pioneer trader, was an Edinburgh Scotsman who had been shot and killed in error by an Indian vagrant.

Potts moved easily from the councils of his mother's people to the white man's bawdy settlements. He had the killer instincts of both societies – he could track and bend a bow like an Indian and shoot like a hired gunman – and was especially dangerous when he had a bellyful of rotgut whisky. He was a laconic, independent, mysterious, fearless character with a chronic cough, and despite all his foibles, an honest man.

"Old Jerry" had an uncanny, intuitive sense of direction on the treeless plains, day or night or during a blizzard. He steered Walsh's party 200 miles through Peigan country to the Missouri River with the loss of only fifteen of the very weakest horses in the snowdrifts. They came to an agreement with a rancher to accommodate and feed the remaining sixty-five animals until spring. Potts guided Walsh back to Fort Macleod, where he had found a home and his true calling. His interpreting was hardly prolific; his drinking certainly was – he was always thirsty – but to the NWMP he was a bonanza.

The average policeman, payless for months, in tatters, in debt up to his ears, often sick, was daily facing the temptation of desertion. Eighteen did, in fact, take off, fully armed. Remarkably, though, life on the Belly River plains settled down. Law and order, and peace, administered by constables who looked in need of welfare, were spreading benignly, and by early 1875 the whisky trade had been compelled to find another major rendezvous point, reportedly in the Cypress Hills, about 160 miles east of Fort Macleod.

Instructions were received from Ottawa to build a post in the hills, the summer fighting terrain of the Blackfoot allies and the Assiniboines, Crees and Saulteaux. Again Walsh received his marching orders. He was to proceed with B Troop into Cypress, find a suitable site, build a substantial fort before winter, name it after himself, take command there, and clear out the wrongdoers.

As could be expected, Jerry Potts was out in front as Walsh and his thirty men started out to institute British justice in the stone-crested border highlands where in the spring of '73 the Assiniboines had been massacred by the wolfers, and where since time unknown the Indian had hunted, councilled, prayed and fought in this geographical oddity of a hundred miles (east-to-west) that emerged from the flatness of the prairies to offer its transient inhabitants deep, narrow ravines for shelter, pine for their lodge poles, game-food aplenty, good water, and in summer, green grass for their precious ponies.

Walsh and Potts hastily decided upon a site close to the massacre ground at Battle Creek, where the valley was broad and the land flat. This was on June 7, 1875. Two days later the first batch of unwelcome visitors arrived. They were Teton Sioux, adherents of Sitting Bull, chased across the boundary line by the U.S. Cavalry. The surprise was mutual and after the initial exchange of enquiry and cordiality some of the young belligerents noticed a couple of Redcoats wearing U.S. soldier garments. It was explained by Walsh, who was sitting at a table in the open, that the uniforms had been bought from traders because their own had worn out.

The explanation did not satisfy the Sioux spokesman. The whites were lying; they were not Redcoats, but Bluecoats in disguise. Walsh countered through Potts, who was trying to interpret, that the flag on the staff behind him was the Union Jack, the flag of the great mother. The whites they saw were her policemen.

The Sioux became increasingly agitated. Most of the police who were cutting and hauling wood for the fort picked up their firearms and ammunition belts and hurried in; the Indians surrounded Walsh and pushed against his table, threatening to eliminate the camp.

"If you try to kill us you will lose many of your own and soon there will be more Redcoats here than there are buffalo and none of you will be left alive," Walsh warned them.

Then, to the relief of the hard-pressed detachment, a large

band of Crees, friendly to the police, were seen in the eastern hills heading for the camp. The Sioux, outnumbered by their hereditary foes, retreated.

In six weeks the fort was finished, barracks and stores forming a part of the palisade. Defensively, it was not in the best of locations. All around were wooded slopes of spruce, pine and poplar where attackers could find plenty of natural concealment for a direct assault. Routine quickly became established, in accordance with Walsh's ways of firmness and despatch. Communications with Fort Macleod became regular; a reasonably predictable ox-wagon service between this southern outpost and the supply bases in Benton also was started.

And what a sight were the Benton bull trains, the passenger and freight convoys ploughing through an ocean of buffalo grass – up to thirty canvas-covered wagons, linked in threes, creaking and bouncing and digging ruts that were to scar the land for a century.

For miles off the dust trails could be seen thinning above the trains, the wagons obscured by yellowish clouds that formed a moving, choking, smokelike screen. Then the oxen came into sight near the fort, as many as ten pairs pulling three schooners like a freight train, the huge animals snorting, stinking, covered with flies and pestered by mosquitoes; then the grimy wagon drivers, bull whips slashing and cracking and profanity flowing from their dry throats with unimpaired fluency.

Walsh and his small garrison could not hope to stamp out immediately all the depredations, theft and killings that had infested the Cypress Hills for years. The pushers of Redeye firewater continued to barter for the skins of the thinning herds of buffalo, and the Indians, too many of them, were willing, quenchless victims of the white man's poison water. Times were changing, nonetheless, and the very presence of the patrolling Redcoats was a deterrent to the Missouri lawbreakers.

Walsh steadily dampened the incessant Indian warfare by appealing to their need for peace and the white mother's justice. (*Maintien le Droit,* uphold the right, was inscribed on the NWMP badge around a buffalo head, the whole encircled by maple leaves and topped with a crown.) He gained their confidence through straight-talking, by switching in on the Indians' own moccasin telegraph, by constant vigilance.

The major, as he liked to call himself, had scoured the trails with his men and in each Indian camp had always observed warriors ready for battle. He believed if he could bring about peace among all the warring factions he could establish a moral position for the "introducers of the law," as he put it, that would gain the respect of all the native peoples. He remarked to one of his officers: "This is an opportunity for a man to do something great and I am going to do it."

He set out to get "five or six of the most savage tribes of the west, always prepared and anxious to meet their foes and avenge the death of some fallen warrior, to lay down their arms, shake hands, smoke the long-stemmed pipe of peace and promise faithful friendship."

On the first day of July, Walsh's persuasive powers assembled the chiefs of the Crees, Peigans, Bloods, Assiniboines and (Yankton) Sioux, and some halfbreeds, at a council site twenty miles west of the hills.

The major was impressively resplendent in his loose-fitting Norfolk jacket edged with gold braid, his white-striped cord breeches tucked into black top boots with spurs, and whitish cork helmet and gauntlets. He stood firmly in their midst with an escort of scarlet lancers, one hand on his hip and the other on the handle of his own cavalry sword, and he told them he had been sent by the white mother into their land to establish order and introduce the law that governed all the people, a law that forbade war.

"Those who obey the law will be protected by me," he informed them with dignified flourishes of purposeful showmanship and authority. "I will always be on the side of the law-abiding people, whether they are white, red or black. I have come here as a friend and I will try to fulfill my mission faithfully.

"You can only be an enemy by disobeying the law, and that is my sacred charge, one which I will defend even at the expense of my own life, and the life of every man in my command."

The pipe of peace was smoked to confirm pledges of friendship among the tribes. Walsh felt he had proved the Redcoats had not come to the country as persecutors but as friends. Years of incessant hostility might be coming to an end. Might be!

The major was in the mind of Little Plume, a chief of the Peigans, one of the great Indian diplomats of the day, as he lay close to death and prepared his spirit for the march to the celestial hunting grounds. He requested his brother chiefs, who stood around him, to send to the major a spotted horse, his favourite, and very much prized by him, so that the Redcoat chief would know that when close to death Little Plume was thinking of him.

"Tell him I die in sight of that beautiful hill where the Great Spirit softened the hearts of so many red men, and where they joined hands as brothers and received so much happiness." Follow his council, he advised them, "and peace will reign in your camp."

The test of the major's words to protect those who abided by the new law came in August. A band of Yankton Sioux, about 700 lodges, approached Cypress from the east, preceded by probing war parties. They overran the hills around the fort, and the few halfbreeds, Assiniboines and Crees in the area gathered near the Recoats' palisade for safety. Three times in one day Walsh mounted his troop and forced the Sioux away from the camps of the other Indians. At night he kept close to them. Before long the harassed Sioux moved back to the American side, down to the Missouri.

Even after only a few weeks it was apparent Fort Walsh was changing the pattern of life on the southern plains. It was becoming safer to travel alone, unhindered if not completely unafraid. Also it was rumoured the Blackfoot had refused to smoke Teton Sioux tobacco that would seal an alliance to wipe out the white soldiers north and south of the line.

At the fort there was a nagging aggravation that prevented off-duty policemen making the most of life in the village that had developed in the valley: the men weren't getting their pay. Walsh, with three sub-constables and Louis Léveillé, trekked through hostile Assiniboine territory to Helena, Montana, to pick up back pay for B Troop and collect twenty remounts. On the return journey the party was hit by the first severe storm of the oncoming winter. The temperature went down to twenty below and the shorelines of the rivers froze over, making the fording of men, mounts and wagon deadly treacherous. Wet clothes were covered with ice and not a stick of wood could be found to light fires. Walsh, sheltering from a blizzard in the wagon, was provided with ample provocation to express his feelings. It was not known for sure whether he was cussing the conditions or the alleged singing of one of his men whose repertoire was limited to "The priest of the parish and his caravan / came over the mountain to visit Susanne."

The small and frozen detachment was able to thaw out under

the bluffs of the Milk River for three days. There they found, beneath the snow, plenty of wood and fodder, and Léveillé, good old Léveillé, brought in two antelopes for anxious appetites. Then on to Fort Walsh and a big pay day for all.

Louis Léveillé, as his sons after him, would be indelibly associated with the infusion of Redcoat power and credibility in this harsh domain of physical and climatic extremes. In his early fifties, tall, spare but unbelievably strong, Léveillé had joined the force as a guide, after a great deal of persuasion, when he met the westward-bound lawmen at a grazing patch near Old Wives Creek (about eighty miles east of Swift Current) on August 21, 1874.

Léveillé, a poor man, had pitied the bedraggled policemen. To him they looked out of place in their ragged finery. The constables, the majority bearded, wore those little bits of round, flat, blue hats with the white bands, no bigger than a plate, standard military "pillboxes." They were useless, providing but a fraction of shade for the wearers whose foreheads, necks and noses were burned almost black. And men and horses were pestered by mosquitoes and black flies – and how insane to bob the horses' tails, thereby preventing them from swishing away the clouds of insects. Léveillé could recognize these crazy things clearly; he was a plainsman.

The winter of '75-'76 was a bitter one for the snowed-in police force. The cold was intense. Patrols were restricted despite disconcerting reports of whisky-trading at the Wood Mountain settlement, east of Fort Walsh. The Missouri go-getters were concentrating on new markets following their retreat from the Macleod district.

From the moccasin telegraph and in official documents the police were also receiving information of increasing hostilities between the Sioux and the U.S. Army. Ottawa was particularly well informed of the latest military strategy along the Yellowstone River. Lord Dufferin, the Governor General, was already predicting strained relations between Ottawa and Washington should the Indians be driven north across the Canadian border.

The salvation of the Canadian plains, it appeared, was dependent on the small, isolated contingents of policemen. Their ability to fulfill their mission was being jeopardized by the bickering between Commissioner French and civilian officialdom. He had never forgiven Government bureaucrats for what he considered the disproportionate allocation of scarce funds for an ill-conceived, jerry-built headquarters at Swan River, near the headwaters of the Assiniboine. Neither did he approve of being so far removed from the action. In mid '76 he resigned to return to the Imperial Army.

If he had not resigned he would have been publicly dismissed. The Government, which was determined to unload this untenable agitator whose frustrations had by now pitted him against Macleod, let him out with his dignity intact.

In July, Macleod was promoted to commissioner. The colonel, which was the title Macleod appreciated the most, nevertheless continued as a stipendiary magistrate in the Bow River district. Lieutenant-Colonel Acheson Gosford Irvine of the Quebec Rifles, who as commandant of the Fort Garry military had marshalled the defenders against the U.S.-based, border-raiding Fenians in '71 and who had been inducted into the NWMP as a superintendent in May of '75, was named assistant commissioner. Headquarters were moved from Swan River to Fort Macleod.

In view of official intelligence and rumours that Sitting Bull's Sioux were being harassed and pursued by the U.S. generals, Macleod sent reinforcements to Fort Walsh.

In June of 1876, when the entire United States was aghast at the annihilation of General George Armstrong Custer's forces by the Sioux and allies at the Battle of the Little Big Horn, Walsh was with his wife and daughter Cora (he had married Mary Elizabeth Mowat of Brockville in 1870) in Hot Springs, Arkansas, resting after his ordeal on the plains. He had suffered quite badly from erysipelas, a contagious and infectious skin disease that produced severe irritation and swelling and bouts of fever and vomitting.

Ottawa suggested he return west as soon as possible, which he did, first visiting the capital to give government officials his impressions of rapidly changing events and circumstances on the plains. He was back with his enlarged Fort Walsh garrison in August, on the trails to Wood Mountain looking for the Sioux.

A Métis, Gabriel Solomon, had reported that another Canadian halfbreed, Laframboise, hunting south of the border, had visited the camp of Sitting Bull and had heard the Sioux leader declare to his council of chiefs:

"We can go nowhere without seeing the head of an American. Our land is small; it is like an island ... We have two ways to go, to the land of the great mother or to the land of the Spaniards [Mexico]."

Sitting Bull – patriot, warrior, mystic, priest, orator, lover and composer of songs – was well into his thirties before his hereditary sphere of skirmishing and war broadened to include the white intruders, the U.S. Army. The Bluecoats, or the Longknives as the Sioux described the cavalry, were destined to learn first-hand about the generalship of the swarthy chief of the Hunkpapa braves. His sagacity as a politician among all those Lakota Sioux who would not resign themselves to the white man's handouts was legendary. He was, in Indian agency parlance, a renegade, a hostile, a bad Indian.

Sitting Bull had no uncompromising desire to foment a direct confrontation with the whites, the sick-looking hairy men. He wanted only to be left alone to follow the paths of his forefathers; he wanted his people to be unhindered to roam the buffalo ranges; and spiritually, because he was a religious man with a holy name, he wanted to make "good medicine," the white man's term for how the Indians communicated with their gods and received visions and signs atop some wind-caressed, secluded bluff. Sitting Bull did not harbour in his soul an irrevocable hatred for all whites. He mistrusted them intensely; he became indignant and angry when he found them in the hunting grounds or near the healing mineral springs of the Paha Sapa, the Black Hills where the people communed with Wakan-Tanka, the Great Spirit, the Grandfather, the Great Mysterious, god of men, animals and birds, the invisible Creator, the guarantor of immortality. His objective was to convince all intruders that these Indian hills were inviolable; the waters were the tears of the Great Spirit; and the earth there, and all it contained, the sacred domain of the Creator.

In his marauding expeditions near the Canadian border where the mixedbloods (the Shlota, the greasy ones) raised excellent horses, Sitting Bull drove the white traders to a frenzy. His appearances were seldom uneventful. One of his favorite dallying spots was the store at the junction of the Missouri and Yellowstone Rivers, not much more than a stone's throw from a military post. Soldiers who wandered from the barracks did so at the risk of their lives.

The traders had a delicate and dangerous predicament. To

survive they had to humour their customers without pandering to them excessively or cowering in a corner. One of them gave Bull (an abbreviation coined by the soldiers) a red shirt and suggested he wear it whenever he came looking for trouble. Bull put it on immediately and when he and his warriors were leaving they fired a volley of shots into the walls. At another store, Bull took over after complaining of being short-changed. From behind the counter he examined his compatriots' furs and in the manner of the proprietor pointed out the flaws. He mimicked the trader's bartering habits as he exchanged lavishly the trader's food, ammunition and trinkets. The trader, in the meantime, sidled up to an open barrel of gunpowder, lit his pipe and declared he was prepared to blow up his establishment and everybody in it. The Indians took his threat seriously.

The first white man from Canada to have a run-in with Bull was probably John George "Kootenai" Brown, who surrendered all his clothes but held on to his scalp. Brown was an inveterate wanderer, a trait that transplanted him from the soft green-clad hills of Ireland to the high plains of the Dog Den range in Dakota.

Brown had sold his British Army commission to try his luck in the Cariboo gold strikes where he lost more than his shirt in the rowdy, shantied, bar-roomed mining camps from where he migrated eastwards. By '67 he was riding the mail in Indian country, and when his employer went bankrupt (due mostly to Indian depredations) Brown was stranded and broke. He signed on as a mail carrier for the U.S. Army. His route passed through the no-white-man's-land of the Sioux, close to the Big Bend of the Missouri, a landscape of rocks, ravines and trees – ideal for ambush.

On May 24, 1869, Brown and a halfbreed Santee Sioux companion were riding to Fort Totten, 150 miles east of the Missouri. They were leading a pack mule, Lady Jane Grey, bent with mail. At the end of this long first day out the two riders were nearing Strawberry Lake. Preoccupied with their fatigue and their grumbling about the cold, rainy weather, they were taken off guard by about thirty painted warriors who came charging at them. Brown had time to aim his rifle (a ball and cap breechloader) at the leader, who turned out to be Sitting Bull, but the cap was wet and wouldn't fire.

Bull ordered his braves to strip the captives and take everything, including the mail. They stood before him, shaking with cold and fright.

"Kill them!" the young men shouted. Bull admonished them to be patient. The halfbreed, in a fluent Dakota dialect, boldly berated Bull.

"We are halfbreeds of your own people. Why do you want to kill us?"

The two of them lied profusely about themselves and their job. Brown, his hair as long as an Indian's, said his father was a white man and his mother a Sioux. Bull was apparently dubious. This man he was questioning had a very fair complexion, light blue eyes and thick, brown locks. Most of all, the chief didn't like the idea of anyone doing anything for the soldiers. His band had recently killed and scalped two others for carrying the Bluecoats' messages.

It began raining in torrents and getting dark. When the eyes of the Indians were off them for a moment, the captives made a desperate move for their lives. They rolled out of sight in the grass, zig-zagged down a coulee and plunged on the run into the lake, standing up to their chins in water and weeds.

The Sioux didn't miss them immediately. When they did, they began shooting haphazardly into the water, the bullets swishing and splashing close to the fugitives. The Indians weren't sure their prisoners were in the lake and off they went, complaining, down the trail in the gloom of dusk.

After an agonizing, motionless half hour in the cold water, the naked couriers crept up the bank and sprinted in the opposite direction, back towards Fort Stevenson. Progress was slow that night; they were unsure of their bearings. The next day, warmed by the sun, they made good time and in the afternoon were spotted from the fort's sentry towers. Covered with reddish mosquito welts, and bleeding, the haggard stragglers were heralded as two naked Indians. Soldiers were sent out to bring them in.

The military commander of the area was Major General Philippe Régis de Trobriand, a rich, middle-aged aristocrat from Tours, an author turned infantryman who had fought for the Union Army in the Civil War. When Trobriand saw the state of his two mailmen, he plied them with lavish doses of cure-all whisky (a perennial bon vivant, he had a few himself) and said

38

nasty things about the Government allowing the hostiles to be at large.

"They should be wiped off the face of the earth," he muttered.

"Kootenai" Brown didn't quit the messenger business immediately. The money was needed. He took his chances in the unhealthy environment until he returned to Canada in '78.

The incursions of Sitting Bull's status-seeking fighters grew bolder. They delighted in plundering the mail and seeing the loose papers and letters scudding over the prairie. Their most daring exploit was the theft of forty head of cavalry mounts from Fort Totten.

In the year the whites called 1873, the Tetons, those of them still free from the restrictions and indignities of the agencies, gathered to smoke the council pipe and conduct their ceremonial dances. There was much talking about the disappearance of Pte (the buffalo). The hungry hostiles could do no more than sit in their blankets through a bitter winter and sharpen their arrows. In spring, when the warm wind cleared the snow from the flatlands, visitors from the Missouri agencies brought news of an impending pony-soldier expedition into the Black Hills. It was said the whites were going to search for the gold metal, and the one that the Sioux called Long Hair or Yellow Hair (Custer) was preparing to leave Fort Lincoln, his headquarters on the lower Missouri, to desecrate the Paha Sapa.

Both Sitting Bull and Crazy Horse were hunting buffalo far to the west, and during the Moon of Cherries Blackening (July), Custer's men, a thousand of them, with wagons and artillery, were left alone to search hills and streams for the metal that sent the white people crazy. The Indians had a name for the wagon ruts that Custer's column had left as a pathfinder on the prairie. They called it the Thieves' Road, and they called Custer the Chief of the Thieves.

Outright warfare on the plains broke out in 1876 when the U.S. generals embarked upon a campaign to "bring in" the non-agency incorrigibles who had refused to give up when the snow was so deep not even a pony could have moved on the frigid prairie. The people would have starved at the agencies anyway.

Sitting Bull had run out of forbearance; he was ready for the inevitable. He organized a strike force of warriors among the

Hunkpapa, the White Horse Riders, and during the Moon of Snowblindness (March) he invited all the young men, including former enemies, to join him in the north, still a promised land of buffalo meat, good horses and plenty of fighting. (The Canadian Blackfoot rejected the offer and were duly commended by the Queen and threatened by the Sioux.) As soon as the snow cleared, when there was grass for the ponies, the men prepared their weapons, the women packed belongings and dismantled the tepees, and the families set out for the Rosebud, a tributary of the Yellowstone River in Montana, where game and grass were abundant.

The trails were clogged with warriors; behind came the women, the old men, children, dogs, and horses pulling the travois (two poles with crossbars of wood strong enough to support all the baggage and small children). The great encampment, enhanced by the big men of the seven Teton councils, moved up the Rosebud, the progress interrupted for reunions, dancing, and singing, courting, and reminiscences of great feats and heroics. How good it was for all the people to be together again, free in their own land. And who better to lead them all than Sitting Bull? And so it was decided.

Above all, an Indian was an individual. Within the disciplines of his religion, his superstitions and tribal customs, he acted alone. It did his heart good, though, to participate in this greatest gathering of the Teton Lakotas and their allies and see again a confirmation of togetherness at the sun-gazing dance, a supplication to the Great Spirit by endurance and pain. During this noisy ceremony of self-inflicted torture, self-discipline and sacrifice, Sitting Bull, a *wichasha wakan* (holy man) and already scarred from many other sun dances, had a hundred pieces of skin cut from his arms as an offering to the Great Mysterious, and he danced and chanted for two days while gazing at the full sun, the power of all things and the benevolent smile of the Creator. Then he collapsed into a trance. When he regained full consciousness he said he had had a vision of many soldiers falling headfirst into camp. (*Hoye!* Wakan-Tanka had imparted his knowledge to Bull, and all the people sang with great jubilation.)

It was the middle of the Moon of Fattening (June) when the growing encampment, with Bull and his war chiefs leading the way, moved slowly across the parched, scrub highlands to the broad, tree-lined valley of the Greasy Grass, the Little Big Horn River.

On June 25, on a listless day of heavy heat and dust, it was as if Sitting Bull's vision had become reality. The U.S. Seventh Cavalry, under the command of Long Hair Custer (although in this campaign he was wearing comparatively short hair), was part of a three-pronged attack upon the hostiles. He had about 700 men, including Indian scouts and a few civilians. There was a slogan in the army, "Custer's Luck," and on this day, in this centennial year, it appeared the idol of the Civil War, author and aspiring politician, was in luck again. There, from a ridge between the Rosebud and the Little Big Horn Rivers, his Indian scouts spotted the great Sioux village.

Despite their warning that there were too many Sioux in the valley for his command to tackle – there were probably more than 2,500 fighting men in the encampment – Custer apparently did not wish to believe he could be stopped. He divided his regiment into three battalions so as to catch the Indians by surprise in a sweeping pincer movement, which was the Custer way of fighting Indians. It was ironic that he selected, unknowingly, Sitting Bull's Hunkpapa circle for the opening shots. This was the time-honoured camp position for the Hunkpapa – the People who Dwell at the Entrance to a Camp.

Sitting Bull was visiting when the warning cry went out that the soldiers were coming; then their bullets zipped among the tepee tops and splintered the poles. Limping, as usual, from his old wound, he ran to his family area to get his weapons and horse and paint himself for the fighting.

The Bluecoats blundered into a mass of bloodthirsty fighters, an avalanche of uncoordinated savagery. The warriors were like bees swarming out of a hive. They cut down their attackers mercilessly amid a confusion and crescendo of shots, war cries and shrieks, frantic bugle calls, the bleating of panic-stricken and wounded horses, and soldiers dying or pleading for their lives.

"*Hoka Hey!*" shouted Crazy Horse. "Lakotas, this is a good day to die."

Custer and twelve companies, the ranks liberally sprinkled with recruits experiencing their first real combat, were either eliminated or mauled in the battle; 261 officers and men, civilians and scouts embroiled in the main thrusts on the flanks rotted under the sun. There were no prisoners. The only living remnants of the whites were some of their horses. Bull was kicked by one that he thought was dead.

In the throes of the carnage was First Lieutenant William (Willie) Winer Cooke, Custer's adjutant, a thirty-year-old Canadian, a doctor's son of United Empire Loyalist stock, an athletic man with extraordinarily long, bushy, curly sidewhiskers that drooped to the third row of breast buttons of his military tunic.

Cooke had had the ear of his commander, something of a rarity for someone not in the clannish family confines. (On the fateful expedition Custer had two brothers with him, a nephew and a brother-in-law, all of whom were killed.) From Mount Pleasant, a small community just south of Brantford, Ontario, Cooke was an out-and-out Custer man, his influence enhanced by Custer's visit in 1869 to the Cooke family's ancestral home in Hamilton.

The adjutant died as he had lived, on close call for Custer. He scribbled Custer's last message: "Benteen. Come On. Big Village. Be Quick. Bring Packs. W. W. Cooke. P.S. Bring Pacs." His final moments were anguished ones within a barricade of dead horses, where Custer's body was also found, amid the sun-bloated, fly-infested mounts, their legs sticking out as stiff as wood.

There were two more Canadians with the command – Lieutenant Donald McIntosh of Montreal and Vancouver, and Private James (Jim) Weeks of Halifax. They were in the first charge that fizzled out in the sagebrush. The troops retreated haphazardly to the protection of the timber along the river banks where McIntosh, thirty-eight, proud of the Mohawk blood in his veins, was wrestled from his saddle and clubbed to death.

Weeks, twenty-two, a former labourer, a tall lad and good-looking, was one of the few to get away from Bull's young demons. He swam the river, scrambled onto the bluffs and frantically dug a shallow ditch to shoot from with a knife and a tin cup.

Hemmed in by carbine fire, exposed to the searing sun on the bluff, he was almost maddened with thirst. The wounded were suffering agonizingly and volunteers were sought to run down to the river for water. Without it they would all surely die.

Jim took off like a hare, pushed a canteen into the water as he put his head under, and stumbled back, gasping, exhausted, his legs hardly able to support him. He flopped into his hole.

A captain asked him for a swig.

"Go to hell," Jim rasped, "get your own water."

Young and resilient, Weeks survived.

Sitting Bull ambled up to the Custer ridge on his black stallion to exhort his followers not to vandalize the dead. Some obeyed but hundreds of others, men and women, stripped the bodies of the whites for uniforms and underclothing and took away all they could find: weapons, saddles, tobacco, whisky in water bottles, wallets, money, letters, photos, watches and flags. One Indian joyfully held aloft on an arrow a scalped cheek (probably Cooke's). Others rode with cavalry shirts on the end of their lances to drive away the white man's sweat before putting them on.

The magnitude of the victory, the implications, were recognized by Sitting Bull. Were not the whites everywhere as the buffalo used to be? He knew the soldiers would punish the Indians wherever they could be caught. Where, then, could they find a sanctuary? The Santee Sioux, their cousins who had lived east of the Missouri, had escaped to the grandmother's country after the Minnesota troubles and were allowed to stay. And was it not a fact that some of his Lakotas still had in their families the medals (King George the Third's) for fighting for the white father during the big war with the Americans? Couldn't it be said they were still British Indians? Perhaps they could have peace of mind and spirit on the other side of the Medicine Road where, they had heard, the grandmother's red-coated soldiers were few.

With a thousand warriors at his call, however, it wasn't long before Bull was in the fray again. The soldiers started to build a fort at the junction of the Tongue and Yellowstone Rivers. Bull was infuriated. There were skirmishes because it seemed the whites never learned. He decided to talk to them in their own language, by placing a pen on paper. He dictated a note to half-breed Johnny Brughière who translated Bull's words. (The Indians called Brughière "Big Leggings" because when he ran into their camp from the white man's law, proclaiming he was their brother, he was wearing cowboy chaps.)

"I want to know what you are doing on this road. You scare all the buffalo away. I want to hunt in this place. I want you to turn back from here. If you don't, I will fight you again. I want you to leave what you have got here, and turn back from here. I am your friend – Sitting Bull."

The note was attached to a stick so that the soldiers could see it. They did see it and they were itching for a fight.

In late October, four months after the Little Big Horn, Sitting Bull had a face-to-face meeting with Colonel Nelson A. Miles. Miles, a tenacious Indian fighter, had been moved to the northern plains from Fort Leavenworth to handle the last vestiges of resistance. His Indian spies had kept him informed of Bull's movements.

The colonel, flanked by his escort, an officer and five rankers, stepped out in front of a line of about 400 Bluecoats and artillery. His unmilitary attire – an ankle-length coat with bear-fur trimming – provided the Indians with an instant name for the soldier chief: Bear Coat.

Sitting Bull walked toward the soldier line with four bodyguards and met Bear Coat half way. They sat on the ground.

There was no customary smoking of the pipe. All expressions of ceremonial cordiality were ignored. They sat hunched against the prairie cold, facing each other, Miles getting his first impressions of his infamous adversary; a strong, hardy, deliberate-looking aborigine with large, sharp features, high cheek bones, thin lips, and taut under the jaw, all indications of determination and force. Big Leggings did the interpreting.

Calm and well-mannered, Bull asked Bear Coat why he was in the hunting lands with so many soldiers. Miles replied, honestly, he was after the Indians. Bull wanted to know how the soldiers knew where the Indians were hunting.

"I not only knew where you were, I know where you are going," Miles replied.

"Where am I going?" Bull shot back.

"You intend to stay here three days and then hunt buffalo," said Miles.

Bull rankled at the thought of spies in his camp. His manner changed; his jaw compressed, his lips were thinner. Each man was suspicious of the other's intentions, wary of an enfilading attack or trap. A young warrior slipped a carbine under Bull's robe; others came to sit with him.

Bull berated Miles that the country belonged to the Indians, not the white man. He said the white man had never lived who loved an Indian, and a true Indian had never lived who did not hate the white man.

"The Creator made me an Indian. He did not make me an agency Indian and I do not intend to be one."

Next morning the colonel moved his troops in the direction of the Tetons. Bull walked out again with a flag of truce. The chief came on strongly and demanded the exodus of the whites and their military posts from the buffalo land. Miles responded with a hard line. He demanded the Sioux give up all their horses and weapons, in effect all their wealth, and place their future in the hands of the U.S. Government.

"You will be pursued until you are driven out of the country, or until you drive the troops out! I will allow you to return to your camp. In fifteen minutes, if you don't accept our terms, we will open fire."

The Indians took Miles at his word and ran for their horses. The troops advanced and the shooting started. The Indians replied and set fire to the prairie without being able to gather all their property and dried meat.

One who didn't scatter with them was Big Leggings, once befriended by Sitting Bull. Now he was doing the talking for Bear Coat and persuading some of the chiefs to return to the Missouri agencies, including one of Bull's nephews, White Bull. He and his followers went to the Cheyenne River. For him, and the others, the old life had come to an end. The soldiers took their guns and horses, and again there was talk of white men's trickery, of holding their relatives hostage, of false words.

In November of '76, General-in-Chief W. Tecumseh Sherman, in a report to the U.S. Secretary of War, stated: "Col. Miles reports his purpose to replenish his supplies, to turn north, and follow this last desperate band to the death. The winter is close at hand and there is great danger from the weather in that high latitude but...I trust that we will make an end to Sitting Bull."

The chief nevertheless continued his obstinate and warring ways. The winter was a hard one on the frigid plains; there was no fresh meat, and in the spring the Big Muddy washed away many of their lodges and belongings.

Dispirited, anguished and worn out, but his coveted prestige and independence intact, Sitting Bull looked to the north, toward the stone heaps that marked the border where the *Shaglashapi* (Redcoats) took over from the *Mini-hanskapi* (Longknives).

# ❖❖❖ Survival of the Fittest

❖❖❖ Jean-Louis Légaré, a French Canadian, was the principal resident trader at Wood Mountain. He had established himself there in 1870, in turbulent and precarious times when the Indians were fighting each other and the traffickers and wolfers were preying on natives and animals without scruple and certainly without fear of punishment. The institutions of statutory law and security of life or property were unknown to the indigenous majority and unrecognized by the white minority: in the spring of that year the territory was in an uproar after a contingent of U.S. troopers had set upon a camp of Peigans just south of the 49th parallel and had indiscriminately killed 170 men, women and children.

Any form of fundamental survival demanded unremitting perseverance, caution, tact, courage and resourcefulness. Légaré was blessed with such qualities. He managed to stay alive in isolation – and stay in business. He also managed to stay in good health, for smallpox was widespread, particularly among the Indians, but there were still about 25,000 of them within possible striking distance – and strike they did. His camp was once plundered by two hundred Assiniboines. The whisky-runners and wolfers, while not constant visitors, were everywhere, roving at will in small packs, and they were mostly Americans. These were anxious days – and nights – for legitimate businessmen. There were inflammatory yarns of drink-crazed warriors brandishing buffalo rifles, of settlers on their way north from the States being ambushed and murdered.

Halfbreed traders calling at Légaré's told the story of one frontiersman who was in Benton for supplies. "How's trade?" he was asked. "We're a whoopin' it up!" was the reply. They said that's how the whisky fort, the focal point of lawlessness, got its name.

Drastic changes were in the offing though. Little did the whisky-peddlers realize, during the zenith of their transgressions, that they were in the throes of impending disaster. That destiny could not be imagined in the early seventies. How could it be? The desperado trespassers, to use a phrase of a Bay company employee at Fort Qu'Appelle, were rampaging and rampant.

Jean-Louis, as he was known to the Indians, halfbreeds and whites, appeared to be immune to the upheaval around him. A tall, dominating and handsome figure, a bushy black beard emphasizing his swarthiness, Légaré was a rather dignified and quiet person. His size and his silence gave him an image of a square-dealing man close to his religion. In business for profit, he was far from avaricious, being a courteous and often unselfish benefactor of destitute Indians. His door was open to all comers. In his mid-thirties, he had been away from home (St-Gabriel-de-Brandon) for more than ten years. A descendant of the Acadians, the son of a farmer who had many children but few possessions, Jean-Louis had developed a yearning for a better life, for some excitement and some money, and so he took the road to the factories of the United States, wandering lucklessly from place to place before deciding to join two uncles at a settlement known as Little Canada near St. Paul, Minnesota. Eventually he got a job as a fur trader's clerk, capitalized on his aptitude, and when he became unemployed again traipsed off, alone, but not penniless, into the Dakota wilds, then north in 1870 across the new frontier to La Petite Montagne de Bois (Little Woody).

Légaré had found his world. Next spring, in '71, he escorted fifteen cartloads of pelts to Pembina, a journey of misfortune that took fifty days during which the teamsters ran out of food. They were ready to eat their horses. Légaré and a young companion, diverted by the overflowing Souris River, rode two hundred miles in four days for emergency rations.

That same year Jean-Louis met Manitoban George Fisher at Prairie du Cheval Blanc (St-François-Xavier). Fisher's commercial horizons also extended to the Canadian north-west. Légaré signed on as a partner for one-third of the profits and departed for the wilderness with two thousand dollars' worth of trade goods, mainly flour, tobacco, hunting equipment and a small herd of horses. He found his customers camped at Wood Mountain.

The times were prosperous. There were plenty of hides worth up to three dollars apiece. By the spring of '73 Légaré was one of the well-heeled traders on the prairie. His marriage to Marie Ouellette was remarkable for its style, and the Manitoba-bound honeymooners, their cart decorated with blue cotton, steered a stupendous convoy of eight hundred Red River carts to the hunting grounds, the all-wood, grating vehicles, three abreast, guarded by a small Métis army of captains and sentinels and Cree hangers-on.

Late in '73, when the surveyors were marking the international boundary, Légaré was returning from the Red River with $14,000 in merchandise that he would be trading for furs. Worried that Wood Mountain might soon be placed, geographically, in the United States, he opened a store where he found the surveyors, confident the delineation of the frontier had him secure in the Canadian possession. In May of the following year all his goods were seized by American officials upon accusations he had been evading duty payments. The surveyors, it seemed, had displaced his new store south of their line. Every fur he had collected was confiscated. His loss was about $9,000.

When they heard what had befallen Jean-Louis, the neighbourhood Santee Sioux proposed that all local Americans be killed and the furs restored to their owner. The trader, backed by a roving French-born priest from Wood Mountain, Father Jean-Joseph Lestanc, talked them out of their drastic retribution.

Back at Wood Mountain with his wife, Légaré easily made up his losses. Inflation had pushed up the price of a hide to eight dollars. The market was booming. Also he had government contacts to supply five outposts with 25,000 pounds of buffalo meat (at fifteen cents a pound). Safe delivery would be a problem.

Since the end of September, 1876, NWMP messengers had been flitting back and forth across the boundary with information on the whereabouts of the Sioux, who were being chased in all directions after their defeat of Custer. The U.S. authorities could only speculate about their position; Walsh was of the opinion that a large band, possibly a thousand strong, was within ten miles of the border, eighty or so miles south-east of Fort Walsh, heading in the direction of Légaré's store. It had been reported to him they were meanwhile preparing to attack Fort Peck on the Missouri and Fort Belknap on the Milk River, both in Montana. Walsh sent out his couriers to the two forts, also to Fort Benton, with appropriate warnings.

The Benton newspaper, the *Record*, complimented the major for this action: "The thanks of every white settler in northern Montana are due Major Walsh for his timely notice of impending danger....These generous acts cannot be too highly commended, and we hope they will be properly appreciated by a grateful people." The paper also reported that the major ("the wide-awake commander of the Mounted Police at Cypress Mountains") had made twelve arrests of whisky-sellers in one week. "The major seems determined to carry out the laws...."

In November, Walsh was informed by his scouts that the vanguard of U.S. Sioux were plodding on toward Wood Mountain from the south. The going was slow. The stark, paralysing extremes of winter had come early. Northerly winds swept down the gullies and timbered valleys with a biting ferocity that froze the earth and the living things upon it.

At Wood Mountain the cold continued unabated. In the afternoon of the seventeenth, when it seemed the wind would take the forehead off a man, Jean-Louis was in his drafty log house, which was chinked with grass, buffalo hair and clay, talking with two men of the five Métis families wintering in the immediate neighbourhood. Through the window frame, covered with buffalo calves' skins, scraped until they were translucent, they saw twelve horsemen approaching, all with heads down, bodies bent into the wind.

They came straight to the window and stayed on their horses. They were covered with all-enveloping buffalo robes, the hair inside, and they were attempting to look into the store. Their features were hardly discernible, but they were undoubtedly Indians. A couple pressed their faces closer to the window; stern, dark, sharp-lined faces with big noses, great cheek bones and searching, cautious red-brown eyes. The three whites tried not to pay any particular attention to them.

The Indians stayed at the window, silently and unexpressively, for more than half an hour before one dismounted and opened the door, walked in a little way, looked around, and stood motionless for several minutes, the door open all the while. He was obviously apprehensive and uneasy in the presence of white men. Then he advanced, with an American carbine in his hands, ever-so quietly and slowly farther into the cabin, across the bare floor with the stealth of a cat approaching a mouse, not looking at Jean-Louis or his companions. He sat down on the floor at the far end of the room.

He was an oldish man, somewhat haggard-looking, and appeared not to be in good health. He was wearing a handsome ring. One by one he signalled his furry associates; they too ignored the white men. They sat in a circle. The door stayed open.

Légaré, familiar with the ways of the Santee and Yankton Sioux and impervious to the precautions and suspicion being displayed by his uncommunicative visitors, waited quietly for them to make their next move.

For going on two hours they sat on the floor, shrouded in their buffalo robes as the wintry blasts gusted through the doorway. Then the Indian who had come in first quite suddenly jumped to his feet, walked toward the white men wrapped in their blanket-coats, shook hands with formality, and returned to his place. One by one the others did the same. Each one of them was adorned with booty, gold and silver watches with chains being most conspicuous around their necks.

Then one of the small band stood again, not the man who hitherto had dictated the procedure. This other one was middle-aged, plainly or moderately dressed, and even by Indian looks had very dark-brown features. He was the official orator of the party.

"We left the Black Hills, our country, because the Americans are very bad. We could not sleep, and we heard that the Big Woman [Queen Victoria] was very good to her children and keeps them in peace. We have come to this place so that our children may sleep without worry."

Légaré understood. The Indian spokesman, a sensitive and emotional man with proud bearing, said they wanted to trade, and he told Légaré that if he would give them something to hunt with – powder, ball and caps – and some tobacco they would trade with him. Légaré gave them about $30 worth of goods and they left.

The twelve horsemen turned away from the lonely cabin and rode back to their camp near the international boundary. They had been sent northwards to scout the land, to see if there were enemies in the immediate path. Légaré, accustomed as he was to all manner of Indian drop-ins, had no idea who his customers were. He was used to such official oratory and ceremony, the procedure of the Indians. He had just shrugged.

A few days later he met Walsh on the Cypress trail and the major told him that he had in fact been introduced to the vanguard of Sitting Bull's piecemeal army. Up till then, Légaré hadn't even heard about the fate of Custer's command. It was therefore with some trepidation that he returned to his Wood Mountain store to tackle an uncertain future.

Walsh had also informed him that the Indian who had preceded the others into his store was Little Knife, still a dashing and gallant leader despite his ailments; the official spokesman was Crow, a friend of Sitting Bull, an orator of note amoung the tribes.

Little Knife's account to the council of his session with the white trader encouraged seventy families of Teton Sioux to move kit and caboodle around Légaré's post. In two days the encampment had mushroomed to about 500 men, 1,000 women and 1,400 children. Their evident wealth consisted of more than 3,000 horses and thirty or so U.S. Army mules, the trophies of their skirmishes with the Longknives during the meandering into Canada. This dangerous array of fighting strength shortly moved to the protection of the timber, four miles east of Légaré, next to the established village of 150 lodges of Sisseton (Santee) Sioux who regarded White Eagle as their chief.

The Sissetons had crossed the border following the Minnesota Massacre and had established themselves peacefully, and although they were related to their newly arrived neighbours, they did not greet them with open arms as brothers. White Eagle, in council with the Teton chiefs, took it upon himself to warn his distant relatives, as best he could, that unless they were prepared and willing to abide by the laws set forth by the Redcoats they would not be welcome on Canadian soil – by him or the authorities.

Two days later Walsh was on the scene to lay down the details of the law. He was saluted by White Eagle, who said he and his followers were uneasy being so close to their Teton cousins, but felt the Tetons would not be troublesome, even taking into account that their numbers included several war chiefs who were dedicated and uncompromising foes of white men.

The major, with White Eagle, called an immediate council, and in the absence of Légaré (he had been called to the side of his wife who was dying in Cypress after being thrown by a horse) all the Sioux dignitaries and warriors of distinction gathered in his store. Walsh, with his own men, and White Eagle, were in the centre. All around the Redcoats was this formidable mob of war-hardened and embittered hostiles. White Eagle spoke the first words. He introduced Walsh and explained the purpose of his visit.

Walsh, most determined to create the impression that the police could be firm and fair, displayed his best soldierly manners and instructed them, at the outset, that they would have to obey the laws of the great white mother when in her country. Through an interpreter, he said he was going to ask them questions and their answers would be carried by him to the great mother's great chief.

"Do you know you are in the country of the great white mother?"

"*Hou!*". . ."Yes," says the interpreter.

"What have you come here for?"

Many voices are heard. The interpreter breaks in: "They say that they have been driven out of their homes by the Americans and come here seeking peace....They say that their grandfathers fought beside the soldiers of the white mother and long ago had told them they would find peace in her land....Their relatives, the Santees, have found the truth of this many years ago."

The interpreter told Walsh that Black Moon and all his people, and everyone else in the camp, had not slept soundly for years. They wanted a place where they could live peacefully. They were tired of being hunted.

Silence. Walsh looked around the cabin.

"Are you going to stay north of the boundary during the winter and in the spring go back to your own country to fight again against the Americans?

"No!" was the emphatic reply (no interpretation needed).

Then more animated remarks were directed to the interpreter. "They all say they want to stay in this country....They ask the red-coated officer to ask the white mother to have pity on them."

One by one, several of the chiefs, among them Black Moon, Little Knife, The Man Who Crawls and Long Dog, made their own pleas for the people of their bands. Walsh told them they would have to be as law-abiding as the Sissetons and all other Indians enjoying refuge in Canada. They all affirmed they intended to obey the wishes of the Redcoat chief (Macleod). Walsh stressed they would not be allowed to make war on the Americans and then return to Canada for sanctuary. If they had such thoughts they had better go back now and stay there.

The next day a group of leading chiefs, with White Eagle as their spokesman, called upon Walsh, and after the usual exchange of greetings, and the smoking of the ceremonial pipe, they asked the major for a small quantity of ammunition. They said all the people were hungry and their hunters had only makeshift lances (knives attached to long sticks) to kill the buffalo. Some of them were using bows and arrows and others were even trying to lasso the animals to kill them with knives. They said many of the women and children were close to starvation.

Walsh said that the great mother did not want anyone in her country to starve. After an assurance that the ammunition would be used only for hunting and in no circumstances would be sent to the hostiles south of the line, he agreed to leave instructions to Légaré to provide them with bullets, powder and balls. When the Tetons heard this they were elated and thanked Walsh profusely.

Actually the trader had about 2,000 rounds of ammunition for distribution, about two rounds to a family, and there was no danger that any would be carried across the border; the refugees needed every round. And by coincidence, for the first time in many years, there were plenty of buffalo in the region.

This meant more furs and robes for Légaré and more ammunition and provisions for the Sioux. There were full stomachs and much rejoicing in the camps. And there were no Longknives to bother them. They hadn't been so well off and happy in years. Légaré found the Tetons to be unrealistic bargainers. For a $4 pelt they would expect up to $30 worth of goods. They were indeed rough clients demanding his utmost patience and discretion.

The major and his party, during their return to Fort Walsh, encountered severe hardship. The journey took nine days, twice as long as the outgoing trek. They were buffeted by immense snow storms and demoralizing cold. The guides lost their bearings time and again and the men floundered hopelessly, tramping about and hammering themselves to keep from freezing to death. The horses suffered terribly, five of them died, and when the men's rations ran out it seemed they would have to shoot the remaining animals for food. Fortunately, they stumbled upon a small herd of buffalo and managed to kill a good fat cow. The sighting of the stockade at Fort Walsh prompted some appropriate, earthy comments.

After this experience it was Walsh's decision that scrutiny of the Sioux refugees could not be maintained from the Cypress Hills. He recommended that a non-commissioned officer and two men be stationed at Wood Mountain and that a similar sub-post be established at the eastern edge of the Cypress Hills.

The East End post, as it became known, would be about fifty roundabout miles from Fort Walsh on the trail to Wood Mountain, which was another 125 miles or so eastwards, when dry. Not far from Légaré's Wood Mountain trading post there were some small log buildings that had been used as a Boundary Commission depot and these were repaired to accommodate the policemen.

Compared to Fort Walsh, this cluster of flimsy buildings was a slum. The log huts had mud roofs and mud floors and there was hardly any furniture. For resting and sleeping, the red-coated Sioux-watchers, and later their guide and interpreter, Joseph "Blackbird" Morin, stretched buffalo hides between a wall and posts driven into the dirt. It was an insecure compromise, as was indeed the entire situation.

There, at the back door of the Wood Mountain post, so to speak, was Black Moon with about 3,000 Tetons including some of the most notorious war chiefs of the seven tribes – Hunkpapa, Minneconjou, Oglalas, Brûlés, Sans-Arcs, Two-Kettles and Blackfoot (the last named not connected with the mighty Blackfoot nation). And Black Moon, who had the stature of a hereditary leader, could be ranked among the most uncompromising, irascible, and in the Indian manner, nationalistic. He had to be, for no man could continue to gather the respect and allegiance of all the hostiles without abiding qualities of strong leadership.

Black Moon was one of the chiefs who would not touch a pen, as some of his kinsmen had done, to submit to the white men's treaties and give away the Indians' domain. "How can men live like cattle on a reservation, surrounded by whites who would even stop them from visiting other reservations to see their relatives?" he asked. A strong man in war and council, a man with the wealth of many horses, a man who could see beyond the soldier-chiefs' promises of amnesty, Black Moon said the Indian was not born to beg for his food or to dig up the soil; he was born to cherish the land, to live with nature and respect it, and to hunt the buffalo so that he could be free and healthy.

54

It was Black Moon, the realist, who saw clearly that the entire nation was being threatened by encroachment and did not have a leader who could gather the people about him to say the things that had to be said, to do the things that had to be done. When the brave hearts and head men of the seven tribes (seven, the divine number) gathered for the long smoke in the sacred circle to talk of the evil days and of the agency chiefs signing away the land, Black Moon proposed that Sitting Bull be appointed war chief of all the hostile Sioux, and that Crazy Horse, the unruly and unpretentious spirit of the Oglalas, the one with the fair skin who was nicknamed Curly, be appointed second in command.

These two incorrigibles rekindled the flames of fury that smouldered in the souls of all those who still longed for the unrestricted ways of their forefathers, but the old loafers, those who pitched their tepees close to the forts and collected rations at the agencies, would not recognize Bull's authority. The young men, though, were restless for adventure and it gladdened their hearts that the Great Spirit was listening to Sitting Bull and Crazy Horse.

Black Moon had encouraged Sitting Bull to commune with the Creator, to purify himself, to seek wisdom, to ask for His pity, and through visions to learn what was best for the nation, and he officiated at the ceremony of the sacred pole when Bull, stripped to the waist, had fifty pieces of sacrificial skin cut from each arm, when he danced and whistled and fasted, as the Lakotas do, facing the sun.

The people then looked around and saw their new strength with pride and hope. No longer would they be few in numbers, dispersed in small groups like easy game for the soldiers' guns.

# ❖❖❖ Prisoners in the Camp

❖❖❖ During the first weeks of 1877 Jean-Louis Légaré, staying close to his Wood Mountain trading post, found himself virtually penned in by the warriors who less than a year ago had inflicted a major defeat upon the pride of the U.S. Army.

His store became a focal point of Sioux attention. Everybody trooped in to gape, trade or gossip. Many of the Indians were getting their first close-up of the white man and his goods. They jammed the floor space, mind-shopping, imperturbably motionless as others came in with pelts and furs to swap. Every day was market day. Before long his storeroom was piled up with robes and his shelves were shorn of the commodities that appealed most to his clientele – tea, sugar, tobacco, and of course, ammunition, butcher knives and blankets.

Jean-Louis, through his natural tact and fairmindedness, established a rapport with his new neighbours. Inevitably there were moments of consternation and misunderstanding. Nevertheless, he was relieved to find that his customers reacted moderately. Although overly demanding across the counter for what they had to trade, they were rarely offensive. He had a way with them.

At Fort Walsh, buffeted by the wintry storms, the commander hunched over his stove pondering the options of how to deal with the refugees. Once the snow gave way it would be as inevitable as the spring grass that the warriors would be testing the mettle of the police, fewer than a hundred of them, mere pin-points on his unreliable table-length map.

What would happen when Sitting Bull, as seemed most likely, pitched his lodges on Canadian territory, on the soil where for generations the Blackfoot or the Crees had reigned? Would the Blackfoot and the unpredictable, unruly Cree chiefs form an alliance to preserve for themselves the diminishing herds of buffalo,

56

or, heaven forbid, would all the Indians band together to scourge the valleys and plains of whites? There was one uncertain consolation. Crowfoot, chief of the ever-dangerous Blackfoot Confederacy, had declared his intention to abide by the laws of the Redcoats. In return, the police, on behalf of the Queen, had guaranteed to protect his interests. But there was no doubt that the influx of the Sioux, hardened by war, would affect the balance of power and could readily upset commitments already consecrated at solemn ceremonies of goodwill and trust.

The testing time was at hand. In March, as the trails and wagon ruts were revealed again from under the covering of melted snow, the traders, halfbreeds and Indians trickled in with consistent reports that Sitting Bull and his followers were slowly en route to Canada. The consensus was that Bull – or "Ol' Sit" as he was identified by some of the frontiersmen – was managing to keep ahead of the pursuing U.S. troops, that he had crossed the Big Muddy, and that his outriders were leading the way to Wood Mountain. By April, the roving informants had him moving up the White Mud River (more like a creek in some places). The White Mud flowed easterly and southerly from the Cypress Hills into the Milk River which meandered and looped south-easterly into the Missouri.

Walsh decided it would be opportune to move closer to the border to determine the number of Sioux refugees, and to be on hand to instruct them concerning their obligations once in Canada. A contingent of police and scouts traveled eastwards for about 120 miles to a point that crossed a trail from the south. Here, near the Pinto Horse Buttes and the Indian Cliff, the westerly extremity of Wood Mountain, Walsh established his base camp, about forty miles north of the border.

The days and nights were cold. The major quickly had his scouts in action scouring the coarse, undulating land as far as the boundary. Not one of them encountered signs of Indian movement.

Walsh was unable to rest. It was not in his nature to just sit there and wait. He was compelled to move intuitively and swiftly in the manner he had dealt with Big Bear, the infamous Cree war chieftain who had threatened to attack Fort Walsh: the major had confronted him with police strength as he sternly lectured him on the virtues of keeping the peace.

Now, in this latest Sitting Bull scare, Walsh decided that if there were no more Indians infiltrating across the line, he would have to cross the boundary with a small party to find out whether the Sioux were in reality moving northwards. He started off with three scouts: Louis Daniels, a Mounted Policeman from his hometown of Prescott; his old-faithful Léveillé; and "Blackbird" Morin, a halfbreed.

Despite the uncertainty of their mission, and realizing they might find themselves confronted by Sitting Bull and his braves who hitherto had not responded favourably to any suggestions of white authority, the four men rode off in a manner that reflected the invigoration of the spring-like weather. It was a thoroughly exhilarating morning, the almost sudden emergence of new life kindled by the warmth of the deep blue sky upon the crusty soil. The prairie that had been burned over in the fall was beginning to display its new crop of buffalo grass, and after a long and arduous winter the scent of spring in the open land gave Walsh and his companions a feeling of well-being and earnestness. The sun came up from behind the peak of Indian Cliff, that landmark of a bluff, bold and stark, and the four horsemen kept it in sight for twenty miles before they changed course directly to the south in quest of the White Mud River.

They stopped at a place known as the Mud House, which was nothing more than a hole dug in the river bank and the front filled up with loose timber dragged up from the river bottoms. The makeshift shelter was used in the winter by halfbreeds from the north who were trading with the Indians. At this point the river bank was about 300 feet high; in places almost perpendicular.

Walsh and the scouts scanned the wind-swept remoteness for any traces of Indian presence, for any speck or flash that would decide for them the next direction to take. They knew a large band of Yankton Sioux, dissatisfied with life on the American agency at Fort Peck, were in the area with notions of settling down at Wood Mountain where they could get ammunition to hunt, a concession that had been denied them by the Bluecoats.

Below was the valley, about a mile wide in places. Through it, along the south-western edge, ran the White Mud, or the Shining River as the Indians called it because of the bright visual effects of the mica deposits embedded in the banks.

The riders, in single file, swayed down a well-used trail leading to a ford. At the river's edge they were still undecided as to whether they should carry on directly southwards or scout along the banks, east and west. From the level of the water, the four men were confronted with the forbidding desolation of *les mauvaises terres,* the bad lands; it was scarcely possible to see beyond a hundred yards.

The major opted to cross the river and split his party into two; Daniels and Léveillé to follow the river, which veered toward the south, and Walsh and Morin to turn westerly. The plan was to make a fifteen mile circular tour and return to the ford to camp for the night.

Six miles out, Morin spotted the first traces of Indian outriders. Close by he detected the main track of a large band – foot and hoof prints, droppings, and travois ruts – that had been moving recently in a northerly direction. Walsh had no doubt in his mind that he was not far behind a sizeable migration of Tetons. Daniels and Léveillé came across the same clues and they turned their horses around to follow them. When they noticed later the horseshoe imprints of their two companions they realized that Walsh and Morin were also on the trail of the band. They spurred their horses to catch up.

Walsh and his scout, bending over the shoulders of their mounts and pointing out to each other the tell-tale marks, kept on the Sioux trail that was taking them closer to the Mud House ford, the point where they had crossed the river. They reached the banks of the White Mud again and were picking their way through the broken ground when they saw an Indian on a hilltop in front of them; another appeared to their right, then one to their left, and before long, out of rifle range, there were Indians all around them. They were moving through outlying pickets and knew they must be close to a powerful encampment.

The two riders passed around the base of a large butte. Beyond were the stone piles that marked the international boundary. There they got their first view of the Sioux band that was just then making camp. Despite the surveillance of the Indian scouts who had known two whites were approaching the lodges, the sudden appearance of Walsh and Morin on the other side of the river alarmed those who saw them first. The women and children started to shout frantically. The men ran for their weapons; the old women hurriedly began to dismantle the lodges that were in the process of being put up. The hobbled horses of the warriors, which were being fed and looked after by the boys, were herded and rushed into camp, and in a very short time there was a stampede of women and children for the hills behind the tepees on the north bank.

The warriors, believing the white intruders to be U.S. Army scouts who had been following them from the Missouri, formed up menacingly at the ford, working their horses back and forth to get them ready for a fight. Walsh and Morin stood their ground on the south side, about fifty yards away from the agitated Sioux.

Fortunately, when Walsh had made the decision to search in two directions he had taken Morin, the Sioux halfbreed, with him. The Indians refused to allow Walsh to cross the stream. Deceived by the blue coat Walsh was wearing, they shouted that the two of them were Americans spying for the Longknives.

Walsh told Morin what to say in reply. He shouted back that they were not American but guardians of the peace for the great white mother north of the line.

While they were trying to convince the Sioux, Léveillé and Daniels suddenly appeared, galloping over the brow of a hill. This further alarmed the Indians. Many of the warriors, expecting at any second to see the blue uniforms of the U.S. cavalry charging at the camp, turned away from the river in a flurry of hooves, dust and war cries and raced up the hills to take up defensive positions. The major, now with his three aides, stayed at the river's edge.

When it became apparent the encampment was not on the verge of an onslaught, the Sioux resumed their shouting conversation across the river.

"Have no fear," Walsh told them through Morin. "We are not messengers of evil." The four horsemen started to cross; the Indians drew their guns and reached for their arrows. Léveillé, indignant that Walsh should be threatened in this way, raised his rifle. The major told him to put it back in his sheath and be patient.

His horse now in the water, Walsh continued his talking.

"Tell them," he told Morin, summoning the most flowery language he could muster, "that we know they have suffered from treachery and raids on their camps and their women have not had a comfortable night's rest for a year....

"Tell them that we know that when they crossed the boundary into Canada they were looking for safety and that when they reached that boundary every heart was filled with joy and every soul thankful for the Great Spirit's protection....

"Tell them we understand why they are thrown into alarm... that we are determined to stay here until we convince them that they have a wrong impression."

With this the four rode into the camp. Suspiciously regarded, Walsh answered many questions. The warriors who had prepared to fight from the hills returned, and the daringly curious women and children came as close as they could to see for themselves these strangers. Walsh persuaded them to carry on putting up their lodges and was able to pacify their anxieties. He asked who was the chief and was told it was Four Horns.

From a group of warriors stepped an old man of fine stature and light features. Tall (about six feet) and upright, he appeared to be at least seventy years of age. Walsh extended his hand and Four Horns grasped it. The superintendent asked him what tribe he was leading.

"We are Teton Sioux of the Hunkpapa band and followers of my adopted son Sitting Bull," he replied. He told Walsh that Bull was still south of the Missouri but also looking toward the land of the white mother.

It had been Four Horns, more renowned as a durable politican than a warrior, although he had been wounded in battle, who had recognized that Sitting Bull, despite the prior claims of his own sons, should be proposed as the principal warrior chieftain because of his dash and bravery in the fights, his peace-making among the Tetons, his generosity with captured horses, and his prophesies which were as true as a balanced arrow.

Four Horns – old Moccasin Top some called him affectionately – was prominent in the ceremonials when Bull was appointed war leader of the recalcitrant Sioux, when the ornamented pipe was lighted with the proper flourishes, the mouthpiece pointed to the earth in a entreaty to keep the people strong, and gracefully towards the four directions so that the people would not suffer from the winds, and then in the direction of the sun for the people to have clear vision to avoid all the dangers.

At this moment it was Four Horns who needed the clear vision.

Walsh assured the chief that he and his three men were representatives of the white mother and that Four Horns and his village were on British soil (probably just a mile or so inside). After a pause for the interpretation, Walsh carried on with his message: there were definite laws to obey in Canada and he wanted to explain these to all the chiefs, sub-chiefs, the elders and every warrior.

Four Horns agreed. He did not know the ways of the white mother and he asked Walsh for adequate time to call a council. The visitors were invited to enter a lodge and rest. It was by now late in the afternoon and the four of them had been in the saddle since early morning. They were glad to find a place out of the wind to stretch their horse-weary limbs for a while.

They had been led to an unusually large tepee made of newly scraped buffalo skins. Walsh, who had an eye for orderliness and cleanliness, noticed immediately the refined spaciousness and handsome interior. He had never before seen anything quite so elaborate and dignified on the plains.

He was actually in the lodge belonging to Little Saulteau. Walsh noted that his host, about fifty years, was likewise a clean individual whose attire included a fine blanket around his waist and feathers of the most valuable kind in his hair. Little Saulteau, although not a chief, was obviously a man of considerable influence within the band.

The lodge was divided into sections and the four guests were surprised by the degree of comfort. They reclined against a wicker back rest made of willow sticks and held together by buffalo sinew, the closest furnishings to a white man's armchair. The guests rested just inside from the entrance, which was covered by a flap of skin.

Walsh observed some of the sections in the tepee were curtained with brightly coloured blankets nicely looped up at the bottom. Rugs and blanket-mats covered most of the grass.

The centre section of the lodge, the one opposite Walsh and facing the entrance, was reserved for the master of the dwelling. In the section to the master's right was the decorated area reserved for his two wives, and Walsh was attracted by their good looks and neatness of dress. They got on well together, were apparently not jealous of each other, and appeared willing and happy to share their household duties. The women purposefully concealed their curiosity, their way of demonstrating good manners.

The next section along was occupied by his two daughters, one about eighteen and the other sixteen. Their quiet demeanour impressed Walsh and he noticed how beautifully turned out they were in long deerskin dresses elaborately designed with quills and beads. They too tried not to pay attention to their father's guests and carried on with their bead work, geometric designs for moccasins.

In the section to the left of Little Saulteau was a young lady of about 20 years, a niece who was visiting (and was stranded) from the Red Cloud agency which was situated hundreds of miles to the south, beyond the Black Hills, close to the white men's forts of Laramie and Robinson. It was the custom for Indians to visit their relatives in other bands and this young lady was with the Four Horns people when they tangled with the Longknives and had been unable to return to her parents.

Her name was White Tooth, he was told, and Walsh agreed that she could indeed be recognized as such. The sight of this young lady created a picture in his mind that he would remember in the years to come. She was one of the most sensuous women he had ever set eyes upon:

"Her black hair, with an auburn shade in it, dressed a well-shaped head and beautiful features. She had dark, soft, mild eyes and hands and feet delicately small and well-shaped; the feet looked as though they had never trodden upon the hard prairie but upon carpets all their life. She was tall and just slender enough to make her graceful. Of fair complexion, she looked as though she had not been much exposed to the sun or wind."

No doubt about it, Walsh was captivated. "Whiter or more beautiful teeth I never saw," he was to recall. "This girl was picturesquely dressed in garments of fine texture – silk, laces and cambrics of delicate shades all harmonizing and becoming to her."

To Walsh the sight of this Indian maiden, in these surroundings with these primitive people, was a revelation. He had always supposed Indian women and girls to be displeasing and unglamorous, very little more than haulers of wood and water, scrapers and curers of hides, makers and movers of tepees, or more basically, the cooks and chattels of the superior warrior-men who had but little respect for them and mistreated them. He had never seen Indian women at home before; now he had a real insight and he thought about these things as he rested.

He dozed off into a slumber of exhaustion and was angry and

irritable when awakened by Daniels who told him the Indians had been assembled to hear his words.

The hides had been rolled up from the bottom of the lodge so that Walsh could turn around and see and talk to the circle of chiefs. It seemed all the camp was there, the women peering over the shoulders of the men, and the children peeking from wherever they could. As he turned around fully to acknowledge his hosts, he could see these people were tired of war.

They were quiet. The councilors sat cross-legged, occupied by their thoughts. The warriors stood solemnly, chins in their hands. Their women waited apprehensively. And the children, it seemed, had forgotten how to play. For the first time they were going to hear from a white man who claimed to be a British chief. Would he try to return them to the land of the Longknives?

Walsh opened the council without ceremony. He addressed himself to Four Horns and asked the chief whether he knew that he and his people had crossed the U.S. line and were now on British territory. Four Horns said they all knew.

Walsh, turning again to his interpreter, said:

"And do you know there are laws here that everybody – white, red or black – have to obey, and that you and your followers will have to obey them or you cannot remain in this country?"

Four Horns, looking in the direction of interpreter Morin, replied:

"We are strangers to the customs of the white man and ask to be informed."

Walsh, sentence by sentence, as he had done at Wood Mountain, laid down the law.

"The laws you will have to obey are made by the consent of three hundred millions of Britons and these laws govern the conduct of every person who stands on British soil and every Briton defends them with his life...

"What they demand of you is that you will not kill man, woman or child, no matter what their colour may be....

"You will not steal....

"You will not give false testimony...."

The heads of the chiefs in the front rank of the circle turned from Walsh to his interpreter and back to Walsh as he continued to enumerate:

"You will not do injury of any kind to either person or property... and property of every kind (horses, oxen, wagons, tents, lodges, guns, robes, or any article whatsoever) must not be injured or damaged or disturbed or removed without the permission of the owner....

"The person of a woman or child must not be violated; it is the duty of every man to protect them – and this, of all our laws, is the most sacred....

"You must not cross from the north to the south side of the line to commit depredations....

"These are the laws you and your people, and all who may come after you, must obey. Upon every occasion you will find us ready to defend our position here, therefore make no mistakes that might turn against you....

"We shall be patient and do all we can to teach you about the conduct you must follow. In return, we expect your respect of our position....

"If you obey our laws your families can sleep soundly here, and you are safe as if walled around by a thousand warriors....

"But if you think you cannot conform to these laws, return to your own land because you cannot live on British soil, no more than fish can live without water."

Four Horns stood up and shook hands with Walsh. Then, with a sweeping gesture of an arm towards his compatriots tightly packed around the lodge, he said:

"We are tired. Our women and children are crying for rest. We want peace....

"We ask only to be allowed to hunt the buffalo.... Your words we take into our breasts; we will obey them.... Our fathers told us we were British Indians. In our families we have the white father's medals. We do not know why the white father gave us and our land to the Americans...."

As Four Horns was finishing his remarks an Indian courier rode into camp. He had come from the Missouri River and presented himself to the council, which is the way all important messengers are received. He shook the hands of Four Horns and the others forming the inner circle. He then stood before Walsh, stared at him impertinently, sat down opposite him and said nothing. He was evidently a man of some esteem, bold and aggressive, and in this instance, intent on making trouble.

His demeanour was sufficiently provocative and annoyingly

confident to alert the major to impending difficulties. Walsh knew enough about Indians to instinctively adopt an attitude of ridicule. These wild spirits could face bullets, but not ridicule.

Walsh smiled with a sort of sarcastic twist upon his lips, not overly offensive but certainly sufficient for the troublemaker to perceive. The messenger flushed under his dark skin and the anger grew in his face and this was seen by the Indians in the circle. No redman can stand to be ridiculed, especially in the midst of his brethren. Walsh realized that he too could not afford to be ridiculed. This would mean that he could not rule, even if he did get out of the camp alive.

The messenger spoke:

"How! The first time I met you was at Buford, on the Missouri. The last time was on the Yellowstone at the camp of Bear Coat [Miles].... You tell these people you are a Redcoat.... You are a Longknife American."

He stood up and pointed to the four directions of the earth, and called upon the people to listen to what he was going to say. He spoke rapidly in Sioux and Walsh got the gist from Morin. This arrogant upstart warned everyone not to be deceived by the white man's words; that he knew him; that he was an American spying upon the camp and wished to murder people while they slept; and that he and his companions should not be released until the country between the camp and the Missouri had been well scouted.

The messenger's words were received by the Sioux as the foreboding of a storm. There was restless consternation.

Walsh retained his composure and maintained his appearance of ridicule. He made sure everyone could see his contempt. He spoke up:

"I have been talking to you for a long time.... You heard all I said....Now if this man has told you the truth then I have deceived you.... But who is this man?...Does he belong to your tribe?...Do you know him that well?...Are you sure he is a Teton and a friend and not an enemy or traitor?"

Turning to face the courier, Walsh continued:

"What is your purpose in trying to deceive these people?... They say they have crossed into this land to rest from war...to let the smile return to the cheeks of their women...to let the children learn again how to play and amuse themselves as children do...Are you sorry to see them reach this condition?...Are you afraid that your occupation will be gone if they remain north of the Big Road?...Do you want to encourage these people to commit some crimes so that they may be refused shelter here and placed between two fires?...What have they ever done to you that you wish to destroy them?"

Walsh paused a moment, thinking of what next to say:

"Man, if you are not a devil look upon these poor women and children....If you have a heart, pity their tired and worn-looking faces....They are people of your nation and blood; I never saw them before today....And I pity them....With all the power at my command I will protect them from such men as you...."

Walsh paused.

"You may be mistaken in identity, deceived, and have taken me for some other person you saw on the Yellowstone River.... If so, I forgive you."

"No!" the Indian shouted. "I know you!"

"Know me?" Walsh lashed back, losing some of his calm.

"Yes!" replied the unflinching courier.

Walsh jumped up, pointed an accusing finger at his adversary, and forcefully called him a liar.

"You are a traitor and enemy of these people," he shouted. Then turning to Four Horns, he said:

"This man – I don't care who he is – is your enemy ... I advise you to keep a close watch on him."

Léveillé, who insisted on being close to Walsh at all times because of his attachment and a phobia that if anything happened to the major the Government would blame him, was getting more upset by the minute. He precipitated a tense moment when his fury exploded and he too called the Indian accuser a liar. The other three quieted him immediately.

The tenseness was acute; the silence unbearable. The two policemen and their two guides were surrounded by hundreds of desperate and embittered natives. What else could they do but stand their ground and display a conviction that their story was the true one?

No one moved; no one spoke. Then Four Horns, who in his earlier days had been a warrior to heed among all the Tetons, everwhere, motioned to Walsh.

He indicated he wanted him to remain in the camp.

"Why?" Walsh countered.

"We are alarmed by what we have heard here," Four Horns replied. "We thought we could sleep soundly tonight but the hearts of our women and children are beating with fear."

Walsh, slight in frame but firm in countenance, blatantly bargained with the old chief.

"I shall remain upon one condition – that you do not allow that man (pointing toward the courier) to leave the camp until tomorrow when I shall show you a rascal!"

This was agreed to. Then Walsh came up with another condition.

"I want to send a message and to hire two or three of your young men to carry it.....I shall pay them....They shall ride twenty miles southeast of here, across the line, to a place known as the Ruined or Burnt Timber [a bluff of timber that had been ravaged by fire]. There they will find a camp of Sioux under Medicine Bear and Black Horn who are Yankton agency chiefs....

"I want these young men to go to Medicine Bear and Black Horn and tell them that you have in your camp...and are detaining him as a prisoner...the White Forehead chief of the country north of the Big Road."

Four Horns heard these words with disapproval and grunted. He said he would send the messengers but did not want the word prisoner used.

"Oh, yes, I am a prisoner in your camp," Walsh countered. "If I tried to leave the camp your warriors would attempt to stop me....I don't want to bring trouble upon you by any disturbance, so I remain."

There was a brief Indian council and a small party rode off to the southeast.

The major, worn out by a hard day of riding and harangue, asked that the police horses be herded with those of the Sioux and watched over by the herders. This was done, and the four men were treated to a meal of baked buffalo meat. Then Daniels, Léveillé and Morin were led to a nearby lodge for sleep while Walsh retired to the Lodge of Little Salteau and White Tooth. A bed of robes had been prepared by one of the daughters.

It was with some relief and satisfaction and expectation that the Redcoat chief prepared for the night. He was banking that Medicine Bear and Black Horn – the latter in appearance and spirit a storybook Indian, in Walsh's eyes, and a character study for James Fenimore Cooper – would secure the next day.

He knew that outside his lodge there were guards; what he didn't know was that on this day he had confronted and had negotiated with the uncle of Sitting Bull.

Walsh slept in. Such comfort, such pleasure, such tiredness, he had not experienced in several days and his host had told the women of the lodge not to disturb him and to go about their business quietly. About ten o'clock in the morning, judging by the position of the sun, he stepped out into the Indian village and beheld a panorama the likes of which he could not have visualized.

From the cloudless blue sky the spring sunshine enveloped the camp, the surrounding hills, and the river. It was one of those rare mornings on the prairies when the softness of the air overcomes the chillness of the bones and a feeling of renewed strength and contentment combine in the human frame and spirit to encourage an effusion of goodwill and good health.

Walsh saw hundreds of hobbled horses feeding on the green spring grass, warriors sitting in groups on the little hilltops, young ladies in their brightly coloured dresses, quilled and beaded, walking about the camp with the grace of princesses. Whichever way he turned he saw women arranging their lodges, and others of them pegging hides and stretching them to dry under the sun, boys playing with bows and untipped arrows, little girls fondling and talking to their dolls and playing house with make-believe tepees, old men lounging and councilling in the shade of the lodges. It was truly a rare day.

Then, from somewhere down the valley, came the shrill cries of Indian war whoops. The effect was instant. The warriors on the hills jumped up. Just about everybody in the camp ran, lurched or stumbled up the slopes to join them, the old fat women puffing and panting to get a good view of the oncoming procession. Everybody, that is, except Walsh and his men. They stayed together close to the guest tepee. The major was hoping, and was now optimistic, that the newcomers were coming to save his second day in the camp.

They came into sight, Black Horn and Medicine Bear, the Yanktons, with the Teton couriers at their flanks, and behind about 200 armed, feathered and war-painted young men. It was a picture of unusual grandeur and flamboyant pomp, this war party moving along the grassy valley of the curving stream fringed with rose bushes and willows; the braves controlling their prancing mounts, plumed headdresses of natural colours flowing almost to the ground, and young riders putting on exaggerated displays of horsemanship for the benefit of the girls who ornamented, in waving groups, the backdrop of hills.

Above it all the hawks were sweeping the valley, red-tail hawks with big, broad wingspans, swirling round and round and screaming with high-pitched harshness. Into Walsh's mind flashed his boyhood stories of Attila and the Huns.

The last time Walsh had encountered Medicine Bear and Black Horn was during the first testing weeks at Fort Walsh when the Yankton war parties spilled over into the Cypress Hills, when he talked them into returning peacefully to the Big Muddy country. Now, after a brief greeting by Four Horns and much pointing in the direction of Little Salteau's lodge, the chiefs and the warriors, and behind them old men, women and children and dogs, moved to where the beleaguered Redcoats were waiting. Walsh braced himself, but he couldn't be prepared for what was to happen as the redskins approached. Black Horn, recognizing the major, heeled his horse into a trot, dismounted with great agility, ran towards Walsh and embraced him.

Nothing was ever more wild; nothing could be more grand. Again, the Walsh party was surrounded. Black Horn turned to acknowledge the hundreds of bystanders.

"Where is the man who said the White Forehead chief is a Longknife?" (Walsh received this name from some of the Indians because his forehead, sheltered by the pointed peak of his police helmet, was pale compared to the remainder of his sun-burned features.)

Everyone looked about. Not a voice was raised. Black Horn continued to harangue and Morin whispered the translation to Walsh.

"Let him come forward!" No one stepped into the circle. The Missouri messenger was nowhere in sight. He was not even in the camp. Realizing the folly of what he had said, and fearing the consequences when he saw the Yanktons arrive, he had fled with the help of a few of the young Tetons.

Four Horns was livid. Black Horn calmed him down.

"It is just as well."

"My friend," said Black Horn to Four Horns, as he took the arm of the Teton and nodded in the direction of Walsh, "this is the chief of the land north of the Big Road. His word is the law."

To make it official a council was called and the chief spokesman was Medicine Bear.

With the dignity befitting his stature in the inner circle of wise words, and with the sagacity of a disgruntled chief who wanted to court the favours of the Redcoats, Medicine Bear reiterated that Walsh was a British chief and that to live in the country north of the line they must obey the law as laid down by him and any who thought they could not do so would be advised to return to the Missouri.

"No man escapes justice and remains in the land of the White Forehead."

Black Horn was called to speak next.

"My friends, I came here prepared for war. When your messengers told me of what happened here and I asked them to describe the white man, I told them White Forehead was my friend and I gathered the warriors and left for your camp.

"I am glad to find no cause for me making war. The White Forehead has no hard words to say against you, and my heart is glad, for had he been injured this camp would not be standing now.

"Listen to his words; his tongue is not crossed."

Four Horns, a Teton elder with the gift of profound oratory, respected as a sensible head man among the people and close to the hearts and souls of the Hunkpapa, felt the moment was appropriate for a review of the last half century of Sioux history; the times he had lived through, times of great hunts, wars against their enemies (Crow and Arikara and Pawnee), the incursion of the white men into the hunting grounds, the disappearance of their brother the buffalo, and their 25-day flight from the Powder River to the great mother's land. He said they had lived on horse flesh for the past 15 days because the Americans were so close behind they couldn't stop to hunt.

With dignified solemnity he concluded with pledges to obey the laws of the Redcoat chief and apologized for doubting Walsh's words, and asked forgiveness.

Walsh, who had the upper hand, said to the council he accepted Four Horns' apology although he was displeased that the mischief-maker, the Missouri runner who bore a false message, was allowed to escape. Nevertheless, in view of what Black Horn had threatened to do to this man, Walsh said it was best that he did get away.

The council ended with more expressions of goodwill from Four Horns.

In late afternoon, when the sun cast long tepee shadows to the east, Walsh and party started their return journey to the police camp that the major had set up between Wood Mountain and Cypress. Men and horses well rested, they travelled quickly and rejoined the escort late the same night. The next day the contingent broke camp and headed for home, Fort Walsh, where for a week or so the scouts found themselves, with great willingness, the story-tellers of the adventures of the Mounted Police among the ferocious Teton Sioux, and how Walsh had walked into the domain of Four Horns and had walked out the chief of the Sioux.

The Tetons under Black Moon, who had been at Wood Mountain through the winter, heard all these things on the moccasin telegraph, from the runners of Four Horns, and it was good medicine, good that a great chief of the Hunkpapa had smoked the pipe with the British. Four Horns, they said, was a wise man and looked after all the people.

# ❖❖❖ The Meeting

❖❖❖ *Shaglashapi...* Wherever he had been in the midst of the Sioux, Walsh had heard the word constantly. Simply translated it meant Redcoats, or British, or the whites who lived north of the line under the protection of the great father (a king) or great mother (a queen). The major was surprised and worried to learn that the Sioux regarded themselves, conveniently, as British. They showed him the medals presented to their grandfathers with the blessing of King George for having fought for the Redcoats against the Americans. They recounted to him the promises made to their forebears that the Sioux would always be welcome on British soil.

Their affinity to Canada, however politic in their adverse circumstances, appealed to the pride and patriotism of Walsh. It also appealed to his sensitivity and to his prejudices.

By this time he had mixed with many of the Sioux leaders in two sizeable camps and had rather enjoyed the experience irrespective of those lingering moments of uncertainty and tension. He had a feeling he could talk their language; he was pleased with the respect that had come his way; he sympathized with them in their misfortunes.

Having chased the whisky-runners about the countryside and having heard an inkling of the complaints of the Sioux, Walsh found himself critical of U.S. actions, past and present. He rankled when the American press described the Indians as infernal devils. He said that it was this approach of so many Americans towards the red men that forced them, in self-defence, to act like devils. He could sympathize with the Indians' inherent desire for freedom in the land that had always been theirs: the untrammelled land of perfumed lilies in the spring; summers of bountiful contentment on the trails; autumn hunts of buffalo and antelope; and winters of relaxed comfort when the winds buffeted the overlapping lodge skins and the people moved closer to the fires to hear again exciting stories of brave men, the legends and the songs.

Nontheless, he knew that for safety's sake, and for the purpose of his official tasks, he would have to be firm. While he had so far been able to be master in the house, he had to consider the reactions of those Canadian tribes who would regard the Sioux as invaders of the land and poachers of the buffalo, and while it could be said the buffalo were plentiful in this spring of '77, the great herds might not be in the region next year, or ever again, and what then?

It was obvious the numbers of buffalo were decreasing alarmingly, the outcome of willful and wanton massacre by whites for the furs and by Indians for the whisky cups. Often the meat was left to rot on the plains, a feast for the wolves. In one year, 250,000 full-size hides were shipped from Benton to St. Louis. Even the Métis were known to slaughter up to 800-head in one day.

If stomachs were empty, and the children were crying for food, it would be unlikely that a handful of policemen could control the passions of Indians who had been warring for centuries to reserve the buffalo ranges for their own requirements. And the worst was yet to come. The main body of Sioux, the warriors of Sitting Bull, were on their way, but where?

Scouts reported that Four Horns had resumed his journey northwards along the White Mud and was intending to join up with Black Moon in the Wood Mountain area. In late May, Walsh learned that Sitting Bull, having crossed the Missouri with his large camp, was approaching the boundary line. This was the information the superintendent was expecting. He was soon packing saddle bags again, as were Sergeant Bob McCutcheon, three constables and two scouts, one of whom had been with the major the last time out – the ever-ready Louis Léveillé. The other scout was Gabriel Solomon.

The small party rode out of the fort in the direction of Pinto Horse, about fifteen miles east of a northern branch of the White Mud, a two-day ride. Here Walsh intended to unload and await Sitting Bull. However, when they reached the river it was obvious to everyone that there had recently been a great deal of activity in the area; there were signs of a recent Indian camp (trampled grass, tepee circles, cooking sites, grazing areas and droppings) and a wide, new trail. They also came across a grave; that of a warrior, Walsh subsequently found out, who had been wounded in the Custer battle of last June and had died on the trek from the Missouri. His relatives and friends had kept the body to bury it on British soil.

Bull was farther into Canada than Walsh had anticipated.

The policemen followed Bull's trail into the Pinto Horse Buttes, which formed a western buttress for Wood Mountain, east of Snake Creek, a tributary of the White Mud.

Tents were put up for a night among the buttes and in the morning they took up the hunt again. There was no need to dismount; the evidence of a large movement of people, horses and travois could be clearly discerned and the ruts were easy to follow. The patrol was catching up quickly and Walsh sent out his scouts.

After three hours in the saddle the police noticed they themselves were being tracked. Indians began to appear on the hilltops, and as the patrol pushed on, their observers increased. Walsh told his men not to pay attention to the outriders who were surrounding them. The Indians kept their distance and did not attempt to communicate, which was fine with Walsh. He wanted to get into the camp before talking.

Because of the hills the patrol found itself among the outlying lodges without visual warning. The party halted, dismounted, and calmly set about removing saddles and unfurling tents.

The nonchalant attitude of the visitors and the casualness of the Indians camouflaged the anxieties of both sides. As the red-coated lawmen watchfully busied themselves unloading their gear and tethering the horses, scouts Léveillé and Solomon, who could converse in Lakota, strolled about the lodges (the outside hides painted in red figures of men and horses to record personal battle feats) and chatted with the people, learning about the camp and telling them about the Redcoats and their purpose. The two scouts confirmed they were in the company of Sans-Arcs (No-Bows) Tetons, so named because before they had guns they armed themselves with lances rather than bows.

In short order the policemen were approached by a group of warriors, from the look of them chiefs and sub-chiefs. The one leading the way stood out. At the first sight of this man Walsh knew he was about to meet a figure of considerable importance. He introduced himself as Spotted Eagle, a war chief of the Sans-Arcs. He shook hands with a firm grip.

Spotted Eagle had a striking physical appearance. He was tall, slender and agile, and muscular; a fine specimen of prime manhood, probably early fortyish, but in appearance younger. His skin was copper-hued, his slightly chubby face unlined by the northern air, and most noticeable were his eyes and eyebrows, which were extraordinarily light for an Indian, a striking contrast to his skin. His black hair, parted in the middle, was in two plaits and each was covered with animal skins and flopped over his chest. Attached to his hair at the back of his head was a large, solitary feather. He had gentle features and manners, a broad poutish mouth, and he smiled easily, and exuded a certain informal grace that touched the awareness of Walsh and his partners.

The Sans-Arc warrior turned out to be eloquent of tongue as well. He said that the policemen were in the camp of Sitting Bull – and it was the first time in his life that he had seen white men (soldiers or scouts) walk into Sitting Bull's circle and settle down with such lack of concern.

After more introductions and hand-shaking, another party approached and in the lead was a broad figure of a man who was limping, although not to a degree that seemed to handicap him. He was of medium height, somewhat shorter than the men with him, and had a sturdy bearing.

Sergeant McCutcheon, wearing his red jacket with the three stripes on the sleeve, was standing to the front of Walsh and thus became the first Canadian official to shake the hand of Sitting Bull.

Then it was Walsh's turn. Here, on the fringe of Sitting Bull's very own camp, he was facing the most notorious, incorrigible and feared Indian leader of the American West. They shook hands, the irascible representative of the great mother and the swarthy chieftain of all the warring elements of the dreaded Sioux nation.

So this was old Bull, the strong-willed fighting gypsy of the plains, the man who had unalterably affected the pattern of white civilization, the man who for ever would be held accountable for inflicting a grievous and humiliating defeat upon the elite of the U.S. military machine.

Walsh introduced him to all his men. Bull smiled with a great charm and his features, for a moment, lost their severity and their creviced cragginess. He could smile easily and sincerely. He had a broad and a high brow, a mouth that gave Walsh an impression of grimness and determination and revenge, and eyes that penetrated; eyes that also hinted of some measure of sympathy or pity.

Behind the parting of his hair, two eagle feathers gave him extra height (one of them was dyed red to indicate he had been wounded in battle). Two long braids hung over his chest, wrapped in what looked to be weasel skins.

Walsh was surprised; he had expected someone much more fearsome, although he could see Sitting Bull was prideful, a forceful man who could command loyalty.

The major, as he had done on other similar occasions, explained why he was in the camp. Bull replied that he had buried his weapons before coming to the land of the white mother and desired to learn about her laws. It was agreed that a council of the chiefs and the police would be held in the late afternoon.

At the council Walsh was to be confronted with another attribute of the chief of chiefs; his philosophy, which he could expound convincingly with a guttural flow of fluency. From Walsh's standpoint, such oratory would explain how Bull could be so powerful among the tribes and among the people who were not by nature meant to follow the edicts of others. It was true the Indians had their own unwritten laws (they had no written language as such), that they abided by traditions and customs, but they were naturally independent, not at all inclined to follow a foolish or untried man.

At about five o'clock the chiefs took their places in the council lodge, Bull being the last of the Sioux to arrive. Then Walsh entered accompanied by his chief scout, Léveillé, and the interpreter, Solomon. Walsh sat in the centre of the group and reiterated the purpose of his visit. Afterwards, Bull immediately took the floor, moved forward and shook Walsh's hand, and started his oration.

With a profound flourish of voice and arms he outlined a history of his people, as handed down from the grandfathers. From his own memories he recounted the treaties the Teton Sioux had made with the grandfather in Washington, how these had been broken, how their camps had been attacked by the soldiers and the people plundered and murdered – the Longknives "hurting me like wild animals seeking for my blood." He assured Walsh that he and his followers had crossed the line seeking peace – "the grass in Canada is not stained with blood" – and they wanted to rest, to be relieved of war; it was their hope that the white mother would deal gently with them.

As the other chiefs made corresponding pleas and pledged strict adherence to the law, Sitting Bull contemplated, as he revealed later, how for the first time in his life he had submitted to the white men's wishes. His heart was both gay and sorrowful; gay because there was peace and he had met white men whom he believed he could trust; sorrowful because he wondered whether the audacity of these policemen who had walked into his camp, but whom he did not have to curse and fight, had relieved him of his powers.

Spotted Eagle again impressed the superintendent with his deep-throated rhetoric. He said that they had all been hounded by the soldiers and that for the sake of the women and children they had no choice but to ask for sanctuary in the far northland.

This was an admission that did not come easily to the war chief as he stood before Walsh holding the biggest and most ghastly Indian tomahawk he had ever seen – three long blades of pointed steel set into a wooden shaft, an instrument that no doubt had cut down some of Custer's men in the melee when the soldiers, their guns jammed with the heat, hopelessly fought for their lives with knives and rifle butts.

When the chiefs had finished, Walsh asserted his official presence in conciliatory tones, stipulating the fundamental laws concerning life and property in Canada, and there followed a sort of question-and-answer period with Walsh using the occasion, as he would in the months to come, to propagate the official puff designed to influence them to return to the United States: that only a minority of the white people there wanted to fight them and that the Americans wished to deal kindly with the Sioux and place them in a position that when the buffalo and other game disappeared from the earth they and their children could carry on.

Turning to Bull, the superintendent told him that the lawless characters he came in contact with on the frontier did not represent the sentiments of the American nation. These men were, in many cases, criminals on the loose from justice and were using him, his relatives, his friends, and his people as a barrier against arrest. Those men who thought it fun to shoot at, or kill an Indian, dare not show themselves to the white population of the east because they would be hanged or put in prison.

The council ended with Bull doing the speaking again. He said this had been the first time he had been instructed about the laws of the whites. While he had a very bad heart against the white man, an intense dislike of some of them, he now recognized that they had better laws than the Sioux and he would like to hear more. Would the *Shaglashapi* chief return? Walsh agreed to.

The police patrol bedded down for the night with the intention of getting an early start the next day. They were up at first light, and after breakfast, when they were about to leave, horses saddled and the gear packed, three Indians came up the trail leading five horses. Solomon whispered to Walsh he recongized the three as American Assiniboines from the Missouri agencies and that one of the trio was White Dog, a notorious hostile (when outside the range of army superivision). White Dog was regarded as a great warrior and it was said that in '76 Sitting Bull, who had adopted a young Assiniboine as a brother some years ago, had offered him 300 horses if he and his fighting men would join up with the Sioux for the summer.

Solomon sauntered across to the new arrivals, who were talking to some Sans-Arcs, and casually had a look at the horses. There was something about them. He believed that three of the five belonged to Father Jules Decorby, one of the Catholic priests who ministered to the Métis in and around the Cypress Hills. Father Decorby, referred to by the Indians and Métis as the Priest Who Speaks All Tongues, kept a herd of horses and was inclined to give some of them away when he felt someone had a real need, but that someone would not be a hostile.

Walsh asked Solomon if he was positive they were Decorby's horses. Solomon nodded. Walsh instructed Léveillé to wander over. He too recognized the horses. The major sent both of them to look again, to be absolutely sure. They were convinced three horses were "little" Decorby's. Walsh called Sgt. McCutcheon over, told him what was going on, and ordered him to take two constables and the interpreters and arrest White Dog and his companions.

"We'll give an observation lesson to the Sioux to show them how we treat horse thieves," said Walsh.

The popularity and prestige of White Dog among the Tetons was unquestionable. By this time he had more than fifty warriors around him as he expounded on his latest exploits. McCutcheon moved to the centre of the tight circle, imperceptibly parting the listeners. He stepped out firmly to confront White Dog. "The three of you are under arrest on a charge of stealing horses."

When the interpreter relayed the message, the bystanders stood incredulously aghast. White Dog couldn't believe his ears. Arrest, here, among his friends the Sioux and only these whites to do it! White Dog truculently denied the horses were stolen, said they were his, and that he would not give them up and would not be arrested.

At this stage Walsh and the other constable stepped in; Walsh did not want McCutcheon to have to move out of the throng for further orders and lose the initiative. One of the scouts had slipped away to fetch the stolen horses, now out of sight behind a growing audience of Sioux who were getting excited and agitated.

The major acted decisively. "White Dog," he said to the hostile, "you say you will neither be arrested nor surrender these horses [which were now at hand]. I arrest you for theft."

Walsh put one hand on the warrior's shoulder and with the other pointed to the other two Assiniboines.

"I'm arresting you and you."

He ordered McCutcheon to take their arms. Before the trio could move to get away the sergeant and the constables had disarmed them.

The effect was uncanny. The three prisoners were speechless and paralyzed; the Sioux stood and stared in bewilderment, not even a whisper passed among them. Never had they seen the likes of this.

One of the constables had gone to get the shackles from a pack horse. Walsh took these and holding up a pair of leg irons said to White Dog: "Tell me where you got those horses, how you got them, and what you intended to do with them, or I'll put these irons on you and take you to Fort Walsh."

White Dog wilted. He said he was passing over the plains east of the Cypress Hills, saw the horses wandering on the prairie, and took them. He added, apologetically, that he did not know it was a crime to do this; along the Milk River it was the custom to take such horses into camp and return them to the owners if called for.

That statement, as false as it could be, was accepted by Walsh because he had no real desire to transport these Indians into captivity and perhaps jeopardize the lives of the policemen, although the onlookers, by now in the hundreds, did not make one move to interfere.

Said Walsh: "White Dog, never again when you are north of the line violate property, no matter where or how it is found."

White Dog was crestfallen, disgraced in front of the Sioux. He had been ridiculed, and to the Indians there was hardly a more culpable insult or degradation. His eyes exuded resentment and viciousness. As he was about to walk off he muttered something about seeing Walsh again and getting his revenge.

The interpreter picked up the words and told Walsh. The superintendent shouted at White Dog to come back. Walsh repeated what he understood White Dog to have said. The Indian, already humiliated to the core, did not deny his remarks.

"Withdraw these words," said Walsh, "or we'll take you to Fort Walsh."

The Assiniboine said he did not mean his words to be a threat.

Another lie, but no matter. Walsh had secured his victory. The fugitive Sioux had seen for themselves how the Assiniboines – reputedly the most unyielding and bravest of hostiles – had shown fear when faced with the uncompromising fact of Canadian law.

The policemen commandeered the horses and told everyone they would be returned to their owner – and they were.

Walsh, henceforth to be known among the Assiniboines as The One Who Ties, knew White Dog would have to be watched. The word of his defeat would be spread to many camps. His name would be mocked and slandered around the fires. Sitting Bull certainly heard, and the very fact that his visitors had brought White Dog to his knees in his camp of 600 warriors convinced him the Redcoats were determined to enforce their rules. So impressed was Bull that he came to Walsh as he was leaving and asked for further and immediate instructions on what he could or could not do. He also asked for permission to trade for ammunition for the hunts, a request that seemed reasonable to Walsh, provided not a round or ball would be used for fighting the Americans.

The Redcoats, saddlebags well stocked with fresh meat obtained from the Sioux, started off for Fort Walsh. When they reached the first foothills of Cypress, Walsh ordered the scouts to make camp for a few days to keep an eye on the movements and activities of this latest batch of refugees. The policemen resumed their journey with words of precaution to Léveillé and Solomon.

On the rest of the tedious, bumpy, saddle-sore way they exchanged impressions of their observations of the Sioux fighting force. They had all noticed the prevalence of U.S. materiel, saddles and saddlebags of Custer's Seventh Cavalry, and carbines and ammunition belts. Walsh recalled the weapon carried by Spotted Eagle; the equivalent of three axes or spears. It could rip a man apart. He speculated some poor devils on the Little Big Horn had felt its tearing wrench with their last gasp of life. No wonder it appeared that the naked bodies on the Big Horn ridge had been mutilated.

Irrevocably, Spotted Eagle had made a tremendous impact on Walsh. "Spot" was an anomaly. Obviously an unswerving hostile, probably chivalrous in battle, he appeared to be a compassionate and understanding man, especially in his own camp circle, willing to listen and compromise. He had a sense of humour too and had mastered the white man's diversion of winking. Walsh had found him to be an accomplished talker and a patient listener.

Spotted Eagle had indeed listened in 1874 when Custer, the Long Hair, was an unexpected guest of the Sans-Arcs. The tribe was camped east and a little north of the Black Hills that summer, as is the custom at that time of the year, when a column of Longknives, with many wagons, was seen heading for the holy places. Spotted Eagle, who did not believe the whites were bent on trouble, organized a council with the soldier chiefs at which Long Hair smoked the Buffalo Calf Pipe, the most sacred pipe of all the Teton Sioux that was in the custody of the Sans-Arcs, its bowl of red stone representing the earth, the wooden stem representing the things of nature that grow from the earth, and the 12 eagle feathers hanging where the stem fits into the bowl representing the highest-flying and holiest eagle and all the winged creatures.

When they smoked, the civil and war chiefs of the Sans-Arcs and the soldier chiefs, it was a tacit promise of peace, but when Custer's men found the yellow metal in the hills there was no regard for the sacred places as thousands of spoilers came to disturb the spirits and chase all the Indians away from their birthright.

So much for promises. Sitting Bull, whom Spotted Eagle had supported with other great men of the Tetons to be the principal chief, was right again.

# ❖❖❖ The Virtues of Quick Action

❖❖❖ Continually on duty at the fort after his visit with Sitting Bull, Walsh had but little time to relax. More often than not the garrison was surrounded by thousands of natives – the Crees, Blackfoot, Assiniboines, Saulteaux and Sioux who had heard buffalo were plentiful in eastern Cypress. Their lodges sprang up overnight like mushrooms. They came and they went, a shifting (and often shifty) populace augmented by dozens of halfbreeds who congested the little village north of the compound. Police patrols moved in and out, and so did wagons filled with supplies and itinerant characters. All this activity demanded a great deal of police vigilance; resources and tempers were pushed beyond the limits of normal endurance.

Walsh was feeling the pressures; he was not an entirely well man. The severities and anxieties of the job, the rough living conditions, the extremes of weather were a ceaseless aggravation.

Near the end of May he was confronted with an urgent crisis, precipitated (again) by some haughty south Assiniboines.

One of the most co-operative chiefs the Mounted Police had dealings with was Little Child (he was at least six feet tall) of the Saulteaux. Chief OK, as Walsh nicknamed him, was regarded as a true friend. The police found him to be a very intelligent, broad-minded individual who constantly sought reassurances that the Redcoats would protect his comparatively small following from marauding bands of hostiles.

Little Child came in with a tale of woe that his small band of about fifteen lodges had been overpowered and sacked by a large contingent of U.S. agency Assiniboines, about 200 lodges, who were up on a buffalo hunt. They had demanded he conform to their hunting rules and obey their instructions. This was a dictate of prestige. When Little Child refused, 150 war-bedecked hostiles tore down the Saulteaux tepees, shot their dogs and scattered the people into some wooded hills northeast of Fort Walsh.

Little Child, whose fighting force consisted of only thirty warriors, had attempted to stand up to Broken (Crooked) Arm, an Assiniboine war chief, saying that he was a British Indian on British soil and the only chief he obeyed was the white chief at Fort Walsh. This infuriated Broken Arm.

"When your Redcoat friends come to my camp you will be there to see how I use them. I'll pull down their lodges and shoot their horses." He then ordered his followers to tear the Saulteaux camp apart.

Little Child warned that the Assiniboines, strong with their own power, had promised to cut out the heart of the Redcoat chief and eat it if he dared to come to their camp.

Walsh reacted immediately. He didn't appreciate threats. In less than an hour a heavily armed patrol was on the way. In temporary charge was Captain Edwin Allen, a sub-inspector. He had twenty-five or so men, including Léveillé the guide, and a surgeon, John Kittson, there being every likelihood of bloodshed on this assignment. It was imperative that Walsh move quickly and resolutely if he was to retain the confidence of all the Indians he had pledged to protect. The word of the police was at stake, let alone its avowed efficiency.

At seven o'clock in the evening, two hours after Allen's departure, Walsh led another, smaller contingent out of the fort. He had used the time to plan the strategy and prepare the reserves. Inside the barracks, in a state of readiness, were 100 men and four artillery pieces that could effectively cut off the Assiniboines should they try to escape to the south.

Walsh caught up with Allen in less than two hours. His stirrups were hot!

Little Child, a handsome and energetic chief, was popular with the police and Walsh trusted him to scout the route to the scene of the sacked village. Late the same night, at about eleven o'clock, after forty miles in the saddle, they came to the deserted Saulteaux camp, but there were no Assiniboines in the vicinity. Léveillé decided they had gone farther north, and while the policemen dismounted and rested the scouts soon picked up the fresh trail. The entire patrol remounted and slowly and quietly followed the guides for an hour before they halted and unsaddled again until three o'clock in the morning.

As the light of day spread out from the horizon of hills, Léveillé and Little Child sighted the distant village. Walsh cautiously joined them on a hill to survey the layout of the Assiniboines – more than 200 lodges fringed by cottonwood trees on a beautiful green plateau, a little stream running along its base. Not a sound, not a ripple, came from the slumbering camp.

Despite the prospect of having to do battle with hundreds of hostiles, possibly with odds of twenty to one, Walsh decided upon an immediate surprise swoop and peremptory arrest – but not before breakfast.

The policemen, their guns at the ready, resumed their march to within 400 yards of the objective, where, precariously, they had to descend a hill, in full view of the camp, twenty or so scarlet coats brilliantly bright in the pale sun. The silence and suspense were painful. A neigh of a horse, the rattle of a curb, the bark of a dog could be a calamity. The horses moved gently along with hardly a nudge of rein or spur. All was still as death. One by one they passed through the lines of tepees heading for the central war lodge. They surrounded it, dismounted, and at a pre-arranged signal of his own Walsh stepped in with ten troopers, grabbed the chief by the arms before he could jump up, and hustled him outside. Three more leaders were rounded up, and more than twenty braves. Without a shot being fired the Mounties had their men.

The patrol, with the prisoners shackled in pairs as far as there were manacles to do so, moved out almost as quickly as it had moved in and at a nearby butte everyone set to work, in double time, building a square breastwork of stone and earth topped with saddles. The prisoners were made to help, carrying stones. The horses were tied together in the centre. All were expecting an attack. The surgeon had his medicine chest open, bandages in a pile alongside.

The camp was in absolute turmoil; the impossible had happened, their foremost war chieftains spirited away in the dawn, the henchmen left milling around in confusion.

The police interpreters were outside of the improvised fort, but not too far away, trying to get a hint of what was being said by

the minor chiefs as they harangued the warriors to overpower the Redcoat position. Walsh was hoping that with so many hostages under his guns the Assiniboines would not counter-attack. Dozens of them moved menacingly towards the breastwork and stopped beyond carbine range.

Walsh moved to within 300 yards of the mob. He sent word he wanted to talk to the principal chiefs. He told them he was taking Broken Arm and the others to Fort Walsh for trial and a similar fate would befall others if they did not respect the rights and property of all buffalo-hunting bands. They were informed they were on British soil where the rights of all men were sacred, where all men were brothers, and where the police would protect every man's freedom and property.

"The law is the chief in Canada," Walsh told them.

The Assiniboines pleaded for the release of their compatriots, promising never again to commit an offense and to respect the authority of the police. Walsh was adamant. He ordered the Assiniboines to return to their camp peaceably and not worsen the situation for the captives.

They refused. They persisted in demanding freedom for all their comrades.

Walsh repeated the captives would not be released until after a proper investigation at Fort Walsh.

"You won't take these men alive," he shouted at the threatening Assiniboines. "They go to Fort Walsh or they die here. It depends on you."

The Indians counciled and agreed to retire. The policemen prepared for the march to the fort. The prisoners were told they would have to walk, manacled together, unless they could persuade their friends to send them horses – and it was going to be a quick and hard walk to reach the fort that night.

One of the warrior prisoners, Blackfoot by name, called to the Assiniboine crowd to send one horse for each of their friends. Shortly after four young men, unarmed, rode up with sufficient mounts to enable the patrol to ride off to Fort Walsh, special care being taken to establish an alert rearguard. The Redcoats, the guides and prisoners got to their destination just before midnight without incident. The Assiniboines were unshackled and locked up in the guardhouse.

Walsh did in fact set up an investigation at the fort and of the twenty-five prisoners, the majority, the young men, were set free following courtroom warnings about the consequences of breaking the law.

Broken Arm and three other chiefs were retained for the prestigious attention of Assistant Commissioner Irvine, whom Walsh knew was en route from the west. The belligerent instigator got six months' detention with hard labour (with ball and chain); the other chiefs got one, two and three months apiece.

As usual, the moccasin telegraph, with its symptomatic embellishments, carried news of the goings-on all over the hills, as far south as the Rosebud and easterly into the Sitting Bull lodges where the Sioux had already seen the Redcoats in action. Walsh had made his point.

Irvine, having disposed of the four Assiniboine renegades, consulted with the superintendent about the 3,000 fugitive Teton warriors in the territory under Sitting Bull, all of them in the area of Wood Mountain, although likely drifting westwards on the buffalo hunts. Irvine wanted to talk to Bull, to see this formidable character for himself, to get a first-hand impression of the man and his intentions.

The uneasiness over Bull's presence kept Irvine and Walsh talking and planning in urgent sessions. Both had seen Blackfoot bands in the area of Fort Walsh, and concluded that they were moving easterly, also in search of the buffalo. There was therefore imminent peril the Blackfoot hunters would clash with the invading Sioux for supremacy of the buffalo ranges.

By coincidence, the day before Irvine and Walsh had decided to start their journey over the country now familiar to Walsh, six Sioux warriors rode into the compound. They had been sent by Sitting Bull with a message that he was holding (and protecting) three American prisoners in his camp: a black robe (priest), a scout for Bear Coat (General) Miles, and an interpreter. The feeling was so great against the Americans, Bull relayed, that he could not protect these spies for long before they were killed.

The leader of the six riders, the official message-carrier, was One Bull, a scarred warrior in his mid-twenties and already a fighter and wooer of renown. He was Sitting Bull's nephew and devoted to him. Brawny, handsome, with a ready eye for the girls, One Bull (sometimes referred to as Lone Bull) impressed everyone with his savage manliness.

He was proud and somewhat arrogant and boastful. He made no attempt to conceal the armaments he carried, mostly spoils from the Custer battlefield, and he was quick to claim that he himself had killed twenty-three of Custer's men with his war club, a heavy oval-shaped stone with a wooden handle that he showed everyone. He took a delight in pointing to the "kill" notches on the shaft.

His was a believable war story, and he had more to reveal to Irvine on the trail leading to Pinto Horse Buttes where Walsh had first walked into Bull's camp.

Irvine, Walsh and two other officers, Edmund Dalrymple Clark and Allen, and a handful of constables and scouts, and the six Sioux, set out the next day, May 31, '77.

The small party, the Indians bringing up the rear, covered as much ground as they could coax out of their mounts on the first day. The horses were rested occasionally, but Irvine was anxious to reach an Assiniboine camp before nightfall. They had come across a wide path of Assiniboine travois ruts and the assistant commissioner was hoping the track would lead him to the same band that had already sampled the audacity and deftness of Walsh (for which he had been commended by the Government). Irvine wanted to give the chiefs a talking-to.

It rained consistently, and this cooled the horses, and at sunset, when the rain stopped and the prairie was fresh with the scent of buffalo grass, and the warmth of the fading sun put everyone in better spirits, the riders came upon a camp of about 500 tepees.

As usual, they were expected. The little caravan, a curious mixture of Redcoats, guides in buckskins, and feathered Sioux, had been under observation. The recently trodden trail into the camp, and the hills around, were covered with people watching the arrival. The police pitched their tents unconcernedly among them and the curious, by the score, converged to see these strangers and their paraphernalia. For the Assiniboines it was an event. They got a running commentary from the Sioux, their distant relatives. (These two tribes were prone to fight each other periodically but Sitting Bull was currently on good terms with them, although not long since he had been inadvertently attacked by a war party and came close to losing his life. One Bull was with him at that time.)

The chiefs knew that the white police chief who had sent Broken Arm and his henchmen into the house with bars was the leader of this patrol and when they gathered to smoke the pipe with the visitors they told Irvine (their language was derived from

Nakota, the dialect of the Yankton Sioux) that they thought it bad their men should be kept in a white man's prison.

Irvine replied bluntly that he had not punished them half enough.

The next morning Irvine arranged for an early departure, but before continuing lectured the chiefs again about his expectations concerning their conduct while north of the line. There was hand-shaking all round.

Irvine's party was on horseback for two hours before a stop was made for breakfast. Out came the kettle for tea. Buffalo chips (hardened dung) were gathered for a fire – not a piece of wood could be found on the bald plain – and before long everyone was enjoying the hot tea, including and especially the Indians. Then back into the saddle, Irvine hoping to reach Sitting Bull's village that day.

At times Irvine found himself dropping back and on one stretch was riding in the company of the six Sioux, the rest of the party being out in front and out of sight.

He looked around him. The irony of the situation did not escape his perception. Here he was, in the middle of nowhere, riding with six war-painted braves, all of them hostiles and suffi-ciently armed and motivated to do him in right there and then. At his side was One Bull, a graduate, so to speak, of the soldier caste whose expertise would be able to complement his energy with telling effect. One good whack with his club would be good enough!

These were natural thoughts, in the circumstances. It wasn't a case of being overly apprehensive, cautious, or even afraid. It was a matter of curiosity. Who was this war lord he was riding with? What thoughts were churning in his mind?

One Bull, who was the son of Makes-Room (or Welcome), Sitting Bull's brother-in-law, and the younger brother of White Bull, a Minneconjou who claimed to be the actual killer of Custer (among others), had always been closer to his uncle than to his own parents. He had been "adopted" by Bull when a small boy. He was brought up a Hunkpapa in the family household of the chief and it was therefore a matter of course that One Bull would be thoroughly indoctrinated into the grand virtues of hunting and warfare and the politics of tribal management.

The chief often took his nephew along on his recurring adven-tures. When he was old enough he named him as his lieutenant.

One of the most notable or memorable escapades of the pair was a horse-theft expedition through Assiniboine-controlled lands into Canada. The halfbreeds up there were envied for the quality of their horses.

Along the border country, where no man can tell for sure whether he is in the land of the white mother, even if he were concerned about such strange details, Bull's small raiding party scouted a large camp of Crees. When it was dark and the fires were out, and only the occasional bark of the dogs came to the ears of Sitting Bull and One Bull as they lay in wait on the other side of a stream, they slithered into the water, waded across in the shadow of some trees, and crawled into a herd of hobbled horses. The uncle, his finesse in the honoured profession of taking other people's horses being a matter of considerable experience and bravado, sought out the lead mare. The nephew, expecting at any moment the dogs would pick up their scent, moved apprehensively and nimbly among the restless animals to cut the hobble strings. The chief slid onto the mare's back; One Bull mounted a pony. Bull raised his arm. They splashed across the river and scurried into the safety of the night with ten horses. Not bad for a two-man invasion.

One Bull was at his uncle's side, as his bodyguard, at the Little Big Horn. When the great battle was over, when the remains of the whites, all stripped and naked, were decaying in the sun, and after the women and children had seen these foolhardy ones and had shot arrows into their corpses and had cut off fingers and other parts, and when the stench was getting to be overpowering, and after the recitals of great deeds performed and mourning for those Indians recently dispatched to Spirit Land, and after the tribes scattered to escape the wrath of the avengers, Sitting Bull appointed One Bull as his aide to help combat the uncertainties of life in the mother's land.

Who would have thought that young One Bull, of all people, would be given the responsibility of escorting a white soldier, a Redcoat chief, to the camp of his uncle? Not One Bull! Not with all the fair-haired scalps that decorated his clothes.

Irvine was determined to make good time; he spurred the Sioux up to the main party. It wasn't difficult. They sensed they were getting close to home.

When the outlying lodges came in sight, at a spot called the Holes where the Crees and the Saulteaux used to fight, Irvine consulted with Walsh about procedure. It was decided to enter the camp with some commanding display. Irvine, a Quebec-born scion of a military family, a lieutenant-colonel when he retired from the army in '75, was inured to military pomp and majesty. The Indians knew how to dress up for their ceremonials. Undoubtedly they would be impressed.

Irvine, on horseback a seemingly slight figure, approached the camp with a bearing of authoritative, colourful and earnest officialdom. He had finely-cut features and a reddish beard that was always neatly trimmed. The tinge of grey, the sign of a man in his forties, accentuated a demeanour of distinction and stern maturity. (Indians were invariably fascinated by beards. Purebloods, who did not have hair on their faces and very little on their bodies, considered it strange that a white man could have lost the hair from his head and be covered on his face and chest.) At the head of this token police column, with almost all the regalia of fulldress, Irvine made an auspicious entry into the kingdom of the legendary cut-throat. The magnetic spectacle of the two white chiefs attracted hundreds: children running alongside the horses; young girls and old men standing by the lodges; women, most of them on the heavy side, scurrying from their chores to get a glimpse; and the straight-backed warriors, arms outstretched, wanting to shake the hands of the visitors.

Irvine had never seen so many men together of such tremendous stature. When he bent over to take their hands he had difficulty staying on his horse, their clasps were so firm.

The policemen and the scouts rode through the camp as if on parade. At the opposite end to where they had entered they dismounted and assembled their canvas tents. Throngs of Sioux crowded around as they unloaded the pack horses. The children were frightened at first and scampered off if one of the strangers got too close. They had been taught by their elders to be careful of the *washichun* (whites). Irvine managed to chuck a few under the chin and before long he had the boys and girls tugging at his sleeves.

In this happy melee, one man beckoned to Irvine to follow him, and the assistant commissioner, with some of his party, walked to the centre of the village. They approached a group of important-looking dignitaries, massive men Irvine thought, except for the one in the middle, the one he shook hands with first. This was Sitting Bull. Bull had stood still, expressionless, until his guests were just a few feet away; then he smiled, stepped forward and extended his hand. His companions, presumably his body-guard, followed suit. It was clear that Bull had gathered the pick of the fighting crop around him; all these men were tall and very muscular.

Bull uttered his statement of welcome: "At last we have met you; we know today what we never knew before. We know we are safe."

Irvine's first impression was favourable. He liked him. True, Bull was exuding his best charm, but Irvine was particularly struck with this benign rebel. He thought he had a rather pleasant face, a mouth showing great determination, and a fine, high fore-head. He noticed that when Bull smiled, which he could do with-out any strain, his face brightened up wonderfully.

After the exchange of pleasantries, and having determined the three U.S. "captives" were safe and well, the Redcoats enjoyed a meal before resting. Later in the day Sitting Bull arranged a meeting in the Hunkpapa tribal council lodge, a much bigger-than-average enclosure. The Indians were in place when the police were escorted inside; they were directed to a space opposite Sitting Bull where buffalo robes had been spread out for the guests to sit on.

As the others made themselves comfortable, Irvine glanced around him. Behind Bull were younger men; sub-chiefs, war chiefs and bodyguards. They were all bare to the waist, their breech clouts held up by belts adorned with scalps stripped from the heads of Custer's fallen, and the majority clutched the most up-to-date U.S. Army repeating carbines.

Squatting closest to Bull were two Hunkpapa chiefs, one rela-tively young and the other an old man. The elder was Bear's Cap, and he was wearing a complete bear's head that covered his own. Old Bear's Cap, in his best years a noted warrior, was still active and alert for his age, someone to be reckoned with in the councils. The other chief was Pretty Bear, crafty-looking, from appearances more of a politician than a soldier.

The lodge was crammed with about 100 people; the atmos-phere was stifling, and outside there were many hundreds milling around with not a hope of hearing or seeing anything. However, they knew the outcome of the talking could very well herald either a period of needed peace and happiness or a return to the ceaseless skirmishing with the soldiers.

Pretty Bear was responsible for opening the meeting with an invocation befitting the aspirations of the refugees. A redstone pipe was removed from a beaded, buckskin pouch. Pretty Bear assembled it and offered a prayer to Wakan-Tanka, the Great Spirit:

"God Almighty look down on me. Look on me my Grandfather. [Meaning the Great Spirit. All the chiefs and warriors held their hands aloft.] My Grandfather look on me; see the course I am going to take after this. [Hands up again.] Look on me, I am nothing now; have pity on me. [Hands up and grunts.] My Grandfather, you raised me to eat buffalo meat, to be strong. I am nothing now."

Pretty Bear pointed the revered peace pipe to the four directions, starting with the south, the source of life.

"My Mother [the earth] take the pipe. Understand, my Mother, we are going to be raised on this ground; take hold of this pipe strongly.

"My Mother wants me to smoke; we will all smoke. My Mother, make this land to be full of plenty, and a land of peace. I am going to light the pipe straight [with truth]."

The pipe was lit with a buffalo chip. The Indians did not like to use the white man's matches because they were considered deceptions. No one spoke as the pipe was passed around. When it came to Sitting Bull he pointed it to the four quarters and said:

"My Grandfather, have pity on me; we are going to be raised with a new people."

He handed the pipe to Irvine. All the policemen drew one puff, an affirmation of their strongest oath. The ashes were taken out and solemnly buried; the pipe was dismantled and placed over the spot.

The ritual of the speech-making began. Walsh had heard most of it before. Bull proclaimed how badly he had been treated by the Americans. They had all suffered greatly from the Longknives and had been fighting a defensive war for years. They were all British Indians and hoped that the white mother would protect them. Bull spoke slowly in his guttural tones:

"We are going to live in the north with the British. God Almighty has raised us, and God Almighty says that we are going to live with the British without throwing away anything. I came here to hunt nothing bad. My Grandfather said we must shake hands with the British; today I see it all.

"My Grandfather made us shake hands with the Longknives, and we have done it since I was in my mother's womb; I was in my mother's womb ten moons....God Almighty raised me strong ....My Grandfather said he would raise me with a big body and heart; my heart was good....The Americans always ran behind me, and that is the reason I came this way. God Almighty our Father said the Longknives would fight me, so the Americans have our buffalo and trade....The Americans gave us flour in every direction; I said hold on, we want bull's meat....My Grandfather, if I had done what the Americans told me, I would have been no one today...."

Bull paused to gather his thoughts.

"I came here to see the English, and we are going to have a new life. There are still some of us behind yet. On the American side I saw they were running after us in every direction....When I left the other side, my Grandfather told me that this was the place to come to. The Americans gave us flour but no powder and ball...."

The chief looked pleadingly at Irvine: "I have been here a good many days, but have seen none [powder and ball] yet. The buffalo are around us.

"My comrade, we are the same now. I am glad. Let us help one another. Anything I can't do I will ask you [Walsh] for help. You told me if anyone came into camp 'Let me know'. Some Americans came. I did let you know." Walsh nodded.

"God Almighty makes horses. He raised me on horseback. Now I see it. The Americans did not teach me to get on a horse....When I had plenty of horses, the Americans wanted all my horses; that is the reason I came to let you know it. The Americans who came here asked for my gun and horse, and said they would take care of me well. I then told my young men to tell you [Walsh]....The Americans treated me bad. They asked for all my arms...."

In his stop-and-start presentation (to help the interpreter who was having trouble turning sentences back to front from Lakota to English) he referred bitterly to the three Americans who had come into his camp to try to persuade his people to return to their own land overrun with the whites.

The leader of the three was Father Martin Marty who had been starting up schools for Indian children on the Dakota agencies. He was an abbot of the Benedictine Order and a Missionary

Apostolic. The other two were John Howard, who was chief scout for General Miles, and J. J. Smith, an Indian Affairs official. They had been held for eight days.

Marty was convinced that there was only one way to "civilize" the Sioux and that was to educate the children, and the concept of education, repugnant to the Indians, was the boarding school system, taking the children from the parents, cutting the boys' hair, putting them in sweaty trousers, stiff-front shirts and hard boots. Marty had undergone all manner of privation and risk in traversing hundreds of miles in his attempts to induce Bull to surrender. He felt, as a gentle and humane person, that the only hope for the Sioux was their return south where progress would reach them and where, at Standing Rock reservation, the ripples of the white man's world, just as the wind-swept ripples of the Missouri, would overflow and confront them.

Two other chiefs had to have their say....

Sweet Bird: "The Black Hills are the heart of the people; for forty years I was there. Now I listen to the Grandmother's advice. Anything wrong I put aside. I came here with a good heart. I came here to see the mother [Queen Victoria] and the white mother's trader who reads and writes, where there is plenty of ball and powder. It's only the Americans who did anything wrong to me. Since we came, some Americans came behind us to see where we are. What my mother thinks and says I have come to listen to."

Spotted Eagle: "God Almighty raised me on the American side. The Americans ran us every way. Our land on the other side I did not give away. What these three Americans wanted us to do, I did not want to do. My Grandfather raised me with a buffalo robe. God told me so, and that is what I want. From here to the sea the streams go. You thought I did not know! God raised you and me, and what I have I keep. My Grandfather makes me think about it....When we shake hands we trade. That's what we came to do.

"On the other side the Americans destroyed all the trading posts. God told me to trade robes. The Americans destroyed what the ground raised [they burned the grass]....God told me there was a trader north, and I came to see him. I came to shake hands with him who shakes hands with me first. When I came here to shake hands with the English, the Americans followed to shake hands. I don't want that. What the Americans do won't raise me and my children....I have nothing bad towards them. God hears what I

95

say... I come to hunt nothing bad, but what is good, and to raise my family. The Americans who use us so badly have come after us, so we sent for you, and thought you could bring them in here before us [nodding to Walsh]."

Irvine, as Walsh had been, was captivated by Spotted Eagle. His straightforward approach, the context of his remarks and the manner in which he uttered them, and the very figure of the man, touched the chords of admiration and compassion within the colonel.

"You and your families can sleep soundly here and need not be afraid," he said. "The Americans cannot cross the line after you."

As the interpreter relayed these words, the chiefs, outwardly inscrutable as always, looked among themselves with satisfaction and relief.

Irvine told them: "Now that you are in the Queen's land you must not cross the boundary to wage war against the Americans and return to this country. We will allow you enough ammunition to hunt the buffalo for food, but not one round of it is to be used against white men or Indians.

"In the Queen's country, we live like one family. If a white man or an Indian does wrong he is punished. The Queen has a very strong arm, and if her children do wrong she will get them and punish them.

"If anyone comes to your camp like those Americans did, come to the fort and tell Major Walsh. You were right, and I am glad you sent your young men to tell us about these men. As soon as your young men arrived at the fort we started, and I came to see you and shake hands with you. I will go to see those Americans and find out what they are doing here and I'll take them out of the camp with me.

"We will protect you against all harm, and you must not hurt anyone this side of the boundary."

Sitting Bull took it upon himself to tell Irvine what the Roman Catholic priest had told him. Sentence by sentence, with his customary pauses for the interpreter, Bull paraphrased Father Marty in his own staccato style:

"I come with the words of God....I am going to say a few words and go....I did not come here for anything bad. I want you to live, that is why I came here, that is what God told me to come and tell you....The English, maybe, won't have you....If you come with all your people, and the Yanktons, and give up your arms without surrendering, the American hearts will be glad....You think you are going to live on this side. You will get smaller and smaller and die....If you come on the other side I will try and get you a few horses....If you come you will live well; here you won't....Try to do what I tell you. If you live on this side I want to know if you are throwing away your land on the other side?"

When Bull finished, a chorus of grunts came from his companions. The chief looked straight at Irvine.

"Why would I go there?" he asked. "For the Americans to come after me again?"

A pause and more deep-throated murmurs of agreement.

"I have only two friends – The English and the Spaniards. If you had not told me to let you know if anyone came into my camp, I would not have known what to do."

Pretty Bear, who had opened the meeting with a prayer, closed it with a few conciliatory observations.

"You are soldiers; I am no soldier; I am a chief. My Grandfather raised me a chief, and I am so to this day. God raised me to hunt nothing bad. What arms we have, what arrows we have, the Longknives want.

"Our Grandmother has the ground raising good and I came to look. Since I came here I told the young men to put their guns behind them. I suppose these Americans will go back and say what takes place here, and I will listen to anything good.

"I only see on this ground the blood of buffalo, and this is the only blood I want to see. On the American side I never knew I wanted to steal or do wrong. God who raised me loves me, and raised me well. The Americans kept stealing from one side to the other.

"This day you must think our hearts are glad. If you send the Americans away the buffalo will raise from the ground, and my heart will be glad. I don't want to fight the Americans. If we would see each other like friends I would be glad."

Irvine stood up and told Bull he was going to see the Americans and would find out what they wanted.

The council met for a second time that afternoon and Father Marty was present with his own interpreter. Pretty Bear repeated his prayer and Bull smoked the pipe and passed it to the priest – "If there is any lie between us, may all men know it."

Bull was now in a ferocious mood. He glared at the priest, his bloodshot eyes oozing with the frustrations and the hate of his encounters with his white enemies.

"You know, as a messenger of the Great Spirit, that the Longknives tried to kill us. Why did you wait until half my people were killed before you came?"

There were exclamations of approval from the throng for these words. One of the chiefs blurted out: "Did the Great Spirit take our horses and arms from us?"

Bull muttered his concurrence and turned to the priest again.

"Why should I return only to give up my arms and horses?"

Father Marty pleaded with him to go back to his ancestral lands. This remark was a fuse for Bull's explosion. For a moment he contained himself, then with arms outstretched upwards he let loose all his innermost furies with a spontaneous verbal outburst.

"O God, remember this is the land I was brought up on.

"God brought up things from the ground for my children. I was brought up where God made food for me. I sit on the ground and hold it strong now.

"Listen to me," he shouted to the priest. "Look into my eyes. Look straight at me. Do you know what you tell me is going to be so? You come with the thinking of God. Where are you from? Under the ground? Do you know the cause of war? You ask me if I am going to return to your country. It is impossible for me to go back.

"God never told the Americans to come to the land of the Missouri. We were raised on this side of the sea. You were raised on the other side.

"God made my heart strong, but now it is weak, and that is why the Americans want to lick my blood... Why do the Americans want to drive me out? – because they want only Americans to be there.

"God made me leader of the people, and that is why I am following the buffalo. God told me, 'If you do anything wrong your people will be destroyed,' and that is why I came here. I was afraid." Bull still glared at the priest who had no chance to reply.

"Look at me. See if anything wrong sticks to my body.

"I never told what my Grandfather said before, but I am doing so now. You told me you came as the messenger of God. What you told me was not good for me. Look up, you will see God. Look up as I am looking. You come and tell me, as God's messenger, what to do, but I don't believe it. I have nothing but my hand to

98

fight the white men with. I don't believe the Americans ever saw God, and that is the reason they don't listen to me.

"I told the Americans to keep off my land....You are waiting for my people to come to your land so that the Longknives may rush at them and kill them. If you want to make a treaty, give us back our horses.

"God made all Indians out of one Indian, and He came to smoke with the old Indians and make peace....Are you here to ask me if I am going to throw land away? I never thought of giving my land to the American people, and still you follow to bring something wrong to me."

Bull switched his gaze to Irvine and back to the priest.

"I came here to hear from my white mother, and why, if I go back to the Americans, are they going to take all my stock away? Did God or the Queen ask you to tell me to give all my stock to the Longknives?...Did God tell you to come and make me poor?.. I never tried to do anything wrong to the white men. My body is clean. I never saw the road [the line] before, but I came on till I got to this side of it. I only think of two people, the English and Spanish. [It had been in Sitting Bull's thoughts to seek refuge in "the Spanish country," that is Mexico, if not in Canada.]

"I am between them. The Americans tried to cut me up, and that is why I talk to the chief there [Colonel Irvine].

"I am afraid of the cross you spoke of. Unless you use your influence with the President to send back the bad men to where they came from and leave the good men, there will be no peace."

The priest spoke up, briefly, denying he had come to give any advice – "If you remain here it is all right; if you come to America you will have to give up your arms and horses."

This statement further upset the chief. It sparked a hot ex= change:

Sitting Bull: "The thing you told me is not here; tell me today what you said yesterday."

The priest: "I don't want you to come back, but if you wish to come I would try and make it as easy as possible."

Sitting Bull: "It is not the same as yesterday what you are saying now; I have told the chief here what you told me yester-day."

The priest: "After hearing all this talk and what these British officers say, I would think you were better off on British soil. If you wish to come back, I pledge my life that your lives and liberties will be safe. You will not be killed or made prisoners."

Spotted Eagle butted in: "Have the Longknives on the other side talked it over and sent you here?"

The priest: "I am not sent by the Government, but I am assured that what I promise will be carried out. Do you intend to return to the other side or remain?"

Bull turned to Irvine.

"If I remain here will you protect me?"

Irvine: "I told you the white mother would, as long as you behave yourself."

Sitting Bull: "What would I return for? To have my horses and arms taken away? What have the Americans to give me? Once I was rich, with plenty of money, but the Americans stole it all in the Black Hills. I have come to remain with the white mother's children."

That was that! The council ended and the policemen felt they had achieved their principal objectives – to determine the immediate intentions of the Sioux, to affirm the strength of the law, and to rescue the Americans.

The Rev. Marty showed Irvine letters he was carrying from officials in Washington. The scout, whom Irvine distrusted, was despised by the Sioux.

The assistant commissioner invited the Americans to an evening meal in his tent. Other Redcoats, feeling secure among newly found friends, took a tourist's delight in strolling around the camp.

It was everywhere obvious the Indians also regarded the council as astonishingly satisfactory; a happier people there couldn't be! There were laughs and smiles in and around every lodge, especially among the women now that they felt the Longknives would not be allowed to come into the mother's land and attack them.

Sub-Inspector Clark went to see the dancing – the tight little circle of men beating one drum as they chanted the high-pitched calls strange and fearsome to his ears, and the gyrations of the warriors dancing round and round, stamping and swaying, stooping and rearing. It startled and fascinated him. Everywhere he saw evidence of the Custer battle; horses and mules bearing the brand of Custer's regiment; U.S. Army ammunition pouches and saddle bags; even a bugle hanging up outside a lodge. Everything was left unattended or unguarded. It appeared no one ever entered the lodge of another without an invitation.

Rejoicing was widespread, but Clark noticed that Sitting Bull was more reflective, almost sad. Clark saw him wandering about the camp preoccupied with his own secret thoughts. He went up to him and offered him his pipe. Bull flashed on one of his ready smiles, accepted, and smoked.

At about eleven o'clock, the drummers still pounding, their nasal chants intermittently drowning out the tom-tom like a banshee in a thunderstorm, Clark turned into his blanket and lay reflecting. Fate had brought him to an isolated Sioux encampment housing the most notorious braves who were being held in check by the whims of but one chief; here he was listening to their weird, devilish songs and about to sleep – or try to – in safety. Sleep he did.

Just as Irvine was getting ready to retire for the night there was a tapping at the entrance to his tent.

"Come in," bellowed the colonel, thinking it was Walsh or one of the scouts. In stepped Sitting Bull. Irvine motioned Bull to sit alongside him and he called for an interpreter.

Bull was wearing his smoke-tanned buckskin shirt decorated with quill work and human hair. His leggings and moccasins were also of tanned buckskin. Irvine noticed again his broad, lined face, his heavy jaw and his thin lips, and he detected a look of concern rather than absolute power.

Bull, it became apparent, was in need of some consolation and sympathy. He sat on the edge of the cot. Irvine, the military man, turned the conversation around to the Battle of the Little Big Horn. Bull said he knew for twelve days that Custer and his troops were on the way to attack his camp, and that when the fight was joined the soldiers found that their carbines jammed and they could use them only as clubs. They had to rely on their revolvers because they were not carrying swords. The Indians pulled the troops off the horses and killed most of them with knives and stone clubs.

Bull said he never saw Custer but others recognized him before he was killed when the soldiers' defences splintered and the Indians moved in to finish them off. "He did not wear his hair long as he used to wear it. It was short and the colour of grass when the frost comes."

101

When it was time to leave, Bull took off his beaded moccasins and presented them to the colonel as a memento. They shook hands and Bull walked away in his bare feet.

"Poor people!" Irvine noted. He knew American troops usually had orders to "kill all who talk."

Irvine was satisfied the Indians understood what was expected of them. He prepared to return to Fort Walsh with the three Americans. Walsh was going in the opposite direction, to Wood Mountain, as it had been decided to bolster the force there to twenty men.

Irvine and his party moved westwards along the streams of clear water that interspersed the ravines of Pinto Horse Buttes and then out onto the plains where the ragged grass was as high as a man's knee. And then came a swirling snow storm, in early June, and all had to shelter for a day behind prickly bushes in a ravine.

Irvine continued his journey to Fort Walsh without any further incident, then moved on to Fort Macleod where he relayed appropriate messages that in his opinion Sitting Bull would be law-abiding. Commissioner Macleod, despite this, recommended to the Government that Ottawa inform Washington that the Teton Sioux would not be recognized as British subjects, that reserves would not be allocated to them, and the Canadian Government would not assume the responsibility for their upkeep.

The commissioner was concerned that such a concentrated conglomeration of Tetons on the fringes of the hunting grounds of their ancient enemies, the Blackfoot and the Crees, must inexorably lead to a major clash, particularly as the once limitless buffalo herds were vanishing. In these circumstances the police would be powerless to halt what would be an Indian war on a grand scale, both the Sioux and the Blackfoot being by instinct and upbringing prodigal and uncompromising fighters. Macleod wrote Prime Minister Mackenzie that an attempt should be made at once "to get these Indians to recross the U.S. side. The longer it is delayed the more difficult it will be."

The commissioner continued: "I believe the U.S. Government have set apart large reserves for these Indians, and have made very liberal appropriation for their support."

The U.S. Government itself was equally unhappy at the prospects of continually dealing with thousands of warriors who would be in a position to mount hit-and-run attacks from the north upon the boundary settlements and retreat to a sanctuary that would be out of bounds to U.S. pursuers. This would lead to a series of international incidents that neither Ottawa nor Washington was anxious to foment.

The Americans, in their concern, most co-operatively waived the customs regulations to allow passage to Fort Benton of eight train carloads of boxes – each box was three feet long and two feet deep and was marked, "Merchandise – Canadian Government." The merchandise? Emergency supplies of ammunition for the NWMP.

Sitting Bull, meanwhile, who had been a model refugee but nevertheless was still king of the Teton realm, was hoping his subjects would receive the same consideration and concessions that were accorded the Santee Sioux when they fled to Canada following the Minnesota massacres.

The official Ottawa viewpoint was that Sitting Bull and other U.S. Indians should be induced to return to reservations...induced, not compelled.

From the U.S. standpoint, persuasion was the only possible alternative if the Canadians were not prepared to use force. And the next persuader in Sitting Bull's lodge was another religious person, Father Jean-Baptiste Génin of Ottawa, liked and indeed respected by many among the Indian bands who criss-crossed Dakota Territory and followed the herds into Montana. To the Sioux he was known as the Black Gown who had been "adopted" by Chief Black Moon as a nephew.

In '76 he had started to set up Catholic churches adjacent to the Northern Pacific Railroad. The last thing he wanted to see was recurrent warfare. The Indians were obviously bitterly opposed to the iron horse cutting their remaining hunting grounds in two.

He was making his own personal crusade to influence Bull to surrender to the U.S. authorities. Bull listened politely, in compliance with the instructions of Irvine and Walsh, but absolutely refused to consider the priest's suggestions. The missionary returned to the south with definite opinions about the Mounted Police: "I regret sincerely that the Canadian officers of police petted Sitting Bull so much instead of reinforcing our work by advising him to surrender and put an end to all the trouble."

❖❖❖ The Blessings and the
Temptations



❖❖❖ The hot, listless days of late spring and summer came as a blessing to the Tetons. Their hearts were good in the safety of the hills and valleys of the white grandmother. They could hunt; they could eat and sleep without having to look over their shoulders for Bluecoats. There was tranquility in the lodges and around the cooking fires, a relaxed time for friends, for courting, for games, gambling and horse racing, a time for composing and singing songs, a time for copulation.

Bull could concentrate more on his wives and children. He liked to play with his children, all children, to carry them piggyback around the lodges, running and cavorting with the energy of a bronco.

His heart was noticeably gentle as he urged all his people to get along with their Wood Mountain neighbours, the French-speaking halfbreeds. Life was a delightful, lingering holiday. There was food aplenty for every family's kettle.

To coincide with the period of the month when there was eternal light, when the moon was full, Bull dutifully organized a great looking-at-the-sun dance to give thanks to the Creator, to receive His blessings and to test the strength of the young men. There were eight days of feasts and vows climaxed by a profound spectacle of torturous worship. The sacrifical cottonwood pole was ceremoniously selected and put up in an area near where the Métis had built cabins and corralled their horses.

Forty aspiring warriors, carefully selected and anxious to emerge into manhood in the ritualistic manner, were stripped to the waist and painted red and black, and purified in the three ways: by the smoke of the sweet grass, by the steam of water poured on hot stones, by the rubbing of their bodies with sage. They lined up to the west of the holy tree trunk. When the drummers responded to their own rhythm with the sacred chants, the "graduates" swaggered to the unvaried beat, bodies gyrating, necks straining, heads tilted upwards, the breath that was left going into their holy-voiced eagle-bone whistles, the shrill, squeaky tones a harping, unharmonious contrast with the fast, deep, monotone pulse of the drums, each beat the voice of the Great Spirit. They danced in a circle, symbolic of the shape of the sun and the full circle of all life.

Hovering about them was a holy man, a combination high priest and master of ceremonies who raised the pipe with both hands to the deity for the blessings. Encircling the active participants were the chiefs, the war chiefs, other dignitaries of the councils, and alongside and behind throngs of happy spectators in their very best finery.

The young men danced all day around the pole, without food or water, and through the night until dawn when the ritual of self-sacrifice started, an event anticipated with considerable veneration and expectation. This would be a profound ceremony for the holy man; a divine act for all the Tetons.

One by one the braves moved forward to lie under the pole. The priest cut and pulled up the skin from their breasts or turned them around to cut into their high backs and pushed wooden or bone skewers into their muscles. When these were in place, protruding through the flesh at the ends and the blood flowing down dusky bodies and dripping onto the legs, the holy man fastened each skewer to a horsehair rope that was tied to the top of the pole. The boys with skewers in their backs were joined to heavy buffalo skulls.

When all were attached to the pole or skulls, the drummers worked themselves into a vocal frenzy, the beat accelerating and the spectators reacting predictably, trance-like, with shouts of encouragement. The dancers deliberately tortured themselves by stepping jerkily, by springing, twisting and leaning backwards, tugging with their bodies so that the skewers were slowly tearing the flesh, the tissues gradually softened by excruciating pressure. The more they tugged, the tauter the ropes and the greater the pain. The young men, their bodies a mass of blood, gritted their teeth and bore silently the dedication of their tussle with the skewers until after several hours the climactic finale, and with one bursting wrench the skewers tore through the flesh with a splurge of blood, and sprung out, and the ropes went limp at the pole.

The boys had given their bodies to Wi, the sun, to the Great Spirit without the sin of one cry. Such was the making of a brave (and scarred) man. The proud families dressed their heroes' lacerations with moss from the creek banks.

The Métis were putting on a show of their own. They delighted to tease these hardened Sioux with the speed of their horses, racing them spectacularly for prizes. The warriors watched with envy. The jealous ones had been warned by Bull and his soldiers, who in their day had been the leading protagonists of the honourable profession of rustling, that horse-stealing forays were forbidden. In these circumstances the underemployed braves were finding the adjustment to the Redcoats' law an almost unbearable imposition. Since childhood they had been reared and trained to ride off with the wealth of others to gain their feathers. It was all right for the old men, the big bellies, to change the tune; they had their glories. How could the young men get their share?

The temptation to run off some sleek Métis horses became overpowering for Gray Eagle, brother-in-law of Bull. Gray Eagle and three companions arranged for the disappearance of a hundred head.

It was obvious to the Métis that the Sioux were the culprits. They complained to the police and Walsh went to see Bull.

The wily chief, alarmed that this incident might set back his campaign for a permanent settlement in Canada, promised that the offenders would be found and punished in the Indian way. It didn't take him long to uncover the ringleader, Gray Eagle. Reluctantly, Bull called in his own policemen, led by One Bull, to carry out his sentence: "Put him on a horse, run him to the top of a bluff. If he falls off, shoot him. If he stays on, let him live."

This was drastic retribution for a relative. Bull's heart was heavy and sad.

Gray Eagle was taken from his lodge and put on a horse without saddle or rein. One Bull, with Brown Eagle, Little Horse, Bob Tail Bull, Killed Plenty and Brave Crow, stampeded Gray Eagle to a high bluff and when the pony got to the brink it reared on its haunches. To the relief of the six "executioners" Gray Eagle hung on – for his life.

He was sent out into the hills to bring in the stolen horses, but could not find anywhere near the hundred. The chiefs, the owners of most of the horses in the camp, had to deplete their own herds so that the correct number could be returned to the Métis.

Bull was further displeased about this sacrifice and ordered Gray Eagle before him to demand the identity of his accomplices. His young relative, who had always been loyal and had fought in battles with distinction, could not refuse. He revealed three names: Good Crow, White Bird and White Cow Walking. Bull authorized their arrest and punishment.

Each horse-taker, including Gray Eagle, was to be tied to two upright stakes by the ankles and wrists, their legs and arms outstretched, the ankles to be tethered to the bottom of the poles, toes barely touching the earth, and their wrists above their heads. They were to be naked and to be strung up during daylight for seven days and allowed only water for sustenance. At night they were to be cut down and imprisoned in a lodge.

When Bull's wives heard of this there was much wailing and protesting for had not their brother already been punished and confronted with death? Bull relented, but the other three, not yet punished, were subjected to this week-long torture, in full view of everyone, and guarded by Bull's police with his threats that should one of the prisoners escape the sentries would take his place to be tormented by the flies and mosquitoes.

At the end of the week, when the young men had come through their ordeal, Sitting Bull and his tightly-knit group of Hunkpapa soldier-policemen organized a feast to honour the three miscreants who had been stretched and burned under the sun. Bull proclaimed that he was proud that his young warriors had taken their punishment with fortitude. They received many gifts from Bull and his cohorts, mostly embroidered clothing.

All was forgiven on both sides. Bull explained his predicament. His generosity and oratory overflowed. The culprits, knowing that in the old days the chief would have praised them for their action, did not harbour bitterness or revenge in their hearts – not then. After all, was it not so that the chief, Tatanka Iyotake, had to shield the people from the clutches of Bear Coat and the Americans and look to the Redcoats for protection? Indeed it was true.

Walsh had set up his temporary headquarters at Wood Mountain during the summer of '77 so that he could personally supervise the police detachment that had the day-and-night burden of making sure the Teton Sioux behaved themselves. The various bands were enduringly nomadic, which meant the Redcoats were continually patrolling, sometimes well off the trails, to ensure the young men were heeding Sitting Bull's advice. And besides, Walsh could not really convince himself Ol' Sit had suddenly become, permanently, a law-abiding citizen. He needed watching, from a short distance.

Furthermore, Walsh was getting messages from the fort that the Nez Percé Indians, whose inherited and legitimate domain was the Valley of Wallowa in Oregon Territory, had refused to be moved onto a reservation and were fighting their way towards Canada over and across more than a thousand miles of mountains and plains. Fast on their heels, or trying to head them off, were converging columns of U.S. cavalry and infantry.

Walsh started to patrol the country south of the border. There was some sketchy information that a few of the Nez Percés were in advance of the main band nearing the line.

The major had two scouts with him, Léveillé and Culbertson, the latter a recent addition to the eyes and ears of the force. They were moving westwards, parallel to the line and thirty miles north of it when they saw in the haze about twenty lodges seven or eight miles south. It was Léveillé's opinion they were Nez Percé tepees. Culbertson agreed. It was the consensus they should approach with caution.

They got going at a gallop. Lévellé had trouble keeping pace and when Walsh looked back from his saddle after riding a mile he saw that both scouts had fallen well behind. He didn't think anything of this; probably they had stopped to tighten their saddle girths. The terrain was uneven and Walsh lost sight of the two men as he pushed on.

Within a mile of the camp he halted to have another look at the lodges with his field glasses. He turned around again and saw only one horseman, far behind. It appeared to be Léveillé on Culbertson's mount. Walsh rode on another half mile, and after concluding the lodges were American Assiniboines or Crows he rode into the camp. They were Assiniboines. He dismounted, sat on the grass with them, and enquired haltingly about the possible route of the Nez Percés.

At this point everybody was startled to see a horseman (it was Léveillé) riding at full whack up the gentle slope to where they were seated. His carbine was out of the holster, ready to shoot. He abruptly reined his horse, which was panting and white with foam, jumped off, and full of agitation, ran to the major.

"What's the matter?" Walsh asked. He half expected to hear that something had occurred between Léveillé and Culbertson and that Léveillé had shot him and taken his horse.

"I thought these people were Nez Percés and I would find you dead!" Léveillé replied between gasps for breath.

It had happened that Culbertson had refused to catch up with Walsh, and Léveillé, who had an inferior horse, had forced Culbertson to change mounts – "I'll kill you if you don't!" – so that he could close the gap. He could have been cut down, as he thought the major had been, but such was the impetus of his loyalty.

From that day on Léveillé had no respect for Culbertson, "one of those men, full of courage, who talk about the number of Indians they've killed."

On the prairie, in Indian country, nothing was quicker or more usually reliable than the native runners. It was certain therefore that Sitting Bull and his war chiefs knew about the plight of the Nez Percés.

Under the astute and courageous direction of Chief Joseph they had been able to beat back or evade their pursuers, as the tactics demanded, to reach the Bear Paw Mountains, less than 100 miles south of Fort Walsh.

The major, alert to the natural sympathies of the Sioux toward the harassed Nez Percés, counselled Bull and his henchmen to weigh their blessings and not be foolishly drawn into any plan of military assistance. Before leaving for Fort Walsh he warned Bull to keep his warriors north of the line.

As the Nez Percés edged nearer to the border, and the lines of communication became shorter, the spreadeagled Sioux encampment became alive with scouts and messengers. The Sioux knew exactly what was going on, that their mutual enemy Bear Coat Miles had the Nez Percés in a trap, at the Place of the Manure Fires, and that the refugees were hoping that Sitting Bull would ride out of the north with thousands of warriors to sweep the soldiers into the Missouri. Just as soon as Bull's chiefs got the latest information so did Walsh's trusted informants; the superintendent had made sure Fort Walsh was hooked up to the moccasin telegraph.

When Walsh was tipped off that the Sioux soldiers were getting out of control and preparing, hopefully, for war, he cut short his business and hurried away again to Wood Mountain. He got back just in time. A more intense display of frenetic savagery he had never before witnessed.

Small groups of older men were crouching around the rawhide drums, thumping them with a rapid beat, one hand cupped to the sides of their mouths to amplify their high-pitched chanting. The effect of all the wild reverberations upon the young men was startling. They were ready for battle, hundreds of them, bare to their breech clouts, faces and bodies painted in stripes and dots. One war chief, Rain In The Face, his body black from the waist up and his ribs garishly outlined with white paint, was a frenzied participant. They were going round and round, lithe bodies prancing from one foot to the other in a disarray of physical contortions.

Walsh could see the war dances were nearing a climax. He hastened to Sitting Bull and called a council of war chiefs to reiterate his warnings that they would be endangering what they were now enjoying if the firebrands were allowed to follow their instincts.

The hot spirits might yet be controllable, but their cries were undiminished – "to the rescue...to the rescue!"

The Sioux had sent out about fifty scouts who were coming back and forth with the news. Mirror signals flashed from the hills to the south. In the unofficial councils, where groups of warriors gathered to hear the latest graphic accounts from the border, the verdict to attack the Longknives was clamorous and unanimous. The chiefs, realistically, were listening to Walsh.

"Canada will no longer be a place of safety for you if you let the young men go on the warpath," Walsh warned them bluntly. "One man who crosses the line with hostile intentions, just one man, will sacrifice for ever the safety and shelter that everyone in this camp cherishes.

"The man who crosses the line from this camp, from the moment he puts his foot on American soil, will be our enemy. And if he comes back we shall be to him what he says the Longknives are – wolves seeking his blood."

The major's pronouncement, uncompromising and clear, was

acted upon. The war chiefs forbade their warriors to prepare their horses with the lucky charms of battle. No one left the camp, not even a runner.

Walsh and his troop had pitched their tents on the south side across the track to the border. This was a deterrent though hardly a barrier. The only people on the immediate trails were the returning scouts, and their observations were carried directly to the council where Walsh was sitting with the chiefs to discuss the up-to-date information on the plight of the Nez Percés and to speculate on their actions.

A grey dawn was appearing on the second day when Walsh was finally able to retire for a few hours' sleep. At that time the Sioux had learned that White Bird, a Nez Percé war chief, a man of clear perception and quick decisions, had broken through the American encirclement and was leading about 100 men, 50 women, about as many children, and 300 horses, towards Wood Mountain.

When Walsh awoke he found the vast conglomeration of Sioux in a reinvigorated state of fury. He was visited by Spotted Eagle along with other chiefs who wanted to know how the Redcoats would receive White Bird's refugees should they come to the Sioux for food and shelter, and what the lawmakers would do should the Longknives cross the line to capture the Nez Percés. The major informed Spotted Eagle that all refugees would be safe on British soil. This statement seemed to pacify, once more, some of the agitators, although they were all itching to mount their ponies and rush south to settle a legacy of old scores.

Emotions ebbed and flowed, and then when it seemed Walsh had reimposed, via the chiefs, the wisdom of restraint, something happened to rekindle the urge for retribution. The continuing crisis, the day-to-day ups and downs of diplomacy and persuasion, had gone into the first week of October, and on the eighth day some Sioux scouts, highly disturbed, their horses shiny with sweat, galloped around the camp shouting warnings of many whites coming form the south.

It must be Bear Coat Miles and his soldiers out to punish the people now they were all together!

Panic, uproar and outrage were instantaneous. Warriors ran for weapons and horses in their impulsive eagerness to do battle; the women, accustomed to emergencies and frightingly determined to save their families' belongings, moved quickly to take down the tepees; the children and the old people helped where they could; and the hundreds of dogs scampered in and out of lodges barking and getting in the way during all the hectic confusion and commotion.

Walsh and his men managed to keep the horde at bay until the chiefs were informed their scouts had probably come in with the wrong information. Walsh offered to ride out and see who these invaders were. And he did, with 200 warriors.

A more incongruous spectacle, in those times and on those plains, would be difficult to contrive; a faint blur of red coats and white helmets engulfed in an onrushing wave of a painted, feathered mob galloping full out with piercing yells and war cries to investigate reports of an American invasion. By the time the irregular column had reached the border territory, Walsh found himself the commander of nearly a thousand warriors, a commander who would have had no control at all if the U.S. Army had appeared before them. The Sioux, in their mood, would have swept forward into a fight with the inexorable flash and fury of a prairie storm.

What they encountered, before they reached the invisible line of the boundary, stopped them short with exclamations of anger and pity. These were not whites coming towards them, these were Indians, a distraught, straggling, decimated band of White Bird's Nez Percés.

There were about 200 of them in this first group; unyielding, grim-looking warriors and their families, and some ponies. Even by crude and hard Indian standards these people were in a pitiable condition. When the Sioux greeted them there were wailed cries of disbelief, shouts that there must be revenge.

Many of the children, who had their arms and legs broken and shattered by bullets, were tied to the saddle horns; haggard women, clothed in tatters, wept silently for their children or with their own pain. (One mother had been shot in the breast and the ball had entered just below the nipple, turned upwards and passed through the side of her head. She was on a pony and had a baby strapped to her back with a shawl.) The warriors were in rags, groaning with wounds; one man, naked to the waist, was still bleeding from a bullet gash in his chest. Everyone was destitute.

All these people had crept up the ravines and through the U.S. lines at night while negotations were going on for the surrender of Chief Joseph and all Nez Percés. When they were clear of Bear Coat's sentinels they were soon riding or running northwards, convinced that the Bluecoats would undoubtedly be chasing them. They crossed the border late on the second day and on the third were evidently spotted by Indians to the north. These were the Sioux who thought, from a great distance, that the oncoming blobs on the hills were the vanguard of General Miles's army.

Sitting Bull was touched.

"Before Long Hair (Custer) died, we killed four Nez Percés. Now I want to be friends. You can stay with us as long as you please." The grateful strangers gave Bull eight horses.

Hospitality being as important to Indian philosophy as fortitude and bravery, the Sioux cared for the Nez Percés as if they were long-lost relatives.

They carried most of them back to Wood Mountain, took them into their lodges, fed them, clothed them, nursed them back to health and restored their respect. And when the Nez Percés were well enough the Sioux provided lodges so that they could lead their own lives again. Bull slipped quietly away with a scouting band of Sioux and Nez Percés to the battle site. They brought back some ammunition the beleaguered refugees had buried.

Walsh's sympathies had been aroused by what he had seen in the last few days. His admiration for White Bird, even as he met the chief in complete desperation at the end of his 1,600-mile running battle, was profound though officially guarded. He did not want to make a hero out of White Bird, yet as he looked at these people he was moved in a grand but melancholy way to make comparisions with the glories and the depression of the stories he had read in his youth of Greece and Rome. He felt the saga of Chief Joseph's people, and White Bird's successful retreat, would one day outdo Ben-Hur and would show Europe that North America also had its heroes.

The Nez Percés had been among the first of the far western tribes to welcome the white men and extend their hospitality. The explorers they encountered were in the Lewis and Clark expedition, during 1805; shortly thereafter came the French-Canadian and halfbreed traders and trappers, the contemporaries of David Thompson whose search for new and expanding fur concessions lured them into uncharted mountain territories.

A question Walsh and his men asked themselves was a common one: How did these Indians get their name? There was nothing to indicate the Nez Percés, the Pierced Noses, ever pierced their noses or nostrils for ornaments or for any purpose or reason. Perhaps they used to when the French Canadians bestowed upon them a tribal title that invariably sounded like "Nezz Purses" in English.

The Nez Percés had felt the full, confining force and might of white power and encroachment in May of '77 when Chief Joseph, Echoing Thunder to his own following, was given marching orders and only thirty days' notice to gather and move all his people's stock and possession onto an undesireable reservation.

General Oliver Otis Howard, the one-armed soldier chief, had been given the instructions to move the Indians, although in his heart he knew the Government action was a wrong one – and he said so, privately. However, he had his orders and when Joseph asked for more time, the anguished chief was warned by Howard that if they were just one day late with the move his army would force them from the valley. Additionally, all their livestock, including their horses, would be taken over and distributed to white settlers.

What irony! Here was Joseph, a chieftain more inclined to live in peace and adopt the white man's ways then most native leaders, being unconscionably dispossessed. The Nez Percés were indignant and bitter.

Deceptively mild-mannered and demure, White Bird, now safe in Canada, bared his story and his soul to Walsh.

"Our people were living in a beautiful valley [of the Wallowa River]. Our herds, cattle and sheep covered every hill. We lived in houses, and we had churches and schools; we were starting to grow our food and had given up the hunt. Our children were being educated and our people christened and no period of our nation's life was more prosperous than the year that Howard came to move us from our houses.

"The chief of our nation was Joseph. He had succeeded his father, Old Joseph [the name given to him long ago when he became a Christian]. Old Joseph was a good man and very fond of the whites and anxious to have them settle around him. Most of the people did not feel the same way.

"I remember the first white man to come to our country and he asked to remain among us. Joseph was pleased with the idea, and consented, and gave him horses, cattle and land. I was then a young man and loved Joseph, but I had a sort of suspicion of white men, and told Joseph of my feelings. He said I was wrong, that we should encourage the white men to come to us because there was much we could learn from them in growing grain, vegetables and working the soil.

"He wanted his people to improve; they must have instructors. Before many moons had passed another white man came, and Joseph held out his hand as he did to the first. I again protested against whites joining us and told Joseph that the day would come when he would regret taking them in like brothers, that the white men would deceive him and bring misery upon his people. He said I was blinded.

"I could not quarrel with Joseph, but in my heart I felt he was leading our people into danger. Year after year white men came and located in our country. Poor old Joseph was happy and always their friend.

"He knew the white men did not please me and often he talked to me and tried to make me believe – and hard did I try to believe him – that it was good to have the white men among us. But I could not see his way.

"Poor old Joseph died and his son became chief and he too liked the whites. We were happy and prosperous. More white men came but could find no room. Our hills and valleys were full with the herds of the Indians and their white friends, but the white men saw our good grass and the thousands of animals, and their hearts grew hungry.

"They asked the great chief at Washington to give them Joseph's country and to move the Nez Percés to a reservation. It is a beautiful country and should be open to white people, they said. Let the Indians be moved over to the other side of the gravel range; the country there is good enough for them.

"The white chiefs said, 'Yes, move Joseph.' Our people were told of the decision. Sadness and bitterness filled every heart. Were we going to be driven from our country, torn from the homes our fathers gave us?

"Joseph's head was bowed and upon him the blow fell heaviest. 'O my Father,' he said, 'what have we done that this happens to us?'

"Joseph called a council of all head men of his tribe. He was crushed in spirit. I objected to the decision from Washington and advised Joseph to protest immediately. He did so, but a reply soon came back, that it was settled and the Nez Percés must move. Another council was called.

"Joseph, always peaceable and obedient, said that the Government's commands should be obeyed, but I could not agree with him and asked him if he fully realized what such a move would mean – were not the hills covered with our stock; was not our fortune in those herds; were we after years of toil by ourselves going to throw this country away? Who are richer than Joseph and his people? No, we shall not give away our rights, our country handed down from our fathers whose graves mark a possession of 200 years. We will not surrender! No man has a right to tell us that we must do so!

" 'The chiefs at Washington want lands for their friends,' I told him. 'There are miles of it, unsettled, in other sections. Send them to it; let them do what our fathers did here, make out of it homes for their children.'

" 'If I have to leave this home, I shall never accept another south of the British line.'

"Joseph, who had promised his dying father that never would he sell the earth that held his bones, still wanted to surrender and said that because of our families we should accept the change and move across the mountains to the new territory selected by the Government for us. I said, 'Joseph, I shall never do anything to injure you, but before you move your families you should gather your herds and send them to your new country, and when they are all moved there, then move your house.' Joseph agreed to do this and instructed the young men to go into the hills and gather the horses and cattle and drive them to the new land.

"Two changes of the moon passed and not more than one third of the stock was moved; the cattle and horses, like the people, did not want to leave their homes and would wander back during the night half the distance they were driven forward during the day. The young men, disheartened and worn out guarding the herds, said it was useless; the stock could not be removed from their native ranges, and they called upon Joseph to ask Washington again not to move the Nez Percés from their houses.

"Joseph talked with me. 'Joseph,' I said, 'are you blind to the purpose of the white man in taking you from this country? He sees those valleys and hillsides covered with thousands of horses and cattle. To him this is precious like their yellow metal. It is not your land he wants, it is your herds. He knows these animals cannot be kept from these ranges where they have been bred for generations, and with you gone, the whites will possess them. Joseph, when you leave this house, you leave all your possessions, as well as the bones of your fathers.'

"Joseph met with Howard [in May of '77] and protested again the bad things planned for the people. Howard's ears were closed. He replied, 'You must move and your departure must not be delayed.' Howard left us, and Joseph was so oppressed he knew not what to do. To go to the new reservation [Lapwai, the Valley of Butterflies, in Idaho] would mean the Nez Percés would become poor; to resist the orders of Howard would mean war and killing.

"I said, 'Joseph, I shall never submit to this robbery; I will not give up my right to this home; I will never surrender. It may be all torn from me, and when I leave I will leave all I possess, except my family; they will accompany me. Tomorrow will separate me from these hills I love, from my fathers' graves, perhaps forever.'

" 'In what direction will you go my friend?' Joseph asked.

" 'North,' I replied, 'to the Redcoats' country.'

" 'You don't know these people,' Joseph said.

" 'Yes, my fathers and your fathers knew them well, the soldiers in the red coats.'

"Looking Glass, a chief with forty warriors, said he and his people would come with my people.

"The following day, with women's hearts breaking, children weeping and men silent, we moved over the divide that closed our eyes to our once happy home and we became wanderers. We who yesterday were rich were today beggars, made so by the order of the Christian white chiefs of justice at Washington."

White Bird hoped to cross into Canada by the Big Hole Pass through the Rocky Mountains, but Howard declared him and all the others hostile and he pursued them.

The fighting had started after a small group of warriors, during darkness and in a spate of drunken revenge on the resented march to the Lapwai reservation, killed at least fifteen white settlers, plundered their property and assaulted their women. Joseph, who had nothing to do with this episode but knew that all of his following would be victimized, was now unalterably committed to stand and fight with his people who were divided in their opinions over the killings. General Howard was more than ever determined to obey his instructions with briskness and a religous zeal. He had no desire to be branded in the army as an Indian lover.

After an incredibly skilful running fight across 1,500 miles that brought him to within less than fifty miles of Canada, and safety, Joseph surrendered. A figure of dignity in his extreme adversity, he stood before Miles and Howard to announce he was tired of fighting.

"Our chiefs are killed....The old men are all dead. It is the young men who say Yes or No. He who led the young men [Joseph's younger brother Ollokot] is dead. It is cold and we have no blankets. The little children are freezing to death...." Pitifully he proclaimed, "Hear me, my chiefs, I am tired. My heart is sick and sad. From where the sun now stands, I will fight no more forever."

White Bird was determined to fight to the finish. His heart was sad too, so while Joseph was giving in, White Bird guided his followers away with him into the darkness, past the sentries, through the snow; they were so sick with cold and hunger that even the wild animals had more in their stomachs and on their backs.

After White Bird delivered the remnants of the people to the Sioux, a great depression came upon him. "I have no country, I have no home, and I feel I have no people," he told Walsh.

He confided that he prayed to the Great Spirit morning and night asking to be taken away from this life to join his comrades in the hunting grounds of the Creator.

Walsh, after hearing White Bird's saga, commented that he must be the greatest Indian soldier who ever lived – "history does not tell us of his equal."

White Bird reciprocated with compliments. He said he had always been taught that there were two white peoples who treated the Indians honestly – the English and the French.

What of the future? Some of the warriors, with their families, wanted to stay with the Sioux; others who liked the way of the whites expressed a desire to move into the Cypress Hills, nearer to the traders' village; others, Walsh thought, might still want to return to the side of Joseph in the United States because their

118

relatives were there. Three of these would be Joseph's daughter, his only surviving child, and her husband, and Joseph's nephew, Yellow Wolf, whose face was drawn with worry, whose memory retained the history of his people, whose lust to kill white settlers was not yet satisfied.

Unknown to Walsh, Miles sent two emissaries into the Sioux camp to demand the return of White Bird and his exiles. One of the messengers was a white man, the other a treaty Nez Percé. The first impulse was for the refugees to kill them. Fortunately, Bull found out about these truculent, foolhardy visitors and on the sole basis of his pledge to Walsh, intervened and rescued them from certain execution. He arranged for their escape a couple of days later.

Now it was up to Walsh to reveal the news all the Nez Percés had been waiting for: yes, they could remain in Canada on condition they stayed within the bounds of the law, which Walsh, for the umpteenth time, summarized.

There was no such leniency for Chief Joseph. He and the survivors were moved, as if they were cattle, to Fort Lincoln and on to Fort Leavenworth in a territory the whites called Kansas. They were uprooted once more, to the Indian Territory (Oklahoma), and lodged in a swampland where many of them died of malaria and heartbreak.

Miles protested solicitously; the authorities overruled him. These Indians had to be punished, and indeed they were. Miles was especially incensed. "The Nez Percés were the boldest men and the best marksmen I have encountered. I acted on what I supposed was the original design of the Government – to place these Indians on their own reservation – and so informed them."

Far away to the north their relatives heard of such treatment. They were sick with sorrow. Sitting Bull and his comrades talked of these bad things happening to the Indians, of how they were being persecuted.

As for Walsh, he could accept some self-congratulations without endangering his affinity for perspective. If the Sioux had been allowed to attack Miles to rescue the Nez Percés, the law of averages would have opted for the destruction of Bear Coat's force – and the end of his much-publicized reputation.

# ❖❖❖ The Adversaries Meet Head-on

❖❖❖ The dispatch from the Secretary of State, the Hon. R.W. Scott, to the commissioner of the Mounted Police on August 15, 1877, was headed Immediate and Important.

It stated:

> Important that Sitting Bull and other United States Indians should be induced to return to reservations. United States Government have sent Commissioners to treat with them. Co-operate with Commissioners, but do not unduly press Indians. Our action should be persuasive, not compulsory. Commissioners will probably reach Benton about 25th inst. [August]. Arrange to meet them there. Reply.

The telegram was sent via the Benton trading company, I.G. Baker, and the contents underlined the uneasiness in Ottawa concerning the embarrassing and dangerous presence on Canadian soil of the redoubtable Sitting Bull and his allies. The reference to persuasion was hardly related to compassion but to realism. If Sitting Bull refused to go who was going to make him?

First Government-level rumblings of anxiety over the cost and danger of encouraging the refugees to linger in Canada had been sounded by the Lieutenant-Governor of the Northwest Territories, David Laird, a maverick politician who had helped bring down Macdonald in '73. The Privy Council, in June of '77, through the British chargé d'affaires in Washington, Sir Francis Plunkett, suggested the Americans should persuade the Sioux to return. U.S. Secretary of State William M. Evarts dallied a month before replying, bluntly, that because the Indians were political offenders seeking asylum, the U.S. Government did not have the legal right to seek extradition, neither was it prepared to offer concessions of inducement.

120

Prime Minister Mackenzie, who had visions of having to feed these disrupters at an enormous cost or, alternatively, fight them, made the next move. Undiplomatically, without consulting British officials, he sent David Mills, his scholarly Minister of the Interior, to Washington with informal messages for President Hayes urging conciliation and justice for the Sioux. Mills reported back with optimism that the Americans would appoint a commission to negotiate with the exiles. Mackenzie, by now in a tougher mood, was thinking out loud, in conversation and in letters to Macleod and Dufferin, of inviting U.S. troops into Canada to conveniently eject their evasive enemy.

In Washington nobody wanted to be saddled with the responsibility (or the expense) of the commission. The ideal solution would be for the Canadians to disarm the renegades and force them across the border, or at least to remove them far to the north. By mid-August, after three cabinet meetings, the President authorized a commission but had difficulty staffing it. Eventually he had to call upon Brigadier-General Alfred H. Terry, who as military commander of the Dakotas had directed the '76 campaign of chastisement against the hostiles. Co-commissioner was soldier-diplomat General Albert G. Lawrence. They had authorization to offer the fugitive criminals a presidential pardon, and reservations and cattle – on the condition they surrender weapons and horses.

Ottawa was most anxious to ensure success, the point being stressed by Mills in a letter to Macleod:

"These Indians, while engaged in hostilities with the United States, were reported to be guilty of acts of such barbarous cruelty that should they again return for the purpose of scalping women and children, their conduct could not fail to excite the indignation of the government and the people of the United States against this country. It is therefore important that you should use your influence to promote, so far as you well can, the object of the U.S. commissioners in securing the return of these Indians to their own reservation."

Macleod had his orders. He had to wait until past mid-September for more tangible information.

On September 11, Terry wired the U.S. War Department from St. Paul he was ready to confront Sitting Bull.

"I am directed to suggest," Terry noted, "that the Canadian authorities be asked to induce Sitting Bull and his chiefs and headmen to come to Fort Walsh to meet the commission....If the Indians should accept the terms offered them, it would be extremely desirable on many accounts to bring them in as early as possible. We shall expect to reach the boundary on the 29th or 30th."

Ottawa telegraphed instructions to Macleod to meet the U.S. commission at the border with a police escort.

The telegram further stated: "It would facilitate communication if Sitting Bull and the other chiefs and headmen would meet the commission at Fort Walsh."

When the news filtered through that Terry, notoriously referred to as "Star" in the Teton councils, was to be at the head of the negotiators, Walsh knew he was scheduled for an excercise of deceitful diplomacy. The Ottawa pen-pushers had done it again! Old Terry and Bull facing each other, and Terry asking the chief of chiefs to come home and take his medicine on a reservation. Hell, that would be something to see!

Why were the Americans sending Terry? Walsh wondered.

There were probably three reasons: his area of command included the great Sioux reservations; he had been on a previous commission dealing with the Tetons (which was an acrimonious failure); and he was a personable individual, not exactly a soldier's soldier, not wedded to the manual.

Macleod wanted to reach Fort Walsh with time to spare so that he could personally make sure all preparations were satisfactory for the Bull-Terry confrontation. It was his intention to be at the head of an official welcoming party for the U.S. commissioners at the border. He set out for Fort Walsh on September 28, realizing only too well the challenge of his diplomatic assignment. Had he known about the events that were about to take place in the Bear Paw Mountains, of the impending Nez Percé disaster and the Sioux reaction, he might not have felt inclined to chat so cheerily with his travelling companions.

The commissioner had ordered thirty men to accompany him: Inspector C. E. Denny, Staff-Sergeant Steele and twenty-eight non-commissioned officers and constables. Out in front, almost out of sight, heading east, was the ubiquitous Jerry Potts, the official guide and interpreter and unofficial mentor of the force.

The weather was delightful on the first few miles from the Blackfoot Crossing on the Bow River where the disunited, uninformed or confused Blackfoot allies had just signed away their heritage for money and medals. When the police were approaching the junction of the South Saskatchewan River the low, black sinister clouds rolled in, as they are liable to do in that part of the country at that time of the year, and when it started to snow and blow the policemen found themselves once more completely dependent upon the faultless sense of direction of Potts, a slight frame on a big horse, leaning into the blizzard, somehow guiding everybody through a white hell with the unerring accuracy of a compass. It was hard to believe he had not traveled this snowbound route before.

The storm lasted for several days. The trick was to let Potts do the tracking by himself, unhindered, ahead of the column and just within sight of it. He reminded Macleod of a centaur, half man and half horse, following some unseen guideposts. No one wanted to ride alongside, or talk to him for fear of disrupting his instinctive knack for going the right way and finding, God knows how, sheltered sites for overnight camps.

It was an arduous four-day trek to the stockade in Battle Creek valley. Macleod was especially gratified to ascertain that the personnel there were well advanced with their preparations for the conference despite the inevitable wags in the barracks who could not believe Sitting Bull would be coming at all.

Walsh wasn't in the barracks, or even near Fort Walsh, but he could have been excused for thinking the same way as the doubters. And nobody in the force understood Ol' Sit better than the major, who had been embroiled in the Nez Percé crisis, restraining the Sioux from pouncing on Miles, and then escorting these latest refugees to Bull's main camp, along with the hundreds of embittered Teton sympathisers.

When Walsh first mentioned to Bull that the American commissioners were on their way to negotiate his return, wanting to confer with him at Fort Walsh, the chief jettisoned his anger with a tirade of abuse against the Americans.

Walsh had Léveillé and Morin to interpret for him, but Bull spoke so rapidly and with such vehemence that the pair of them had trouble translating. Bull was overflowing with damnation and protestation.

He said he couldn't understand how "Star" Terry could be coming to ask the Sioux to return when they had just driven White

Bird out of his homeland, and taken Joseph away as a prisoner, and had been shooting the women and children. He pleaded to Walsh:

"I will do anything for you but I can't do this."

Bull threw up his hands; his broad forehead was furrowed.

"What have Joseph and his friends done to be treated so badly by the whites? I look upon them as almost white. They drive Joseph from them today, and tomorrow ask me, who they call a wild man, a hostile, a killer of white men and a hater of Americans, to come back! They say they will give me and my people a home and clothe and feed us. How can I not be suspicious of these men?"

What could Walsh say? The inconsistency was all too evident. Exile Joseph in captivity and invite Bull to become chief of his own reservation?

Bull continued to protest indignantly. While Walsh's sympathy might be with the Hunkpapa chief, he had orders to get him to talk to Terry. Walsh muttered a few words to his interpreters. They all retired and left Bull with his anger.

The major changed his tack. The next time he went to cajole Bull he let Léveillé and Morin do the talking for themselves. Both of them were natural diplomats in their dealings with the Indians. They expounded Walsh's views with native conviction, and threw in their own opinions. They reassured Bull that the police had no intention of "surrendering" the Sioux to the Americans; they merely wanted the chiefs to talk to the commissioners.

Bull said he didn't trust the motives of the Americans, that they were out to kill him and destroy his followers, and he had no intention of saying anything to them or of listening to them.

Walsh's patience and plans were being severely strained. What next? He knew there were two Métis staying in the camp, both of whom were liked and respected by Bull. Walsh got hold of this pair, Antoine Ouellette and André Larrivée, informed them of his intentions and difficulties, and persuaded them to help him get old Bull to change his mind. Another cautious conference took place; there were indications the chief was now beginning to soften his opposition. Walsh repeated his emphatic assurances of police protection, all of the time.

Bull finally consented. Reluctantly, and slowly, with about

twenty-five of his closest associates, he struck out for Fort Walsh in the company of a small contingent of Redcoats, Walsh leading the way, riding reassuringly with the pick of the Sioux leadership.

At about the same time, in this second week of October, and unknown to Walsh, Macleod was heading for Wood Mountain. There had been a delay in the projected arrival of the American commissioners at the border. Terry was held up in Benton, his escort having been commandeered to carry supplies to Miles. Macleod, with time to spare, had decided to give Walsh a hand in the persuasion of Sitting Bull.

Walsh and the Sioux met Macleod's party about halfway between the fort and the Indian encampment at Pinto Horse Buttes. The commissioner of police was relieved that Bull was actually on the way. They all camped together that night, providing Macleod with ample opportunity to assess this much-publicized king of the Sioux, this elusive and awesome pirate of the plains who was sharing the food with the police and enjoying their company.

Bull tersely told Macleod that he and his companions, despite the assurances of safe conduct, were uneasy.

"There is no use talking to these Americans," he said. "They are all liars; you cannot believe anything they say. No matter what their terms, we cannot accept because we don't believe their promises."

Next morning the march was resumed, the police, Indians and interpreters riding amicably together; the police, the brightness of their red jackets dulled with wear and dust; the Sioux, a colourful array of feathers, blankets and beaded outer garments; and the halfbreeds, in their "uniform" of buckskin shirts and dirty, weather-worn slouch hats.

The police did their best to keep the Sioux talking, to distract them from conversing among themselves. There was always a threatening possibility that they would change their minds. It was slow going. The Indians stopped frequently, dismounted and went off for an informal powwow. Every time they did this Macleod and Walsh wondered whether the latest smoke was going to bring about the decision to reverse direction.

Late in the afternoon, as they were getting near to the fort, everyone sighted a small herd of buffalo. One of the Indians spurted away and expertly killed a cow, full of the goodness of the summer grass. The only squaw with the party, one of the wives of The Bear That Scatters, deftly skinned and butchered it and cut the meat into strips.

Camp was prepared, a fire lighted, and before long the tempting aroma of broiling buffalo steaks put everyone into a most happy, contented mood. The policemen got the water boiling, and at sunset all the party were munching steaks and stirring mugs of strong tea. Late into the night they sat around the fire, white and brown faces staring into the darting flames; there was much friendly talking, and unintelligible singing and continuous feasting and tea-drinking by the Indians. The police marvelled at their gastrointestinal capacity and endurance. Each one packed away several pounds of the well-done, digestible buffalo meat.

When the fort came into view Macleod and Walsh exhanged glances of relief. The commissioner had stressed repeatedly to Bull that he need not be fearful of the U.S. Army. He was in Canada. His enemies dared not cross the boundary to attack. As long as the Sioux behaved themselves they would be protected. Bull said he believed everything he was being told.

The Sioux, accordingly, approached the post with pride, riding with noticeable grace and dignity. When they reached the fortification, however, Bull became suspiciously obstinate again and wouldn't go through the gates. He said he had never once been in a white man's fort and he would prefer to set up his lodge outside the walls. And he did, north of the palisade.

Macleod, adept in the manifestation of flattery, quickly arranged for the garrison to come out and pretentiously greet Bull and his hierarchy; the Indians were delightedly overwhelmed and complimented by the welcome. After further assurances that there was not one American in the fort, they went inside for a brief tour.

Things were going well for the Redcoats. Bull was in the fold, so to speak, although not eager to stay; then, almost to the hour after his return to Fort Walsh, Macleod received a letter from Terry, via one of his exclusive $500-a-round-trip U.S. messengers, that the peace commissioners would probably reach the border by October 14.

Terry and his party were escorted by a company of the Seventh Infantry and three companies of the Second Cavalry who had been in the final battle against Chief Joseph. Terry and Macleod reached the boundary at about the same time during the afternoon of October 15. The Americans stopped near the ford on the Milk

River when they saw riders approaching from the north. Through his field glasses Terry could identify the distinctive jackets and helmets of the North-West Mounted Police. The general spurred his horse on, followed by his aide, Captain E.W. Smith, and the commission secretary, Captain Henry Corbin. Close behind were two newspapermen.

The New York *Herald* would describe the meeting of the two men this way:

"Colonel Macleod, whose fame as a gentleman and officer had reached the commission far below this latitude of 49 degrees north, approached General Terry on horseback, and clad in his scarlet uniform at the head of a small but brilliant retinue, passed the stone monument on the left of the road and paused on United States soil to receive his guests. General Terry saluted him and both dismounted and shook hands."

The commissioners were introduced and a hearty hand-shaking session followed as Redcoats and Bluecoats mingled. The colonel was determined to put on a bit of a show, and as he and Terry and the Americans rode into Canadian territory, a platoon of police lancers, with red and white streamers fluttering conspicuously above the dun-coloured prairie of the fall, were lined up on one side of the trail to "present lances" with barrack-square precision. Terry saluted.

Three of the four companies of troopers with Terry remained just south of the line to await his return; the infantry company brought up the baggage train. Macleod and Terry rode side by side at a fast clip, the pace being continued the second day, so much so that some of the U.S. army mules flaked out and wouldn't move another inch. Terry was resolved to reach the safety of Fort Walsh before nightfall.

At sunset the international contingent reached Battle Creek. The Americans' first sight of Fort Walsh was described euphoniously in the New York paper:

"Suddenly Fort Walsh came into view, lying low in a charming valley. No more romantic spot, no wilder scene could impress a traveler at the end of a monotonous journey than the one that met our eyes. The fort, built by Major Walsh only two years ago, is notwithstanding its excellence of form and aspect so quaint and old as to remind one of the stories of the early Kentucky stockades.

"It is in fact an irregular stockade of upright logs enclosing all the offices and buildings, which are likewise built of logs, necessary for the accommodation of the garrison. Whitewashed on every part, except the roof, the fort nestles between the surrounding heights. A scraggly but picturesque little settlement adjoins it."

The commissioners and their staff were graciously received, housed and entertained in the fort; their infantry escort put up their comfortable, stove-heated tents close to the southern stockade, out of sight of Sitting Bull. There were other lodges nearby, though: those of the transient Indians who stood and glared at the Bluecoats and their Springfield rifles.

One face familiar to the Indians – and police – was John Howard, a well-informed Englishman who was chief scout for Bear Coat Miles. An Indian-baiter, he had been one of the three men rescued from Bull's camp by Irvine earlier in the year when Rev. Marty's life was in jeopardy.

The face-to-face meeting between Bull and Terry was arranged for the next day, October 17. Walsh went to inform Bull, and the chief asked him to stay, to discuss the immediate future, the implications of his intransigence, the attitude of the police.

It was apparent the natural politician in Bull could be gauged by the profuseness of his rhetoric. He said they would gladly listen to the advice of the great white mother, but they did not wish to leave her land. There was no shedding of blood in her country. They hoped to remain under her protection. Astutely, he suggested a military alliance;

"If the white mother will protect us we will be ready at all times to assist her."

Walsh and his companions declined an invitation to stay for a feast, buffalo meat washed down with tea which was laced with black tobacco, supposedly a stimulant for the war dance to follow.

In the fort, Terry was explaining to Macleod the U.S. apprehension of Sitting Bull and his hordes sweeping suddenly down on General Miles's command. It was imperative, he said, that the Sioux return to their country, give up their arms and horses, and proceed to the reserves allocated to them.

The largest quarters in the fort, the officers' mess, just inside the gate, had been furnished for the conference. Buffalo robes were on the floor for the Indians; opposite were two tables for the commissioners, the recorders and the press. The senior police officers would be seated between the two factions, at the side. The stage was set.

Sitting Bull was the first to appear, at about three o'clock, remarkably poised and pleasantly relaxed and exuding the confidence of one who was entirely prepared and organized for the events to follow. He was looking his best, his hair neatly parted in the middle and the braids placed forward, dangling over his chest. Part of his head was covered by a wolf-skin cap – recently he had been wearing a red band around the forehead to signify he was in mourning for a son. He also had on a very conspicuous shirt, black with large white dots; a blanket was tucked in around his middle covering most of his leggings; his footwear was ornate, moccasins with coloured beads threaded into symmetrical patterns and embellished by porcupine quills.

He looked about him, smiling in the direction of any policeman he saw, then he sat down near the front edge of the buffalo robe opposite the commissioners' tables. Calmly, without a word to anyone, he removed his pipe from its decorated holder, joined the bowl to the stem, filled the bowl, and started to smoke.

Taking a place next to Bull was Spotted Eagle, the defiant war chief – and he looked the part. In a knot of hair at the back of his head he had a solitary eagle's feather. He did not have a stitch of clothing from the waist up, but carried a belt of rifle cartridges across one shoulder. He had dabbed himself with white paint upon his chest and arms. Around his neck he had a charm of coloured plumes. His waist and legs were obscured by a magnificent silken robe. And he had brought with him the hideous weapon Walsh had seen before, the three-pronged tomahawk with a studded shaft.

Also close to Bull was The One Who Speaks Once, wife of The Bear That Scatters. Iron Dog, a Hunkpapa dignitary, sat in the front. He was one of the original backers of Sitting Bull for head chief and war chief of all the Sioux; he had agreed that when Bull said "make peace" he too would make peace. In war Iron Dog had always fought strongly for Bull and was with him when he attacked a camp of white men before crossing the line. They ran off some horses on that day. Others who were present were Bear's Cap, Crow and Little Knife, all known to the police and Wood Mountain traders, and Flying Bird, Storm (or Hurricane) Bird,

Yellow Dog, Nine, who was a Yankton Sioux, and The One That Runs The Ree, a Santee. Behind were twelve minor chiefs.

General Terry and his companions sat at their tables, ignored by the Sioux. When Macleod and his officers entered, Bull jumped up eagerly to shake their hands, requesting politely that "outsiders" be removed, all those bystanders who had infiltrated the officers' quarters to witness the confrontation. ("One of the most extraordinary scenes in the intercourse of white men with American savages," a reporter jotted down.) Some tables were moved aside so that all the Indians could see the Americans face-on.

General Terry was the first to speak after Macleod's opening remarks. Terry pushed himself up from the table casually, leaning on his elbows to unwind six feet plus. Erect, well proportioned, he habitually fondled his "Uncle Sam" beard and moustache. He carefully positioned his interpreter, Constant Provost, known as "Old Provo," between himself and Bull. Old Provo, an uneducated, coarse frontiersman, had been briefed with extreme care; he needed to be. He had been rehearsed on what Terry was going to say. There must be no misunderstanding.

"We are sent to you as a commission by the President of the United States at the request of the Government of the Dominion of Canada to meet you here today.

"The President has instructed me to say to you that he desires to make a lasting peace with you and your people. He desires that all hostilities shall cease and that all shall live together in harmony. He wishes this not only for the sake of whites alone, but for your sakes too. He has instructed us to say that if you return to your country and refrain from further hostilities, a full pardon will be granted you and your people for all acts committed in the past, and that no matter what these acts have been, no attempt will be made to punish you or any of your people; what is past shall be forgotten, and you will be received on as friendly terms as other Indians have been received.

"We will explain to you what the President means when he says you will be treated the same as other Indians who have surrendered."

Old Provo was a competent interpreter and translated Terry's sentences slowly and distinctly. The chiefs listened impassively.

"Of all the bands who were hostile to the United States, your band is the only one not surrendered; every other band has come into the agencies. Of the bands that have come in, not a single man

130

has been punished; every man, woman and child has been received as a friend, and all have received the food and clothing supplied for their use. Every one of you will be treated in the same manner.

"It is true that these Indians have been required to give up their horses and arms, but part of these have been sold and whatever money has been received for them will be expended for their benefit. Already 650 cows have been purchased for the use of the Indians on the Missouri River. If you abandon your present mode of life the same terms are offered to you."

Give up horses and arms! When Bull heard this from the interpreter his lips curled with a cynical smile. He lost some of his imperturbability although he remained seated and silent. Spotted Eagle was seen to wink at the police delegation.

"The President cannot, nor *will* he, consent to your returning to your country prepared for war," Terry emphasized, with the most kindly tone he could impart. "He cannot consent to your returning prepared to inflict injuries as you have done in the past. He invites you to come to the boundary of this country and give up your arms and ammunition and go to the agencies assigned to you, and give up your horses except those required for peace purposes."

Bull winced again.

"Your arms and horses will be sold and cows bought with which you can raise herds to supply you and your children long after the game has disappeared. In the meantime you will receive clothes and provisions the same as the other Indians have received.

"We have come many hundreds of miles to bring you this message; we have told you before that it is our desire that we should all live in peace; too much white and Indian blood has already been shed, and it is time that bloodshed should cease. Of one thing, however, it is our duty to inform you, that you cannot return to your country, or your own people, with arms and ammunition in your possession, and should you attempt to do so you will be treated as enemies of the United States.

"We ask you to consider carefully what we have told you and to take time and weigh the matter well....We shall be glad to meet you and await your answer."

Terry sat down, hoping the Sioux would be relieved to return on such terms. This was the cue for Sitting Bull.

Bull rose composedly from his crossed-leg sitting position,

tidied his blanket and moved forward. He was dominant. His features were creased with consternation and contempt that he would not, or could not, conceal. With a familiar sweeping gesture of his arm, upwards, in front of his face, his dark, bloodshot eyes flashing, he began to speak:

"For sixty-four years you have persecuted my people. I ask you, what have we done that caused us to leave our own country? I will tell you. We had no place to go, so we have taken refuge here. It was on this side of the boundary I first learned to shoot and be a man. For that reason I have come back. I was kept ever on the move until I was compelled to forsake my own lands and come here. I was raised with the Red River halfbreeds and today shake hands with these people." He paused, strode towards Commissioner Macleod and Superintendent Walsh, shook hands with them, returned, and continued. "This is the way I came to know these people."

Bull spoke deliberately, concisely.

"We did not give you our country; you took it from us. See how I stand with these people [pointing to the police]. Look at me! Look at these eyes and ears! You think I am a fool, but you are a greater fool than I am. I have ears; I have eyes to see with. This house is a Medicine House [the house of truth] and you come here to tell us lies and we do not want to hear them. I will not say any more; you can go back. Don't say two more words. Take your lies with you. I shake hands with these people. The country we came from belonged to us; you took it from us; we will live here.

"I intend to stay here and raise people up to fill it. I shake hands with these people [and he did, for the second time] and here I intend to stay. I want you to go back."

Truculent, defiant, Bull sat down. His rebuke of the American commissioners was impressively bitter. They were taken aback; the police officers were most embarrassed.

The chief then introduced a Santee Sioux – The One That Runs The Ree (Ree meaning Arikaree). "I was born and raised with them," said Bull. "He is going to speak." The Santee repeated Bull's complaints.

"Seven years ago I came here to escape you. For seven years I have not had to fight with your people. That is all I have lost by staying in this country....These people [the British] taught us to shoot for the first time."

A Yankton Sioux called Nine had his say:

132

"The police are good. Everyone here shakes hands. I intend to live here. With bullets here we intend to kill meat and hurt nobody. They let me trade here; everything I get I buy from the traders. I steal nothing. You came here to tell lies."

Bull managed his people expertly. His timing was admirable. He took a vindictive delight in grandiosely introducing a wife of The Bear That Scatters, a most unusual procedure, another prearranged gambit to insult the commissioners, for women were normally barred from participating in Sioux councils.

The woman, The One Who Speaks Once, tall, full-bosomed and in the prime of life, was diffident. The interpreter was puzzled as to how to convey her words to the commissioners. After a pause Old Provo said quietly; "She says, general, you won't give her time to breed!"

She told the Americans to go back where they came from. "I come to this country to raise my children. I am going to stay with these people."

The unpleasantness continued for the uneasy commissioners. They were finding it increasingly difficult to sit through the calculated insults, the ridicule, the dirty words. (There were no godly profanities; the Sioux did not have such words in their Lakota dialect.)

The Indians wanted to end the conference. Terry told the interpreter to ask them if he was to tell the President that they refused the offers made to them.

Sitting Bull confronted him.

"I could tell you more, but this is all I have to say. If I told you more you would not pay attention. This country does not belong to your people; all on this side belongs to these people. You belong on the other side. I belong here. You can take it easy going home" – meaning the Americans would not be attacked by the Sioux.

Meanwhile The Crow sidled up to Commissioner Macleod and Superintendent Walsh and embraced them. Breaking in on the harangue of Sitting Bull, he exclaimed to the commissioners:

"That is the way I like these people. How dare you come here to talk to us! This country is not yours. All this country belongs to the police. The Great Spirit does not want us to do bad things, and these people hide nothing from us. For sixty-four years you shook hands with our people, but we have had nothing but hardships. You can go back to where you came from and stay there.

We are on this side of the line to live under the great mother, to live in peace and rear our children."

General Terry said he had nothing further to say. He ended the council with one more question:

"Do you refuse?"

Sitting Bull turned suddenly, and nastily, upon him:

"I told you what I meant; that should be enough."

Terry, amiable through it all, turned to Macleod.

"That is all; I think we can have nothing more to say to them, colonel."

"I suppose you are right," replied Macleod.

He turned to Old Provo. "Tell them there is nothing more!"

Sitting Bull disdainfully ignored the Americans as he turned to shake hands with the police officers, expressing his deep affection and respect for Macleod and Walsh. He and his retinue left the room for their lodges, outside the fort. They intended to hang on for several days before returning to Pinto Horse Buttes.

Macleod, worried about political reactions, went to Bull's lodge with Walsh as soon as he could. He wanted to see if there was any hope of Bull changing his mind. The conference had failed, but perhaps Bull and the other chiefs would listen to reason. He had to be tough; he had to tell them some plain truths.

Macleod affirmed that although they claimed to be British Indians, he, as the representative of the great white mother, denied this. They were American Indians who had taken refuge on British soil. He emphasized that their only hope of a continuing livelihood was the buffalo; it was plain enough, in a short time the buffalo would be gone. When that happended they could expect nothing from the Government of the white mother except protection as long as they behaved themselves.

He warned that their decision to defy the proposals of the Americans affected not only themselves but their children. It would be well to think about this before it was too late.

Macleod repeated warnings about crossing the boundary to fight; if they did they would not only have the American soldiers as enemies but the Mounted Police and the Government.

Bull was told to carry the words of the chief of the Redcoats to his people, to tell the young men what he had said, and warn them against disobedience. They were not necessarily safe from American revenge on Canadian soil.

Bull reiterated his grievances to Macleod and repeated his relationship with the British.

"I tell you the truth; I have done nothing bad," he said almost apologetically. "The Americans tried to get our country from us....they knew that the gold was there. I told them not to go into the Black Hills. I did not give them our land no more than you would have given it....My people suffer from the Americans. I want to live in this country and be strong and well and happy.... The Americans kill ten or twenty of my children every day for nothing. I like to see all my children alive. Soon you will see more of our tribe crossing the line. The Great Spirit gave us lots of buffalo to live long....I don't believe you will help the Longknives to harm me as long as I behave myself....The Americans gave us sweet words today; they promised me flour and cattle, but if they get me across the line they would fight me....All the Americans robbed, cheated and laughed at us. I could never live there again. They never tell the truth....Everything that was bad always began with them; I have never heard a good word of them.

"Here I hear nothing bad. If they liked me why did they drive me away?...Today you heard one of our women speak; we want to raise children and be big friends with all people here and live in peace with all the Indians; they can come to our camp at any time. We like you and the police very much, and it is only for this reason we came to see the Americans."

Macleod heard the same from the others in Bull's lodge. Spotted Eagle said his people did not give up their land or take annuities. "They are liars; they pretend to know how many of us they killed, but they do not...."

"Look at me and have pity!" Bear's Cap pleaded.

Macleod gave up.

"Carry the great mother's words to your camps – and if these are obeyed your people will be safe."

The commissioner now had to frame reports of the disappointing proceedings for Scott and Mills. His personal feelings slipped in:

"They claim to have been driven off their land by the Americans who, they say, were always the aggressors and never kept any promises made to them.

"It is almost impossible to procure from Indians any distinct statement of facts; they always deal in generalities, and although during my interview with them I was continually trying to keep them to the points I wanted information upon, I could get no satisfactory statement of their grievances.

"It is a matter of common notoriety all through this western country that the Indians are systematically cheated and robbed by the agents and contractors; the former, on a salary of $1,500 a year, have been known to retire with fortunes after two or three years' incumbency in their offices. The Indians know of these scandals and as a consequence have lost all faith in the Government under which such frauds are perpetrated.

"I think the principal cause of the difficulties which are continually embroiling the American Government in trouble with the Indians is the manner in which they are treated by the swarms of adventurers who have scattered themselves all over the Indian country in search of minerals, before any treaty is made giving up the title. These men always look upon the Indians as their natural enemies, and it is their rule to shoot them if they approach after being warned off.

"I was actually asked the other day by an American, who has settled here, if we had the same law here as on the other side, and if he was justified in shooting any Indian who approached his camp after being warned not to advance. I am satisfied such a rule is not necessary in dealing fairly with the worst of Indians.....

"I communicated to the commissioners [Terry *et al*] the substance of my interview with the Sioux as far as it related to their position as refugees from the other side...."

Walsh was given the pleasant duty of escorting the Americans to the frontier. There was much to talk about on the way. The Americans had travelled thousands of miles over rough terrain only to be quickly and acrimoniously thwarted. They certainly knew now where they stood with the Sioux. And they knew where they stood with the North-West Mounted Police, from whom they had received genuine consideration and hospitality. Terry could at least confirm that the police were most anxious to get Bull off their hands and conscience.

As soon as he could, Terry warned the U.S. War Department that the presence of "this large body of Indians, bitterly hostile to us, in close proximity to the frontier, is a standing menace to the peace of our Indian territories." He considered it Canada's responsibility to disarm the Sioux and relocate them. The American press was inclined to gloat over the failure of the talks. The editorialists proclaimed the onus was now on Britain to watch over Sitting Bull's conduct. Good riddance!

One melodramatic rumour that swept the States was that a corporal missing in the Big Horn battle had been seen with the Sioux, a prisoner forced into a marriage with Spotted Eagle's daughter. What a terrible fate! The fact that Spotted Eagle's only child was a teen-age boy could not subdue the public appetite for Custer luridness.

With the American peace chiefs gone, and their soldiers with them, Bull and his companions walked about the fort uninhibited. For their promises to obey the laws they were issued food and tobacco, some ammunition for hunting, and each received a prestige gift of a blanket. An impromptu concert was put on by the garrison, which they attended, and the antics of a conjurer appealed bewitchingly to their inborn sense of the mystic.

They were also fed a portion of unaccustomed food (unaccustomed to them), as the garrison cook provided as much variety as he could concoct. The cavernous capacity of the victims turned out to be a spectacle in the barracks. One could only conclude they were making up for all they had missed in their years of eating buffalo meat. Bear's Cap, who was seen, with amazement, to have an unlimited penchant for plum pudding, devoured a quantity beyond the capacity of his stomach, which rebelled. He "reported sick" to the post surgeon. The treatment, drastic by normal standards, purged the chief of his painful indigestion.

When Walsh returned from the Terry escort mission, Bull and his well-fed compatriots were ready to rejoin their families at Pinto Horse. Their delay had given rise to a rumour that they had all been spirited away by the Americans. The sight of Sitting Bull, Walsh and the others approaching the Sioux camp prompted a stampede of delight, and when the news got around, in degrees of increasing overstatement, that Bull had defeated the American chiefs in council, the lodges resounded with the beat of the drums, the singing and the boastful laughter.

One of the big bellies, an old man, gathered a crowd around him.

"You see a new life before you," he pontificated. "You have heard the words of the white mother. Our old men would not believe them. We advised our chiefs to go and meet the Americans

137

at the fort of the white mother. We never heard of the white mother breaking her word, and we could not believe she would do it this time. You heard the liars in our camp! Now let them be gone, ashamed!"

Ah, to be sure, these were happy days for all of the people. But how long could they last? As long as their brother, the buffalo – but he was elusive, and the pounding of the great herds, the shuffling mass of fur, were but a whisper in the memories.

❖❖❖ The People Still Come

❖❖❖ It was the season of red and gold, of falling leaves, the time for traces of morning snow. When the sun was high and lodge pole shadows short it was invitingly warm enough to sit outside the tepee to sharpen arrow tips and knives with the flat stones and watch the women cooking, the people strolling about, the little girls playing with dolls dressed up in buckskin and beads, the young boys jumping over each others' backs or playing war games with blunted shafts.

It was time of the year, at night, to sit contentedly close to the fires as already the chill winds from the north, the winds that gave the people the strength to endure, swept and swished through the gullies and frosted the lodge skins with a shrill overture that to a relaxed imagination could sound like a lingering whistle of the sun dance.

It was also time for the buffalo bulls, plump and boisterous from the summer grass, to battle for their harems. And from the crest of the hills, where the bones of the people and animals were joined with the sacred earth, the geese were following their pathfinders from the north, taking the thoughts of the people with them to their homelands and relatives far away to the south.

When the red berries in the White Mud valley were ready for picking, the buffalo were grouping and forming into herds, all prime for the kettles and cooking pots. The parfleches, the big rawhide containers in which the women stored the meat, were empty, and the old men and the wives were grumbling. It was time to hunt.

No one could disagree. It was the eternal truth that the buffalo provided everything for life: food, clothes, shelter and utensils. Most vitally, now, meat for the long, wintry moons of snow and immobility when the bands would be dispersed, sheltering along the river bottoms. There had to be sufficient preserved meat – pemmican – to last till spring. Fresh meat had to be dried while there was still warmth in the sun, before the women could pound it into a fine, soft mass and mix in melted buffalo fat, and add a sprinkling of dried berries for seasoning.

During the fall hunts every conceivable edible portion was churned into pemmican. In summer, the time of plenty, the choicest cuts were selected, the rest often discarded for the predators. In winter a shaggy buffalo was a treasured prize, not only for the fresh meat but for its hide, covered with luxurious thick fur that could be fashioned into fur-lined moccasins, or warmers for hands, head and ears. The biggest hides were stretched for capes or robes, soft and comfortable; or they were shaped into all-enveloping sleeping blankets, ample for a man and the biggest of his wives.

Garments for all seasons came from brother buffalo. In the warm months the skin was thinner (adult animals lost nearly all their hair in early summer) and could be scraped and dried for lighter clothes, such as women's dresses, which were long, and men's shirts.

The animal's stomach was converted into a portable water container. Bones and horns were shaped into cups and spoons, the supple bones of the young bent and sharpened into knives. Dew-claws, encased in hide, make excellent ball-shaped ceremonial rattles.

The hide was used for war, for bags to carry arrows, knives, cartridges, signal mirrors, charms (beads, coloured stones, bones, an animal's foot), or it could be cut into thongs and shrunk to secure stone clubs to wooden handles. The thickest hide of all, from a bull's neck, was shrunk over a fire until it was as thick as a man's finger, then shaped on a hoop, suntanned, and painted with symbolic charms for an effective, mystic shield.

Sinews were carefully, painstakingly thinned for bowstrings and thread. Hair was twisted into rope.

Not even the dung was wasted. The droppings – buffalo chips – littered the prairie, ready-made fuel for fires where wood was scarce.

In the fall of '77, when wives and mothers clamoured for a hunt, the young men stirred restlessly with expectation of brave deeds to be boastfully recorded. The chiefs had been so busy with

140

the white-man conferences that little thought had been given to the prayers and ceremonials to ensure the success of the hunters – ceremonials of purification, fasting, endurance and dancing. Therefore the holy men, and the war chiefs among them, took their sacred pipes to the hilltops. When the good earth was shrouded by the night they purified themselves in the sweat lodges, pointed their pipes to the four directions, and to the earth and to the sky, and sang the songs of the hungry people, and prepared the scouts to track the herds whose ancient trails were everywhere around the Wood Mountain hills. The boulders they urinated on and rubbed their backs against to shed their fur were embedded as everlasting, brownish monuments to their presence, the earth around churned up by the pushing of hooves, aeons of hooves.

The people packed all their belongings and followed the scouts. There was no time for resting, no time for cooked meals.

One afternoon the scouts were sighted on their way back. When they signalled that many buffalo had been seen the men went out to greet them wearing their buffalo-horn headdresses, to escort them to the council lodge where the sacred pipe was brought out by a holy man and the bowl filled with bark tobacco and smoked by all the scouts so that they could recount the truth of what they had seen. They had seen many buffalo to the north and west.

"*Hoka hey!*" shouted the onlookers in the lodge. "*Hoye!*" shouted all the people when they heard. Get the horses! Get the lances, the bows and arrows and the guns! Let the chase begin. And it did.

The experienced hunters, the warriors, rode out first to control the impetuous young men. The tactics were agreed upon; one group to charge with the sun behind them, the others to come in as soon as the animals picked up the human smell and started to run. All was ready. The mirror signals flashed. The shout went up. The chase was on.

The buffalo started to stampede, heads down, stupidly and slowly in a circle of panic and chaos, and then quicker as the hunters moved in, the old hands ignoring the tough bulls and going after the fat, lumbering cows and the tender young ones.

The surrounded buffalo were fighting back, stirring up dust with their anger and goring the attackers; the hunters clamped their legs around their horses' bellies, wheeling among the rampaging herd and pumping arrows into their backs until they crumbled into a furry heap under the whirlwind of the pack.

What a great day for meat and robes! What a great day for bravery and horsemanship!

The hunters jumped onto the dying animals to finish them off. The women came running, all panting, shouting and laughing, followed by the old men, and the boys still too young to hunt even the yearlings; they all came eagerly with sharpened knives for the butchering.

The women dug deeply into the carcasses. Skins were cut and pulled back and all the meat sliced in big chunks so that there was hardly a morsel left for the wolves. Before it was dark the pack horses were laden, bloody meat flooping over their flanks, and the travois bulging and sagging with the loads of furs and bones.

The people were in a happy mood, joking and singing their leisurely way back to camp. When they got there the women went into the valleys to collect wood for the drying racks and they cut the meat in strips and laid it out under the sun. They stretched the robes with pegs, the fur facing the ground so that they would dry tautly. Next they began laboriously to scrape the loosely-grained skins to a soft finish, applying lubricants of buffalo fat, mashed-up buffalo brains or warm, spreadable dog manure. (A wet garment, after it had been tanned in this manner, could remind its wearer of what went into the making!) More pleasing to the senses were the tasty treats, succulent roasts of fresh meat being turned over the fires watched by children who darted around pinching mouth-watering samples, the women pretending to be angry and dashing after them with sticks.

That night there was drumming, singing, visiting, gossiping and gambling – guessing games with small bones, sometimes human finger bones, or hit-the-moccasin. The families ate until they were overflowing. In a few days some of the men went back to collect their arrow heads and lance tips, and before they left they turned the buffalo skulls to face the sinking sun, a gesture of respect for their brother who kept them all alive.

When the new skins were dry the families took the surplus to Légaré's store where there were rows of irresistible goods in packages and sacks to barter for. Trading was brisk. There was, thank the Great Spirit, prosperity and well-being in the lodges.

\*　　\*　　\*

142

The bands remained in separate locations, in the steep coulees, to get the best protection from the snow and the winter winds that could not be far off. After the hunts the majority dispersed around Wood Mountain or the Cypress Hills, not too far from Fort Walsh because they had a hunch that Bear Coat Miles was hovering close to the boundary line, plotting an opportunity to strike at them when least expected, perhaps at dawn when the snow could conceal his approach.

As it became apparent that Miles had no such intention, the bands congregated around Wood Mountain where they could have easier access to Légaré's store.

News of the old-style, invigorating life in the Redcoats' land attracted the searching hearts on the U.S. reservations. From Spotted Tail and Pine Ridge, where the Brûlés and Oglalas existed on handouts, confined and dejected within sight of the Black Hills, the venturesome ones longed for the freedom to roam as their fathers had done when the land, all of it, belonged to the people and to their keeper, the buffalo, and to all the animals.

Some of the families quietly uprooted their households and slipped away at night on the arduous and dangerous journey to Canada. They left the Missouri agencies too, small groups traveling the Yellowstone trails through soldier country. More than 150 Sans-Arc lodges tacked themselves on to Spotted Eagle's camp.

Hundreds of newly arrived Tetons were being absorbed, including some 200 lodges of the Crazy Horse survivors who had surrendered with their chief and subsequently fled after he was maligned by jealous compatriots and fatally stabbed by a soldier at Fort Robinson. It was a bad omen when the people turned against each other.

The migration continued into the first weeks of 1878 because the snow was late in coming. The ground was bare and dry and in the buffalo haunts of the Cypress Hills the grass was burnt over; the ever smaller herds were much farther north in search of pasturage.

There was a dreadful snowstorm in January. The centre of its fury swirled around Wood Mountain. The police could hardly open the doors of their makeshift quarters, let alone attempt any patrols.

Walsh was resting in his cabin, stretched out on an old couch. There was a thump on the door, which he never bolted, and in walked two warriors calling him by name. Walsh got up, motioned them to approach, and brought his limited Siouan into practice. Obviously the pair were stranded in the storm and were hoping for a night's shelter. He welcomed them and expressed amazement that they had been able to find his headquarters.

The pair were fine-looking men, handsomely dressed. One of them was about thirty years, and the other four or five years older. Each carried a seven-shot Winchester rifle, and in each of their belts were a Colt revolver and a knife. Walsh, who by now was used to looking into Indian faces and forming instant character references, trusted these two immediately. They had, what he coined, good open countenances.

The elder Sioux said they were sorry to disturb him. They had of course heard of him but had never met him, and this made them feel they were intruding. Walsh replied that his door was wide open to travellers and strangers – as every man's door should be on the plains.

The major called for one of his men, Ben Daniels, a brother of Louis, who was on the cookhouse detail. They were the sons of a Prescott hotelier. Walsh ordered food for the visitors. When the two of them sat down he noticed that the elder one was having trouble with his leg. Walsh asked him about this and the Indian showed him a swollen calf, inflamed from an abcess. He was trying his best to conceal the pain, although he admitted his leg felt as it it were on fire. Walsh ordered a poultice prepared.

"Let me put this on your leg. It will break open the lump and tomorrow you'll feel better. Tonight, though, you will probably have more pain."

He let them sleep in his room. In the morning, the younger Indian, who was called Short Bull, told the major that his friend's bump had burst during the night. The pain had gone, so much so that his friend was still fast asleep. Walsh insisted they stay at the post for a couple of days until the storm abated, by which time the leg would be healed. When they were ready to leave, the elder one thanked Walsh for his hospitality and kindness. He said that perhaps some day he would be able to show how an Indian returns such considerate treatment.

The major's new friend and ally was Stone Dog, an out-and-out Oglala warrior, fierce in battle, gentle in peace. He had a following of fifty braves who had no superiors on the plains.

\*    \*    \*

Any notions that American Indians might not be welcome by the white authorities in Canada never entered the minds of the new migrants. They came in bands, in small groups, and even individually. Bull was glad to have them; he was not about to deny the kindred wanderers the virtues of his generous hospitality. Besides, the more the people the stronger they were, collectively.

Bull's saga of rebellious and belligerent enterprise appealed specifically to those young men whose natural, freewheeling instincts clashed uncompromisingly with the precepts of law and order advocated by the Indian agents on the reservations.

Every society had its habitual criminals, the definition of criminals varying according to customs. Crime, as such, was rare within the homogeneous structure of each tribe. It was honourable and virtuous to steal horses, but never from one's own people. Murder within a band or tribe was very rare. When it did happen it was usually connected with another man's wife, and there were less complicated ways of enjoying a different bedmate without resorting to violence. The punishment for murder was usually banishment.

Brave Bear, whose blood was thick with the inherent and hereditary traditions of his forefathers, was one who became restive on the reservation. His friend, The Only One, was likewise uneasy. Together they disappeared from time to time to forage and steal. Horses, particularly white men's horses, could fetch many fine clothes and decorations on the reservation, away from the administration buildings and the army, and Brave Bear was fussy about his appearance. He liked to think of himself as brave and irresistible to the women – and young Indian women were physically mature and robust at an early age. They responded to male ostentation.

Brave Bear and The Only One, on one of their horse-stealing forays, were caught in the stable of a white settler near Pembina, close to the Canadian border. They shot and killed the two owners and mortally wounded a third, then traipsed into the farm house and attacked two of the wives. Brave Bear was carrying a sword which he used on the head of one of the women. He mistakenly left them for dead.

As it was the Indian custom to boast of one's deeds, the criminals became known to the white agents. They were trapped and arrested. The Only One, knowing that he was destined to finish his life at the end of the white man's rope, wrestled himself free and ran like a deer toward the open countryside. Brave Bear didn't get the same chance; he was hustled off to the guardhouse.

The Only One bobbed and swayed towards some hills, the soldiers firing inexpertly. One sergeant got down on one knee and with instruction-book style killed him with two shots.

The grief of his wife and mother was indescribable. Their self-maiming, the traditional disfigurement by close female relatives of a man killed in battle, was extreme. His wife, a beauty, chopped off all her hair, in fact tore some of it out, gashed her breasts and lower legs until she was covered with congealed blood. The mother did something of the same to herself, and chopped off a little finger, the ultimate act of bereavement. The lamentation, the crying and the wailing went on for days.

Brave Bear escaped from jail. He took his chances on a long, solitary journey to the safety of Sitting Bull in Canada. In the sparsely populated northland, where isolated white settlement was beginning to take hold, he murdered a rather prominent rancher, stripped him of his clothes, stole his money (reportedly $1,700), took his rifle, naturally, and with all the speed he and his horse could withstand successfully joined Bull's camp. He was received with great respect because of his fortitude, one of the cardinal virtues of Indian character. Brave Bear's destiny of violence had not yet been completely fulfilled.

The same could be said for One Elk when he joined the fugitive Sioux. Of below-average mental endowments, he was a good agency Indian. He had declared himself as willing, enthusiastically so, to settle down in one spot, to obey the white authorities. His zeal transformed him into a self-appointed policeman.

His in-laws, the head of the family being Two Bulls, were from the Fort Peck country in Montana. Two Bulls was an habitual roamer, going from one agency to another. When he was at Fort Totten, Dakota, the agent summoned a council to inform all the Indians they could no longer leave the reservation without permission.

Two Bulls could not obey. Gradually he moved his family, including his daughter and son-in-law One Elk, to the western edge of the reservation. There he could hit out for the open country, unnoticed.

One Elk, the reservation zealot, knew what old Two Bulls was up to and applied his own version of the agent's law. Early one morning he went into the lodge of Two Bulls who was asleep, as was his wife and one of his daughters. In his grip One Elk had an axe. The first to die was his sister-in-law; he drove the axe into her skull. Two Bulls was next. The mother-in-law was left for last. He walked out of the death lodge and awoke his wife with orders for breakfast.

One Elk proudly boasted of his exploits in expectation of official praise. Unsettled at being locked up in the military jailhouse, he escaped to awaken the agent, who probably thought he was having a nightmare, with a request he be lodged in the civilian jail.

"Put me in your guardhouse and I will stay," he said. "A Sioux cannot let himself be prisoner of the Bluecoats."

He was returned to the cavalry guardhouse. Day after day he filed at the shackles with a knife he had concealed. When these were off he waited for a stormy night and squeezed through the bars. He shouted the loudest war whoop he could manage, which aroused the guard, and as bullets and balls whined in his direction, One Elk vanished into the darkness, never to be seen again by his captors. He went north, directly, to join up with a Sioux band in the Turtle Mountain district. There he became involved in a life-and-death struggle with an Indian – and lost.

Turtle Mountain was a geophysical oddity in the surrounding plains, a partially wooded natural sanctuary for Indians who were on the run from Fort Totten. The mountain (hardly a mountain at 2,000 or so feet) straddled the 49th parallel. It was west of the Red River and northeast of the gradual westward curve of the Missouri.

The mountain was a haven for disgruntled Indian renegades. It could absorb them, sustain them, hide them, protect them. For someone following the ways of Inkpaduta, a notorious warrior, the mountain could be home base.

Inkpaduta (translated, Scarlet Point) was a minor chief, an outcast from the tribal councils, treacherous enough to be watched, but a valuable ally when all-out war was in the offing. Inkpaduta gathered about him all the others of his kind from a mixture of the bands. No one slept soundly when he was known to be in the vicinity.

The son of a Santee Sioux chieftain called Black Eagle, Inkpaduta had grown up into an ill-tempered, remorseless fighter. He was more than a willing participant in the infamous Minnesota massacres when 2,000 Santee warriors, under the reluctant leadership of Little Crow (who had been converted to Christianity) attacked and killed white settlers – men, women and children – wherever they could be found. The frontier became a no-man's land for whites; homesteads and towns were sacked and burned; the St. Paul-Fort Garry stage was ambushed and drivers and passengers slain and scalped. There were but two guarantees of a safe journey: The Union Jack or Canadian Red River carts.

Almost wherever and whenever trouble was brewing Inkpaduta seemed to know about it. He had the knack of anticipating strife; he possessed the will and wherewithall to invite his participation. In '76 he put up his brightly painted lodge close to Bull's at the Little Big Horn (his son, Red Horse, claimed the distinction of killing Custer) and afterwards guided the remnants of his band – down to about twenty-five families – to Canada, to Turtle Mountain, nostalgically close enough (yet safe) to his old stamping ground. When more of the hated whites came to disturb his serenity he uprooted again and moved farther westwards into Saskatchewan. This is where he died, near Batoche.


Far, far away in Ottawa it could not be expected that the Government could comprehend the exacting realties of the presence and pull of Sitting Bull. They couldn't feel the growing pains of the police; the financial pinch they could feel. Questions were being asked in the House of Commons.

On February 18, 1878, Philippe Baby Casgrain, a Liberal, enquired whether the Government had, or intended to call upon the Imperial Government for the payment of the expenses incurred as a result of Sitting Bull crossing the frontier.

The Prime Minister, Alexander Mackenzie, replied:

"It is not the intention of the Government to make any representation on that subject to the Imperial Government at present. We have had an armed force in that territory for the purpose of enforcing order and maintaining the majesty of the law. Sitting Bull has only contributed to the necessity of the concentration of the force on that particular portion of our frontier. He has, no doubt, caused us some additional expense and may cause more, but we do not think that to be a matter of such serious importance

148

as to justify us in making any application of that kind. The Government do not desire in any matters of minor importance to make any demands on the Imperial Government."

Sir John A. Macdonald interjected: "I do not see how a Sitting Bull can cross the frontier."

Mr. Mackenzie: "Not unless he rises."

Sir John A. Macdonald: "Then he is not a Sitting Bull."

It was decided Walsh should go to Ottawa to escort Fred White, unofficial "governor" and future comptroller of the force, and a batch of recruits back to the foothills.

When the weather loosened its wintry grip, the major started for Helena, Montana, the miners' capital, where he conferred with Macleod. The roundabout route of stage and train, via Utah, was the most comfortable way to travel to the east.

When questioned by the American press en route, Walsh refuted what he considered to be irresponsible rumour-mongering concerning an impending alliance of all Indians in Canada for the purpose of clearing out the whites and invading the United States.

When he got within range of the Chicago papers he was reading stories to the effect that the Canadian police and the U.S. Army would operate together in the event of an outbreak by Sitting Bull.

Walsh read these reports with intense annoyance. He knew that some of the transient traders carried the papers around with them and anything in print concerning the Indians was read aloud to them. He himself had been questioned by the Indians concerning published statements that were attributed to him. A report of this kind, that the whites in Canada and the United States were planning a joint command, could destroy the influence he had assiduously established in the Sioux council lodges.

He feared the chiefs would believe the Americans were using their money to hire the white mother to help subjugate the Indians. From a practical standpoint a joint command would be unworkable anyway. The Indians could make such rapid and frequent movements as to wear out any force attempting to follow.

Walsh boiled.

"We should have no [such] understanding with the United States; we have no interest in common with them," he declared. "Their army on the frontier and their contractors and speculators have no other reliance but an Indian war, and on such a war they constantly depend to build up reputations and fortunes.

"They would be pleased if they could embroil us by making us take common ground with them....The cost of an Indian war in such a country as ours would be enormous."

Walsh felt, though, that if the Indians made a move to cross the line the police had an obligation to warn the Americans – "and we would be doing all the United States should ask or expect from us."

He recommended that the police be redistributed at several points, in sufficient numbers to put up a good front. Seventy men behind a stockade, with sufficient rations, ammunition and a couple of field guns, could resist any attack. He had never known Indians to assault a stockade.

"Those in the United States who have had the most experience with Indians freely state that the mistake their Government has always made has been in using force of arms instead of peaceful measures, and that in having started in that way the Indian will not now trust them even when they mean to do right."

Walsh, on the return trip, was interviewed by a Chicago *Times* reporter. He was quoted that every means would be taken to persuade the Sioux and Nez Percés to return south, but this could not take place in a week or a month. He predicted they would return in small bands, a few families at a time, to see how they were treated.

"It will be slow at first....Indians are independent of each other....Supposing Sitting Bull had said to General Terry 'I will go back.' He would have had to go to his people and tell them that the Americans had made a proposition which he had accepted. The savages would then have probably replied, 'Alright, you go back'.

"If a return of the Sioux could be accomplished it would not only be a blessing for them, but would prove to be an agreeable thing for the people on the frontier, and would cause a happy termination, for both Canada and the United States, of the hostile question. Should they return they would be dismounted and disarmed, and once dismounted would be conquered...."

For the first time, Walsh revealed that Sitting Bull was losing some of his power. Even his own Hunkpapa were moving out, looking more to Spotted Eagle for leadership.

150

The major, with his sixty-five recruits, crossed the prairies into Dakota by rail as far as Bismarck, wild and wide-open, where on May 25, 1878, they rented the flatbottomed paddler Red Cloud, manned by negroes, bound for Fort Benton, a two-week voyage through a grassy desert.

Bismarck, a few miles north of Custer's last "home," Fort Lincoln, had a permanent population of 500. The transients pushed it up to about 5,000, most of whom were either going to or returning from the gold fields in the northern Black Hills.

After resting a few days at Fort Walsh, freshly whitewashed with white clay from the creek, the major started on the last leg of his toilsome travels. On the way to Wood Mountain he and his escort stopped on the bank of a clean-water creek to prepare a meal. When they were settling down, eating and chatting, they were startled by percing yells of "Yihoo" from the top of a bluff. Three Indians careered toward them, horses at full gallop.

The Indians had easily identified them from a distance. Redcoats! (Some of the constables were wearing cowboy hats. Walsh had his U.S. Cavalry patrol hat). The whites instinctively reached for their firearms and didn't relax until the major recognized the trio as Sioux. He remembered the one out in front; it was Long Dog.

A notable war chief, reckless and fearless, a cheery, crazy, turbulent symbol of a charmed life in battle, Long Dog was a middle-aged marvel, scarred and disfigured about his face, chest and back with the evidence of bullet wounds, knife slashes, arrow welts, and sun dance sacrifices. He was a natural practical joker and clown, a leader of men through his bravery which was a legend because of the infinite durability of his protective visions.

When in turn Long Dog recognized Walsh he raised his arms and face to the sky, with typical Indian dramatics.

"*Wakan-Tanka* [Great Spirit]," he exclaimed. "*Walsh-heca* [It is Walsh]."

Long Dog dismounted, extended his hand to Walsh, and embraced him.

He looked to the sky again, one arm outstretched.

"Wakan-Tanka, look down upon me, your son. If what I have done is not good, strike me at the feet of Walsh."

Long Dog and his two friends joined in the policemen's meal. Those who had not seen him before couldn't help but notice the

151

light colouring of his hair, unusual for a full-blood – and that he was a full-blood there was no doubt. He had an alert and humorous countenance; in very short order he was his old self, joking and kidding his companions. He was usually the first to react to his own humour and tricks; he rolled over and guffawed with the unholy glee of an agent from hell – if there had been a hell in the Lakota religion or language. (The place of punishment where the fires were always burning, deep under the earth, was for whites only.)

When Walsh was back into his routine he went from one Sioux camp to another, elated as the chiefs and the people gave him a wonderful reception. When he walked through the camps people followed him about; he had a retinue of admirers; boys and girls ran up to touch his uniform.

East of Pinto Horse, where the word of Sitting Bull still commanded unquestioned attention, the chieftain welcomed Walsh as a brother. Everybody reaffirmed their desire to live under the great white mother, although Walsh had noted a further deterioration in the overall influence of the wily holy man, the most dreaded of them all. Among the young warriors he detected signs of homesickness, a surly restiveness for the warfare that was being denied them. It seemed advisable to increase the complement and fortifications at Wood Mountain. Never since the Battle of the Little Big Horn had so many of the Tetons been so close together in such strength. They were more than ever a military hazard, a potential integrated fighting force that had a capability of creating unthinkable havoc.

One man's dedication to entice the hostiles back to the United States got him into disfavour with the U.S. military (of all people). Father Génin, the missionary, was around the camps again. The black robe, unsuccessful the previous year in his efforts to influence Bull, was rescued by the police on his way to Wood Mountain when caught in an unusually severe spring snow storm. Once more he failed despite his claims that Bull was full of the hunger of discontent in Canada, plotting an attack on the Mounted Police. He was curtly told by the U.S. Army to stop meddling with "any of our Indians."

A more official endeavour to get the Nez Percé refugees to submit to U.S. captivity was initiated by the army following apparently unsubstantiated intelligence that the Nez Percés wanted to rejoin their relatives. Miles arranged for three Nez Percés who had been captured in the Bear Paw battle, plus an interpreter and a scout, to approach and encourage the exiles to surrender at Fort Buford, an infantry bastion overlooking, strategically, the confluence of the Missouri and Yellowstone Rivers.

Walsh feared their presence around Wood Mountain would agitate the Sioux. Consequently a conference was arranged at Fort Walsh involving the three Indian emissaries, an American officer, the police, and eight of the foremost Nez Percés in Canada who had been persuaded to attend by Irvine.

White Bird, who had so formidably led the remnants of the Bear Paw disaster to safety, displayed a rare diplomatic talent at the talks which started July 1, 1878. The proceedings developed into a matching of wits between the persistent White Bird and the American officer, Lieutenant G. W. Baird, who obviously had not been briefed with all the facts of Chief Joseph's fate. Baird had two persuaders with him, Yellow Bull and Bald Head, both co-operative members of Joseph's own defeated band.

Commissioner Macleod, encouraged by the fact that White Bird had rode in to Fort Walsh, suggested that the Nez Percés should retrace their steps. Baird implied that as long as White Bird and his band lived closely to the Sioux they would be considered as allies of the enemies of the great white father, thus impeding Joseph's chances of being allowed to go back to his homeland. White Bird replied that if Joseph were allowed to return to his own territory he would join him.

The Indians, however, decided to stay under police jurisdiction no matter what persuasive evocations came from Macleod and Baird.

"My country is here," proclaimed White Bird. "Joseph is in the wrong direction. Why should I go to him?"

White Bird and his councillors rejoined their neighbours the Sioux. Not long afterward, rumours began to circulate along the trails that the Nez Percés were preparing, first of all, to move westwards into Blackfoot territory.

This was hardly a palatable prospect for the harassed officers to contemplate in the discomfort of their fly-infested log quarters of overcrowded Fort Walsh. All around them were hundreds of

Indian lodges, more numerous than the trees on the dry, greyish-green hills from where keen eyes could look down upon the rock-strewn, small-treed parade ground of the fort to wonder at police activities.

A fortress of huts, a stronghold of discipline, there was always something going on to transfix these nomads. A highlight of a normal day was the afternoon mounting of the guard, an exercise of marching and inspection (helmets, belts and gauntlets were cleaned with white mud). There were numerous other strange spectacles: inter-company football, cricket, running, and attempts at tennis. These were the diversions of frontier life that could subdue, temporarily, horrendous thoughts of the day when the Tetons, the intruders, and the Blackfoot, the incumbents, must inevitably flex their muscles on the buffalo plains as both tribes moved farther afield for the staff of life. This confrontation would have to take its course.

One suggestion, which was not adopted, was that the pick of the Blackfoot, a hundred of the most influential warriors, should be hired as police mercenaries. This would be one way to control them.

The appearance of the Nez Percés in the innermost sanctum of Blackfoot supremacy had not been thought of as a possibility. One could not now reasonably avoid thoughts of a Blackfoot-Nez Percé incident igniting a major Indian war that would sear the dried-out grasslands with its intensity of deeply rooted antagonisms.

Conversely, there had been uncorroborated reports, fomented by scouts and traders who had a monetary stake in the continuation of any hostilities, that the Blackfoot and Sioux were negotiating a joint uprising against white domination. Newspapers as far east as New York picked up rumblings of an Indian conspiracy.

These were days of nagging vexations. The surrounding presence of Canadian and American Indians so close to the fort created a situation of unremitting discomfort and vigilance. Unusual occurrences were being entered in the logs, even the Sioux complaining their horses were being stolen, and the police recovering the animals from a south Assiniboine camp that claimed the protection of the great white father in Washington.

Walsh, in less than a week following his re-indoctrination to the crude accommodation at the Wood Mountain outpost, had confirmed the stories of a meeting between Bull and the one-and-only Crowfoot, battle-scarred chief of chiefs of the Blackfoot confederacy, a warrior since he was thirteen. He also had heard that Bull had been talking to Big Bear, the perennially obstinate and independent chief of the belligerent plains Cree, the fierce, undisputed leader of those eternally dangerous Canadian malcontents.

Crowfoot, responding to Bull's initiative, had sent messengers with gifts of tobacco to the Sioux in the hope of arranging a meeting between them north of the Cypress Hills. The Big Desert country (the sand hills) was how the Blackfoot described the area. Crowfoot's runners told Bull that their chief wanted to smoke the holy pipe for an everlasting peace in view of the many changes taking place on the plains.

Of even greater significance, from Walsh's standpoint, was the tip he received that Louis Riel, the exiled Red River revolutionary Métis leader, currently a U.S. citizen and roaming close to the border in Montana and Dakota, had recently been in the Wood Mountain district to "advise" Bull.

After several Sioux councils it was agreed that they should accept Crowfoot's invitation, apparently with the blessing of Riel, and Bull and his band, including the warriors One Bull, Long Bull, Loves War and White Crow Blanket, and Black Moon and his lodges, moved north between the Cypress Hills and Pinto Horse Buttes, then onwards to the flatlands.

Crowfoot, gangling and conspicuous with glistening, perceptive eyes, a prominently hooked nose, and unbraided, unkempt hair, was waiting for Bull with his sub-chiefs. When the two leaders clasped hands and arms and smoked the same redstone pipe in council the enmities of countless years were eradicated. So profusely did Crowfoot bestow gifts upon his guests that Bull's suspicions led him to wonder whether some act of treachery was in the making. He had been warned that Crowfoot, born into the Blood tribe, had a deceptively mild manner that only camouflaged a very violent streak.

Bull was overwhelmed by Crowfoot's eloquence and his genuine aspirations to induce the Tetons to form a peaceful alliance, not only with his people but also with some bands of the Cree, ancient and recent enemies of the Sioux. Bull promised he would consult his chiefs accordingly, explaining he could not then speak for all the Sioux in Canada because the leaders of the seven council fires of the Lakotas would first have to hear his words. Nonetheless, Bull convinced Crowfoot, temporarily, they would be eternal comrades.

"My children shall be your children; yours will be mine. We shall be friends for ever and never fight again."

After more councils, and some hunting, the two camps separated. As a permanent gesture of his declared admiration, Bull named his eldest son after Crowfoot (*Kangi-Siha* in Lakota Sioux), a name that would be perpetuated in Bull's family. Crowfoot went iarther north, following the buffalo, accompanied by a few Sioux under Black Moon who would inform Walsh of what had taken place.

The major also learned that Riel, nursing his anger in exile, was preparing a revolution, the first blow to be struck at Wood Mountain. Some of Riel's halfbreed friends (mostly of Cree lineage) had been up at the South Saskatchewan River ostensibly to trade but in reality to urge Crowfoot to visit Riel to discuss his proposal for a great Indian-Métis uprising to repossess the land taken by Canada, a plan, Riel said, that had the sympathetic understanding of many Americans. Besides, there were buffalo aplenty in Montana, and ranchers' cattle for the taking.

For the time being Crowfoot declined to meet the mixed-blood visionary.

Riel was doing his own preaching where he was free to operate, in the United States. He was working successfully on the rambunctious south Assiniboines. The cautious Yankton Sioux were resisting his charm and his overtures.

With all this information to occupy Walsh's thoughts, he rode seventy-five miles south into Riel country, to near Wolf Point, on the Missouri, where he knew the Assiniboine followers of Chief Red Stone were camped.

The chief showed Walsh a document that affiliated his band to Riel's alliance. It declared the country belonged to the Indians and their blood brethren, the halfbreeds, and that it would be redeemed through an alliance of all the native peoples. Walsh used his overnight stay in Red Stone's village to talk the chief out of siding with Riel. Red Stone subsequently sent a message to Riel that his Assiniboines had decided to withdraw from the confederation. He refused, however, to hand over the document to Walsh. He had promised Riel never to give it to any man.

156

Riel, predictably and understandably, was outraged, threatening death and destruction. He was not about to give up. To the halfbreeds he was a magnet. They came from police-patrolled Wood Mountain to join him in the Big Bend country where the White Mud flows into the Milk River. If he could get the Sioux to see the legitimacy and the potential of his cause, he would gamble that the Blackfoot, who were in continuing contact with Bull, would wholeheartedly join in the crusade.

There was no denying that Sioux warriors, unaccustomed to an overabundance of the sedentary life, resentfully missing the excitement, challenge and prestige of sporadic warfare, would be attracted by the exuberant oratory of Riel. Furthermore, the Sioux bands were edging southwards where there buffalo scouts had reported long rows of the animals, like an unending coil of black horsehair rope, following the bulls around the slopes and through the grass-softened valleys.

Walsh ordered the traders to discontinue the sale or bartering of guns and ammunition. His next move was to secure pledges of fidelity from the war chiefs in Canada – Sitting Bull, Spotted Eagle, Stone Dog, Long Dog, Black Bull, Black Horn the Yankton, and Broad Trail.

Walsh felt much better when Broad Trail, a Crazy Horse warrior, extended his hands in friendship. (Unusually small hands, Walsh noticed incidentally, for such a fine specimen of an aboriginal in his prime with a handsome, manly and honest face.) Broad Trail, a leader of the Akicita, the Oglala soldier-policeman society, was prominently influential in the councils and had been a restraining influence when the braves were agitating to assist the Nez Percés.

Walsh relied on Broad Trail. With such overwhelming support, with many of the Sioux longing for a fight, of any kind, and the Nez Percé warriors trying to harangue their friends the Crows into warfare against the Americans, the major could easily have mustered the Tetons and Nez Percés to wipe out Riel. He could be forgiven for casually contemplating the prospect.

His approach was more subtle. He let it be known on the moccasin telegraph that if Riel came into Canada again he would be arrested. He suggested to the peacefully inclined Indians to the south of the 49th parallel that they should protest to their agents about the hostiles from Canada, the Indians and the breeds, who were scattering the buffalo and stealing their horses.

The plan worked. The agents complained to the Department of the Interior. The army was signalled to send all the Canadians back to their country. So much for Riel's claims that the U.S. authorities were favourably inclined toward his objectives.

The Sioux were disappointed; they had had hopes of a good scrap or at least a good hunt. They were disgruntled too. There weren't enough buffalo between Wood Mountain and the Cypress Hills to meet the increasing necessities. The food supply had disappeared. The big herds, or what was left of them, were on American soil. There were rumours of huge grass fires started deliberately by the halfbreeds or the American Indians to keep the buffalo from the Sioux.

It was being repeated more and more in the lodges that "the white man's road" was, sad to say, the only salvation. "Oh God," they asked, "is it so that our brother the buffalo has deserted us, leaving us weak on the empty plains to live on gophers and rabbits, berries and turnips?"

Walsh could see nothing but privation and trouble ahead. At every opportunity he was impressing upon the chiefs the advisability of returning to the agencies. He wrote Irvine that more of the Sioux were thinking more favourably of such a movement.

"In fact chief Pretty Bear has spoken so strongly in favour of it that Sitting Bull, who is opposed to the idea, has withdrawn from the camp and has joined the No-Bows. Bull is afraid to go back to the U.S. on personal grounds and opposes the return of the others.

"He and his brother came to the post last week and remained for two days during which time I talked the matter over thoroughly with him and find that he is determined never to return to the United States fearing assassination from roughs about the agencies. He did not think it was the intention of Pretty Bear and his followers to return to their agency, but they would cross the line and roam about the prairie until captured by American troops.

"As near as I can ascertain Pretty Bear has a following of about forty lodges. I have caused a watch to be kept on his camp and in case of his crossing the line I shall despatch a messenger in haste to General Miles, and also warn officers commanding posts along the Missouri River. It is my own opinion, however, that there will be no attempt to cross this fall."

Walsh mentioned he had had several conversations with Sitting Bull's cousin, Watogla (The Wild One): "He tells me he has advocated a return to their agencies as strongly as he dared, but finds he has to be very careful how he speaks."

Walsh had encouraged Watogla to spread the word that by not returning to their agencies the Indians were not only depriving themselves of many comforts, but were actually robbing their children of an inheritance to which they were justly entitled, the benefit of which was being reaped by others.

The major was correct in his assessment that the Sioux, despite the scarcity of buffalo, were not yet ready to give up their freedom. But how long could they ignore the plight of the children? When the meal whistle sounded at the Wood Mountain post the children ran to the windows to watch the policemen eat, to grasp the scraps and tidbits that were handed out when the plates were empty. The women were urging their men to cross over, not too far beyond the boundary line, to hunt from one great encampment that the Americans dare not attack.

Sitting Bull and a small party ventured daringly into soldier territory. They didn't see one Longknife, only hundreds of Canadian Indians – Blackfoot, Blood and Peigan camps – all looking for food. Even the elk and deer were scarce in Canada. Gophers, the rodents of the plains, were being snared by ragged, once-proud warriors lying in wait, forlornly, by the small holes.

The most plentiful commodity close to the forts was whisky, peddled on the sly. In white-man's money Montana Redeye was fetching at least four dollars a gallon; Jamaica ginger cost a dollar for six ounces.

The Indians, in their desperation for food and favours, were becoming violent within their own bands. One hunting party of about twenty warriors came across two of their own men who had been stealing horses. The father-in-law of one of the pair asked where they had got the horses. His young son-in-law replied that they had found them.

"You're a liar, you stole them."

The older man clubbed his relative on the head. His companion got away, temporarily, shouting, "You've killed him; I'm going to kill Walsh."

159

The surviving thief was captured by the Indians in the Crazy Horse camp and held by Sitting Bull, who offered to execute the boy himself or hand him over to Walsh for execution. Summary execution for one of their own warriors for stealing horses! How times had changed!

Walsh assured Bull he wasn't frightened of the boy and instructed him to let him go. As for the father-in-law, he was never arrested for murder because the incident had taken place on American soil.

The hunger on the U.S. reservations was being blamed by the army on dishonest agents, traders and contractors who were rustling beef destined for the impoverished families. This resulted in rumours that more Tetons were moving north. On November 3, 1878, Walsh wrote to General Miles about it: "I don't anticipate a general movement of the Sioux from this side to assist the fugitives. I have most forcibly impressed upon them that by doing so they would jeopardize their rights to the asylum which has been afforded them in Canada. I will keep Sitting Bull and the head men under my own eye."

The major let his emotions trickle into the letter: "These poor, unfortunate people are making the greatest mistake in leaving where they are well taken care of to come here and starve. I cannot see anything else before them as the buffalo are getting very scarce.

"The emissaries who have been from the camps on this side to the American agencies, saying that they were sent by Sitting Bull to see upon what terms they would be received back, are the cause of all this trouble, as their real object has been to induce others to come to this side."

Meanwhile, an incredibly brave band of Cheyennes who had been exiled to a reservation in the southern desert, the land of death from where the winds carry the diseases, were fighting their way to Canada across hundreds of miles at impossible odds.

The outcome was decimation by the Bluecoats.

The grasslands in Canada were lifelessly frozen. Only at the forts and trading posts were there any glimmerings of existence. Bull, and all the people who were once his subjects, sat close to the fires, hungry and miserable.

At Fort Walsh, where the rejuvenated police band paraded and laundress "Nigger Mollie" cavorted – she claimed to be the

James Morrow Walsh, *who in 1890 attempted a memoir of sorts in a long letter (the first three pages reproduced here) to his daughter, Cora, quickly defends the Sioux who have been described in the United States as infernal devils. With his characteristic, impatient scrawl he writes . . . "it was this unkind feeling that so many Americans entertained towards the Indians that forced them in self-defence to act like devils. . . . Such feeling towards men that only wished or asked to maintain the freedom that nature gives as a right – to every man – is foreign." Walsh, immersed in his own memories of the North-West Mounted Police, claims the credit for controlling the hundreds of exiled warriors. "The man that saved Genl. Miles from destruction . . . and the witness thereof, are yet living – but he is not the first of his countrymen who has been god's agent . . . and not published it to the world."*

First commissioner of the NWMP (from 1873 to 1876) was an Irishman, George Arthur French, who had been seconded to the Canadian Militia from the British Army. A Sandhurst disciplinarian, energetic and ambitious, he became, however, blatantly disdainful and critical of federal politicians.

Second commissioner (1876-1880) was James Farquharson Macleod – "The Colonel." He was born on the Isle of Skye, Scotland, into a military family that settled near Toronto. Macleod, a lawyer, had joined the Militia and was decorated for his service with the Red River Expedition of 1870.

Third commissioner (1880-1886) was the first who was born in Canada. Acheson Gosford Irvine, of Quebec City, an engineer and businessman, was attracted to the military life, and while training for the cavalry distinguished himself as a swordsman. To him the Canadian west was "God's country."

Louis Léveillé, *guide, scout and interpreter, was the son of a mixed-blood prairie girl and an immigrant officer of Napoleon's army who was wounded at Waterloo. In his early fifties, Louis was lean, strong and a deadly marksman, and he lived dangerously in Indian country on both sides of the border.*

Jean-Louis Légaré, *a Quebec-born adventurer and trader, combined tact with low-key daring to survive and sometimes prosper in the midst of thousands of suspicious, hostile, warriors. He didn't talk very much, but when he did the Indians listened, as if mesmerized by his penetrating eyes.*

Sitting Bull (Tatanka Iyotake) – *patriot, warrior, orator, lover (he was married eight or nine times) and chief. Revered or hated, he would not be ignored. "A strong, hardy, deliberate-looking aborigine with large, sharp features, high cheek bones, thin lips, taut under the jaw, an indication of determination and force," was how he appeared to a military antagonist. The chief, a priest of the religion of his people, is wearing a crucifix over a white buckskin shirt. This symbol was a gift of a Jesuit, but was regarded by Sitting Bull only as an ornament of dress.*

James Morrow (Bub or Bob) Walsh – *police superintendent, and formerly a machinist, railwayman, dry-goods clerk, stockbroker, hotel-keeper, athlete, fire captain and cavalry officer. The son of a carpenter, and usually indifferent to school or paper work, he longed consistently for a life of action and therefore was among the first to enlist with the* NWMP. *Meticulous about his appearance, especially when in uniform, he could present a stern, uncompromising front, an attribute he used to advantage when the Sioux first overflowed into Canada and came up against the red jackets of the Queen's law.*

The fort that Walsh built alongside Battle Creek in the Cypress Hills
to crack down on the ever mobile whisky traders and to bring the
white man's legislation to the roving bands of war-like natives. Pine
and spruce for the palisade and buildings were abundant on the
surrounding hillsides. An American newspaperman, in 1877, found
the fort as quaint as an early Kentucky stockade. "No more romantic
spot, no wilder scene could impress a traveler." One year later, when
the Blackfoot and Nez Percé braves were restless, police reinforcements
were compelled to tent outside the safety of the overcrowded fort.

Unconventional and flamboyant, Walsh could be the antithesis of
the public's image of a Mounted Policeman. One old scout, who
lived until 1959, remembered him as a "small thin man with a
moustache, goatee and long hair. He looked like a bushwhacker."
On one of his trips to Chicago, where he visited occasionally to receive
treatment for a severe skin ailment, Walsh donned his patrol buckskins
(and his favourite blue felt U.S. Cavalry hat) and posed imperiously
for a studio portrait. Walsh's language could be as spectacular as
his attire. "I thought I was pretty good at cussin', major, but you've
got me skinned a mile," a teamster once told him at Fort Qu'Appelle.

Spotted Eagle, *a warrior chief whose physique, intelligence, oratory and wit immediately impressed the police guardians of the Canadian border.*

**Gall** *was credited with a leading role in Custer's defeat that resulted in the successful escape of Sioux malcontents across the Medicine Line.*

**Low Dog,** *a notorious combatant, resilien and dedicated, sullen and sulky, his wa trophies including a collection of light-haire scalps.*

Crow, *friend of Sitting Bull and an official spokesman, was with the vanguard of the exiles who cautiously approached the white mother's land.*

Crow King, *a hunter and soldier of renown, was rich with horses but unlucky in romance. His first wife, his true love, ran off with another warrior.*

No Neck, *a political maverick, but his allegiance was unquestionable in the thick of the fighting against Crow Indians and whites along the border territory.*

Long Dog, *a scarred and battered veteran of the wars and sun-dance tortures. A legend among the young men because of the infinite durability of his battle-protective charms and clear-sighted visions, he was also known as a practical joker and comic.*

*Sitting Bull's daughter, when in Canada, lived in her father's tepee with her sister, three smaller brothers, and the chief's two wives who were sisters.*

Rain In The Face, *overflowing with revenge, is reported to have cut out and eaten the heart of one of the slain Custer brothers at the Little Big Horn fiasco.*

Superintendent L.N.F. (Paddy) Crozier, *a perfectionist, a manipulator who tackled the Sioux situation with a brand of urgent determination and behind-the-scenes persuasion. He knew the Indians' weak spots and he concentrated on them, talking directly to the vacillating war chiefs and tempting them with organized feasts.*

Hairy Chin, *a few years after he and his followers left Canada to surrender, was persuaded to dress up as Uncle Sam and lead a Fourth of July parade in Bismarck, North Dakota. Two days later, when he returned to the Standing Rock reservation, he died. The Sioux there claimed that for an Indian to parade as a white-man figurehead was bad medicine and thereafter not one Sioux would put on Uncle Sam clothes.*

Sitting Bull (the "killer of Custer") and Buffalo Bill Cody, impresario, are strange companions indeed in this publicity picture taken at a time when the red man, if he couldn't beat them, was joining them – in this case, in show business. The chief of chiefs, an impassive actor, homesick and tired of looking at paleface audiences, lasted one season in Cody's Wild West Show that was advertised by this portrayal of reconciliation. He returned to the Dakotas to fight conclusive battles of words and bullets.

Crowfoot, *young son of Sitting Bull who was named after the chief of the Canadian Blackfoot, shared his father's fate.*

Short Bull, *a rebel and religious leader-to-be, was accommodated by Walsh in his own quarters when stranded by a mammoth snow storm.*

Gray Eagle, *stampeded to the brink of death by his compatriots for stealing horses in Canada, lived to witness the end of a nation*

Kicking Bear *was an ardent disciple of the Ghost Dance religion whereby all the Indians would be free of the white man, the hate of his life. Originally a Crazy Horse warrior who excelled in the last, bloody resistance movement to the north, he later dedicated himself to perpetuate the old, time-honoured ways and traditions through religious fervour.*

Sitting Bull, *the pride worn out of him, was a prisoner at Fort Randall in 1882. Still a "blanket" Indian at heart and in fact, he huddled stoically against the bone-chilling winds that sliced down the Missouri valley.*

first "white woman" in the west – and where harshness and boredom could be drowned out, preparations were in full swing for Christmas Day. Walsh's picture was put up in the mess hut, facing the door. Around the top there were evergreens and chains and underneath someone had appropriately coined the caption, Sitting Bull's Boss, a descriptive commendation lifted from the American press. This adulation was bound to energize the major's spirits. At Wood Mountain he revelled in the compliment and was moved to compose a seasonal message for his non-commissioned officers that he dispatched to the fort.

And so for the 329 scattered officers and men of the NWMP 1878 was coming to an end – with Bull dethroned, perhaps.

On the day before New Year's Eve, Walsh sat down to write his final report of the year. Sitting Bull was very much in the forefront of his thoughts. He had been tipped off that the Nez Percés had proposed a confederation of themselves with the Sioux and the Crows who were fearful of being disarmed by the Americans and were looking to Canada. It was hardly credible the Sioux could ally themselves with the Crows, the depth of their reciprocal hatred and contempt being so fathomless: nevertheless it appeared to Walsh that Ol' Sit, not confident of Canadian friendship, could embrace his former foes with the utmost endeavours and with all the memory lapses and diplomacy necessary to consummate a numerical union of safety.

### ❖❖❖ The Fighting and the Turncoats

❖❖❖ When the rivers were swirling with the floods, in mid-March of '79, and the snow was deceptively, dangerously soggy on the sun-missed slopes, Bull and the people closest to him were on their way, belatedly, to Wood Mountain. The horses and the travois poles they were pulling were dragging in the slush. Bull was impatient with the slow pace, although in good spirits as he bantered with Little Assiniboine, who was as a brother to him. In the Indian manner, that is what he was, a brother.

Twenty or so years previously, during a mild winter spell, a Sioux war party had scouted a lone tepee on the north shore of the upper Missouri where the Assiniboines wandered. The stalkers shattered the cracking stillness with war shrieks as they easily overwhelmed the fleeing family. Sioux arrowheads, at short range, thudded deeply, silently into the husband, his wife and two small children, and drips of blood discoloured the whiteness where they slumped. There remained but one boy to kill, of about ten winters, slightly wounded and haphazardly shooting arrows. The little Hohe (as the Sioux called the Assiniboines) faced the attackers, shaking with fright.

"Mercy, brother!" he quavered in his dialect that the Sioux could understand.

Bull reared his pony. His companions were anxious to get it over with. The boy's scalp would be thick.

"Don't kill him," Bull shouted. He rode up to the lad and stood in front of him. He talked the others into cutting the scalps of the family and rounding up their horses. The chief hauled the little Assiniboine up to sit behind him. When Bull reached home he proclaimed he was about to adopt his brave young prisoner as a brother. He organized a feast, dressed the boy up and dabbed paint on his face, and to celebrate gave away horses to the poor

162

people. From that day on Bull and Little Assiniboine, in accordance with traditional commitments, would be as one person in their thoughts and actions and in their dealings with the Creator. The boy even grew to resemble Bull physically; not especially tall but solid and chunky. He was blessed with a pleasant disposition that ingratiated him to the men and enticed the women.

Little Assiniboine's ancestry was helpful to the Tetons in Canada. At the first meeting with the northern Assiniboines, when Bull was wearing his bear's head (the snout was like the peak of a cap across his forehead), the Sioux were lectured by Little Assiniboine's cousin, Big Darkness. Bull was so delighted that he bestowed gifts of many horses upon the distant relatives of his adopted brother.

"I came to this country to make peace, not to make trouble," he told his former enemies.

Now Bull was taking Little Assiniboine with him for an expected confrontation with Walsh. The small group arrived on March 20. The women put up the lodges close to Walsh's quarters, a low hut with a sod roof. When the "tiger of the plains" declared he and his family were without food the major supplied rations for the duration of their stay and the return journey.

On March 23 they assembled in the superintendent's roughly hewed living quarters, five of them: Bull; Little Assinibone (variously called Jumping Bull, Painted Face or Kills Often); Bull's young son, Crowfoot; his nephew, One Bull; and his brother-in-law, Bad Soup (or Bad Juice). Soup or Juice, no matter, Bad was the operative word. He impressed Walsh as a lean, hungry-looking warrior, obviously brave, callous, outspoken, observant, his known association with Bull going back to their earliest days of stealing horses.

Ol' Sit took the stage.

"I want to tell you why I came to see you. It is to deny a report carried by one of our men, Black Wolf, to the Americans."

Bull said that he had heard that Black Wolf had gone to the lower Yankton agency claiming he had been delegated by the Sioux council in the white mother's country to let it be known that Sitting Bull and Broad Trail wished to be admitted to an agency if terms were satisfactory.

"I want to tell you, and ask you to tell the Americans, that this man wasn't sent or authorized by the council to say such a thing

163

– and neither was anybody else. When Black Wolf was about to start he came to me and said, 'I am going to the lower Missouri for my wife and child.' I said to him, 'You always were a rascal and won't listen to any person.' He was allowed to go."

Bull paused, for effect, and extended an arm towards Walsh.

"What I wish to say to the white mother is that I have but one heart, and it is the same today as when I first shook your hand. When I first entered her country I told you that my heart was pale and that my people had been persecuted by the Americans, and that I came here to sleep soundly and to ask her to have pity on me that I never again would shake the hand of an American."

Bull reminded Walsh that he had gone to Fort Walsh, at his request, to meet the Americans (the Terry Commission), but would never meet them again.

"I have forbidden my people to use my name to the Americans. I have always said to them in council, 'if any of you want to go back tell me!' None of them has done so yet. I am looking to the north for my life, hoping the white mother will never ask me to look to the country I left, although it is mine. Not even the dust of it did I sell, but the Americans can have it.

"I never look at the white mother's children with a side face. I told you before, and I tell you now, I am never going to leave. Those who wish to return can go."

Bull said he hoped that those who remained would be given land to farm, if that is what they wanted.

"I will remain what I am until I die," he asserted. "I am a hunter and when there are no buffalo or other game I will send my children to hunt prairie mice, for when an Indian is shut in one place his body becomes weak."

Bull continued with his oration, with the grunting concurrence of his companions. He said he was at the present camped on the south side of the line, not far over, to hunt food for the children. When the horses were strong the people could hunt there and still camp in Canada, but now they were weak and unable to make long journeys looking for the buffalo.

"I will not remain in the south one day longer than I can help. I do not lie. I have but one mind. Any report you hear that is different from what I now tell you are not my words. All I am looking for is something for my children to eat. I want to see no blood but the blood of a wild animal."

164

He promised he would continue to obey Walsh's orders and tell the young men to stay out of trouble.

Bull ended with a question. He said that for a long time the superintendent had been advising the Sioux to get their living from the ground. Where could they get such ground in Canada?

Walsh replied that the police had managed to grow vegetables and barley and twelve acres of oats near the post, but there was no country superior to the one they had left, that the soil there was rich and abundant, that furthermore the American Government supplied regular rations, clothing, cooking pots and other necessaries that made the lives of those who had worked in the fields very comfortable.

"There is no place where you can subsist easier and enjoy life better than with your own people on the American agencies. You have many friends there; you can see the animals are scarce here... I expect you will return. I don't know whether the white mother will give those of you who are determined never to return a piece of land or not."

Walsh, deciding this was a heaven-sent opportunity to reach all these headmen under the one roof, his own roof, advised all the people who couldn't make a living in Canada to go into the U.S. agencies at once. The Americans would not let them wander around the land at large. If they had a fight with the Americans they would not be allowed to return to Canada. If they did, the white mother would send them back.

The major played all his cards; he was acutely aware that he had his detractors in the force who whispered he was too soft with the Sioux.

"Every year the buffalo is getting scarcer. The Americans will be building a railway along the Missouri, and a fort in Assiniboine country, and there will be a great many more whites along the Missouri and Milk Rivers. Those of you who don't want to starve must prepare yourselves to get your living from the fields."

Walsh aimed his final verbal shots point-blank at Bull. He said he had seen the pipe placed above Sitting Bull's door to invite the young men to his lodge to tell them to prepare for war.

Bull replied that he did not mean he would go out of his way to make war. His people had to be prepared to defend themselves because he had heard the Crows wanted to fight. Not that he blamed the Crows. They were being urged on by the Americans who dared not, themselves, come into the white mother's country to injure him, but could not rest without trying to persecute him.

"If my horses are stolen I will leave it to the white mother to have them returned," he asserted.

Was Bull really losing his grip? The police learned he had sent a poignant message to his relatives at the Standing Rock agency: "Let them know that once I was strong and brave, my people had hearts of iron; now I will fight no more forever. My people are cold and hungry, my women are sick, and my children are freezing. My arrows are broken and I have thrown my war paint to the winds."

There had been some reluctant defections from Wood Mountain recently, 200 lodges of destitution packed and en route to the soldier forts, the headmen carrying letters from Walsh and not knowing what the words said.

The presence of Sitting Bull and his relatives at the post could not pass unnoticed. The hills were alive with Indians and as usual, when Bull was in the immediate area, he placed a sentry on one of the highest knolls a few hundred yards northwest of the police HQ. From there a man could scan the hills to the south; it was Bull's perpetual suspicion the Americans were after him.

Sioux trading parties mingled with the Métis; they liked to hang around the halfbreed shanty settlements and the ramshackle trading establishments. Liquor was being smuggled up from Fort Buford. With so many halfbreeds and Indians wandering south and back again looking for buffalo, smuggling could not be eliminated.

The scarcity of food was disastrous. The tensions of resentment, poverty and hopelessness, and the bewildering calamity of hunger, were gnawing at the souls of the Tetons. It was a man's duty, it was his birthright, it was his prime ambition to hunt and fight for wealth and rank. Now there was nothing to hunt and he was forbidden to fight. A man was no longer a man.

The air seemed to be heavy with clouds of degradation and dejection, and from where Walsh was standing, with a detachment that was undermanned and badly housed, it appeared to him the lightning was going to flash right over Wood Mountain.

Government leaders in Ottawa were irrevocably determined to remove the Sioux from land and conscience by refusing their pleas for sustenance.

On the other side of the border, General Miles, Indian-fighter supreme, proud and pompous, politically influential with relatives in the right places, a conqueror of Commanche, Crow, Kiowa, Apache, Cheyenne, Nez Percé and Sioux, was determining his "delicate" strategy for an early spring campaign to squeeze the marauding undesirables back to their adopted Canada from the Milk River region where there were migratory buffalo to hunt, survivors of the Missouri River currents, every one of them a precious prize.

There was one consolation. Riel was as unsuccessful as before in marshalling the faithful and downtrodden into a significant confederation. After accusing Walsh and Miles of collusion, he gave up, for the time being, and moved away, his influence retreating with him.

All the rumours did not disappear. One that persisted concerned the Blackfoot, who were in a state of absolute starvation, eating all their dogs, and grass, and boiling old hides for juice, and stealing the white man's cattle, and offering the women for prostitution, and carrying their decrepit relatives, living skeletons, to the forts in hope of creating pity and collecting scraps. They were reportedly looking to the mixed-blood partisans for their eventual salvation. Crowfoot denied it.

"I have told my people not to listen to them," he assured the police.

In the sanctity of Ottawa, on April 2, 1879, Sir John A. Macdonald, who had regained the prime ministership from Mackenzie in a landslide the previous September, was resisting suggestions from home and abroad that Bull be arrested.

Arrested?...By whom?...For what?...How? U.S. Secretary of State Evarts had suggested Bull be invited to Ottawa where he could be trapped and locked up easily, without bloodshed.

"It seems to me that some evidence should be obtained of a hostile intention on his part," Macdonald protested. "The mere apprehension of the American Government would scarcely be sufficient." He thought Washington relied too much on their Indian agents and scouts for information. "Many of these people are unreliable to the last degree."

The Americans, anticipating an invasion by the Sioux, incensed that they had not been disarmed or interned, formally put the responsibility upon the Canadian and British governments "for any mischief that may come." Evarts pronounced that henceforth the hostiles, having renounced their rights in the United States for security, subsistence and peace, would be regarded as British Indians, a presumption that was rejected emphatically in Ottawa.

The Canadian position was that the Americans should revise their surrender terms. It was not reasonable to expect that hunters would willingly hand over weapons and horses.

In the remoteness of Wood Mountain, the end of the line for diplomatic messages, tempers were on a thin edge. Police rank and file were disgruntled over a ruling that decreased the pay of men re-enlisting from seventy-five cents a day to fifty cents. One of the constables had a fight with a stick-wielding Indian and ejected him from the compound. When some of the young hotheads, having nothing to do, assembled threateningly as if to attack the post, the halfbreeds sided with the police. Conciliation calmed everyone down. Another kind of tempest struck in April, a prairie fire that came perilously close to the headquarters after burning down eight Sioux lodges. A man and a child were killed during the panic. A local hero who ran in while the populace ran away was Sub-Constable Charles Shepherd, a teenage trumpeter who rescued three children from a tepee surrounded by flames.

Sickness in the ranks was a continuing strain on manpower resources. Influenza, catarrh and rheumatism, commonplace afflictions, could be attributed to cold, damp living accommodation in a harsh climate. Of more anxiety was the spreading prevalence of a lingering malarial fever, sometimes accompanied by the symptoms of typhoid, that had taken hold in parts of the Cypress Hills. This fever appeared at Fort Walsh in '76; by '79 it could almost have been called an epidemic. One of those who died was William "Billy" Walsh, a nephew of the major, an ex-member of the force, proprietor of the village "billiard hall." The disease, known to the non-medics as mountain fever, spread to Wood Mountain and claimed halfbreeds and Indians, mostly the undernourished babies of the Sioux.

A temporary diversion for Walsh, if it could be thought of in that way, was his purchase of one of Custer's horses, a gray gelding of about twelve years with the U.S. 7th Cavalry brand clearly visible. The Sioux had brought it to Canada from the battlefield and traded it to a halfbreed.

Walsh had always been a fascinated listener when Ol'Sit, given the inducements of hospitality and flattery, recounted his experience and impressions of his most notable and exaggerated achievement. By and large the men were hesitant to talk about what they did to the Bluecoats. Bull was no exception. Lurking in all their thoughts was the possibility of retribution, fears that turned out to be well founded.

"The old trooper," as Walsh referred to his latest horse (and there was a shortage of horses at the post), had to be processed through official channels. He wrote a letter to General Terry (not forgetting to mention the "gallant Custer") asking permission to keep the horse, which technically was stolen property. Eventually authorization came from the Secretary of War in Washington.

Walsh had managed to influence Bull (and the other headmen) to relent on one important point: voluntary defection. The chief was an autocrat, when he was allowed to be, and applied tribal laws uncompromisingly. No man or family could legally join or leave his band without permission. Punishment for infractions could be severe, although not a question of life or death. However, Bull had now stated that he would not stand in the path of any people who wished to return to their homeland.

In May a hundred starving families were packing for their journey to the U.S. agencies where they would be eligible for food. They were put in a state of turmoil and last-minute indecision when the moccasin telegraph reported that Bear Coat Miles was parading all the soldiers at a Yellowstone River fort for a do-or-die campaign against the northern hostiles. It was even rumoured he had paid their old allies, the Cheyennes, to track down the Sioux.

Bull called a council. After the smoke and after each of the chiefs had spoken, they concluded that Miles was intent upon their destruction. Bull organized a morale-boosting sun dance, just as he had done prior to the Little Big Horn, so that all the bands could be together to ask the Great Spirit for strength, solidarity and wisdom to turn aside their persecutors. The favoured spot for the ritual of dedication and rejuvenation was Medicine Lodge Creek, twenty miles due west of Wood Mountain, in the heart of the badlands. In early July, fifty young Tetons, all volunteers identified by the heavenly wreaths of sage on their heads, were put through the holy rites of mind and flesh.

Events on the frontier were revolving around Bull into a crisis. After the sun dance, when his spirits were bubbling and some of his powers restored, he digressed to Wood Mountain to trade with the halfbreeds before returning to the Milk River hills to go after the buffalo. On the way back his recently initiated warriors ran off a rancher's horses. Bull wanted ten of the best in the herd before he would consider returning the rest.

Walsh and "Cajou" Morin, and a small group including the complainant, Pierre Poitras, saddled up and tracked down the thieves. The major lost his temper with the chief. The outpouring of rudimentary expletives was beyond Morin's ability to translate, but the tone was unmistakable. Bull responded angrily. The outcome, after Walsh had threatened to co-operate with the U.S. military, was the surrender to the rancher of all his horses; Ol'Sit realized he had trouble enough.

One typical source of trouble was Lieutenant-Colonel Joseph Whistler, a corps commander with Miles's army. Whistler had spoken very bitterly of Bull to Walsh at Poplar Creek agency, accusing him of killing two army mail carriers back in the sixties. Walsh convinced the colonel that if he would produce a warrant charging Bull with murder, he would be arrested by the police and locked up in less than a day for the U.S. Government to file an extradition paper. The warrant never came.

Bull, when he heard of the charge from Walsh, denied the accusation and challenged the American to produce any person who could prove he killed these whites. He scornfully suggested that if the Americans wished to uncover the guilty person they should go and see Spotted Tail, an agency chief: "This villain, who is being fed at the Spotted Tail agency, was responsible. He charged me when I was a young man with this, and other crimes, to put the soldiers on my trail so that he could have me killed to save his own neck."

As Bull and his band were taking their time to the Milk River, pausing on agreeable camping grounds to look for meat, Miles and his mixed bag of campaigners were closing the gap. Miles had already reached Fort Buford where the Yellowstone sandbanks spilled into the murky waters of "Old Misery" Missouri. Two paddlers (the Benton and the Rosebud) transported most of the infantry, and supplies and equipment westwards to old Fort Peck, near the junction of the Milk at a place where the Missouri opens up and becomes a lake, where mosquitoes in the billions darken the evening sun. By the middle of July the Bluecoats, guided by their Indian scouts, were moving towards Canada along the north bank of the Milk, a river of endless bends, snake-like in the arid prairie, its course weaving among the fringe lushness of green trees, bushes and the "itch" weed.

On a summer day when the vivid blue of the sky shimmered down to the dust of the earth and little white blobs of isolated clouds drifted about aimlessly, and the strength of the sun sapped a man's initiative, and baked him, and gave him a thirst that a buffalo stomach full of water could not satiate, a lone Sioux on horseback, just beyond sight of his own camp, was meandering around in search of stray horses.

He saw some horses all right, eight of them, and eight strangers riding them, all Indians. He turned his own pony around and dashed for home, which was Bull's own camp.

"Hey, wait!"

They were shouting in his own dialect. He reined his horse. Out in front he recognized Big Leggings, the breed, once adopted by Bull but denounced and thrown away as pork meat when he went over to the side of Miles. His companions were Cheyennes.

"We want to go to your camp to see Sitting Bull," said Big Leggings.

"If you go there you won't come out with your scalps," the Sioux shouted back.

Big Leggings said he was going in anyway and he rode towards the lodges with two Cheyennes, one of whom could speak the Sioux language and the other, Bobtail Horse, a renowned warrior who had fought with the Tetons.

Bobtail Horse put his life on the line when he informed Bull that he was going back to Bear Coat to lead the soldiers directly to Bull's circle unless he promised to surrender.

The number-one hostile, burning inside, was beyond the extreme of emotional response. He took the threat calmly.

"Let them come! Let the Indian dogs come with them! I'm not going to run away!"

Bobtail Horse kept his word. He guided the soldiers to where he had threatened Bull, but the Sioux had packed up tepees and gone, chasing the migrant buffalo farther into the United States.

Miles had sent out other Indian scouts to bring in all Canadian halfbreeds hunting in the region, and they did, tying the unfortunates to their horses and scaring them half to death.

An odd alliance of reliable Crows and Cheyennes, and recently enlisted Assiniboines, and a few troopers to control the mob, accidentally came across Bull's hunters. The army scouts, with new guns to try out and plenty of ammunition, opened up; the Sioux and their Nez Percé allies, unprepared, retaliated and retreated ten miles to the overflowing Milk River. When they got their families safely across, they swam back to the south side, hanging on to the necks of their war horses, so as to surprise the turncoats with a counter-attack.

The turncoats were no match for the Sioux in the skirmish; Bull killed a sniper with his own sharpshooting.

Miles, a first-rate front-line soldier, took over from his mercenary Indians. When two of his Hotchkiss machine guns opened up, the barrels revolving and the shots cracking with the rapidity of a hundred soldiers shooting accurately, the earth about the Sioux broke up with the impact. They scattered to get out of range, abandoning precous buffalo meat, saddles, lariats, bows and arrows, even ponies.

The noise of the Hotchkiss "panic" guns alarmed Bear Cap's camp two miles away. The commotion was immediate. So much, and such rapid firing, was a clarion call to glory. As the old men, women and children frenziedly decamped, the fighters stripped for war, unhobbled their best horses, and sped off in the sultry heat towards the sound of all the fury, the ponies soon sweating and frothing with the pace.

The fighting became intermittent as Miles used his scouts to do the probing. His smallest contingent were a dozen or so turncoat Sioux still following the warrior chief Hump (short for High Back Bone). Hump had been a fighter of considerable repute, an idol of the murdered Crazy Horse whom he had adopted as a young brother. Hump shifted his allegiance to the Bluecoats, as he had threatened to, when he had failed to persuade the uncompromising hostiles to give up.

After three days of desultory encounters along the slippery, precipitous banks of the White Mud River, which was deepened by incessant summer downpours, the stubborn rearguard escaped into the Queen's land. Their losses in men had been slight – Miles's mercenaries had cut but five scalps. The Sioux put up their lodges under leaden skies as Bull was joined by the chiefs of the other bands to mull over the unexpected opportunity for a unified attack on Bear Coat from Canada.

Miles, with his commanders, rode up to the trench surrounding the boundary stones. Before them, just out of rifle range, were the dusky forms of a bunch of Bull's scouts, lounging on their ponies, watching them mockingly, the sun flashing off their signal mirrors. Miles's scouts were whooping up their excitement, prodding their animals back and forth, impatiently waiting for the word to get 'em!

Would they get the word?

"If Sitting Bull wants a battle he'll have plenty of opportunity from me," Miles had retorted a few days before.

"Won't he take advantage of the British line to elude you, general, if he finds himself too weak?" someone had asked.

"That's one of the troubles of this business," Miles had answered. "Our Government must do something to come to a definite understanding with the Dominion. When the Sioux were driven across the line they were virtually helpless; they had lost almost everything. Now they have fine arms and plenty of powder and lead. They could only have procured these supplies in the British possession."

"Would you respect the boundary line if you whipped Bull and if he retreated across it?"

"That must be an after consideration," the general had replied.

Miles looked contemplatively to his left and right, towards other boundary markers. What a temptation! He thought of the Nez Percé battle and how White Bird had got away. If he crossed into Canada now he knew he could rely on top-level military backing in Washington, on civilian adulation of his exploits and burgeoning support for his glowing predictions of a magnificent, civilized destiny for the plains. Politically, the risk was unquestionably immeasurable although he could probably count on sympathy both in the cabinet and in the Senate through his wife's connections. The press would assuredly be on his side.

If he didn't move northwards he might never get another chance at Bull. His aggressive ego was pushing him on. He had heard his officers say that the line would never stop him when in pursuit of Indians. There wasn't a scout, muleskinner or trader along the upper Missouri who would doubt that Miles would say, "To hell with the border!"

Who could stop him anyway? A handful of policemen in red jackets?

Bear Coat, bold and innovative, physically strong, indefatigable foe of Sitting Bull, made an uncharacteristic decision.

"We'll camp here," he ordered "Picket the horses in the center."

He rode back to the troops. They were staying south of Europe, as the soldiers termed the Dominion. In short order there were fires all over the place; smokey, smelly fires of wet sagebrush and weeds to relieve them from another enemy, the man-eating mosquito.

When the Sioux headmen conferred, the belligerents advocated an immediate assault on the army. The women and children were not now endangered. More than 2,000 warriors could be mustered on the spot, all of them frantically eager to exercise their manly devotions to the collection of coups and scalps.

"Bear Coat will fall before us like dry grass before a fire," Bull proclaimed. "A few hours and the wolf that is seeking my blood will be no more."

Broad Trail, who had taken over as chieftain of Bull's camp while he was foraging in the United States, sent a messenger to Walsh outlining what he had heard from the border and suggesting that the major be present at a great council called by Bull almost within gunshot range of the Americans.

Walsh jumped into action. When he arrived the Sioux were in a fervour; warlike passions were boiling over; every man was preparing himself excitedly for the battle. He could see that 2,500 warriors were ready to strike, the mightiest collection of well-armed Sioux strength ever assembled anywhere, far outnumbering the opposition. He envisaged for Miles the same treatment Custer had received, and whereas he could have looked the other way "if Miles had inflicted upon Canada the indignity of an invasion, as the Americans had done in Mexico to kill and capture Indians," he could not in any way consent to Bull's army sweeping Miles off the prairie when Miles had not yet set a warlike foot in the Dominion.

The temper of the Indians did not allow for jurisdictional niceties or international politics. Death to Bear Coat and all his soldiers and all their Indian turncoats. Revenge!

Walsh got Broad Trail to convene the council. Bull recited the story of his latest encounter with Miles. He said the Americans

174

were moving northwards looking for a fight and they would get it.

"Friend," he said, turning to the major, "not one of the men following my trail today will ever recross the Missouri River. They are hunting me like hungry wolves, but they will find their prey like a rattlesnake with a sting."

Turning to the chiefs he exhorted them to listen well.

"Warriors, you want guns, ammunition, horses and saddles. In all these things you are poor. The supply you got at the Greasy Grass (Battle of the Little Big Horn) is just about gone. The Americans are coming to replenish our supplies and before the sun rises twice the young men of this camp will have the chance to prove themselves. A victory as easy as the one on the Big Horn is before you. The Great Spirit will guide you. Prepare!"

The major, outwardly unruffled, counselled Bull to retract what he had just said. Again he pointed out that such action would disqualify the Sioux from asylum in Canada.

Bull, though, was back on the throne with the resources and the sympathy of the majority of the tribes. Right now, at this place, they could assert themselves to regain their heritage.

"We have been attacked and shot down for no other offense than gathering food for the starving children," the crafty chief pleaded and cajoled. No Indian in the lodge could, or dared, disagree.

For twenty-two hours they argued and listened; then they became tired and hungry and their emotions cooled; and the realities came into focus. Could they afford to give up their sanctuary for the satisfaction and prestige of a crack at Miles? The council agreed, sadly, to be advised by Walsh, and at his request the camp moved twenty miles farther from the border and its enticement.

The major returned to Wood Mountain, to two visitors he had left at the post during the crisis. One was a lieutenant with Miles's 5th Infantry, young John Tillson, who was carrying a letter from the general requesting the arrest of Indian horse thieves wanted for murder. The crimes had been committed in March along the Yellowstone and the criminals were known to have escaped to Canada. His companion was a civilian, Sturms, who was a witness. Tillson was also looking for U.S. Army deserters, a ceaseless problem for the military as the shiftless elements in the ranks, unaccustomed to discipline and hardship, were lured by tall tales from the Montana goldfields or the money to be made in the whisky trade.

Unobstrusively Tillson was absorbing all he could about the Sioux in exile. He had orders to report directly to Miles. Sturms, who had been wounded by the thieves, told Walsh that the five Indian thugs on the wanted list were two Nez Percés (one called White Eye and the other "Johnson") and three Sioux.

The major put his information network in motion. White Eye had recently been killed by the Crows; "Johnson" was among the Tetons. Walsh agreed to take Sturms where he would mostly likely find "Johnson" and the three other renegades – close to Bull. From there he could escort Tillson and Sturms to Miles, whom he wanted to meet anyway.

Ten miles out they came upon the leading edge of the vast Sioux conglomeration that was still edging away from the frontier, in accordance with Walsh's advice. Sturms, when he saw the extent of the Indian sprawl, lost his zeal to uncover the murderers. He had already shaved off his beard and had further disguised himself, a precaution against being recognized later by the associates of the Indians he had intended to hustle off.

Walsh's detachment attracted a mob of inquisitively restive Sioux. It was an unnerving experience for Tillson, who had been surprised that the major would undertake the journey with so small an entourage. The lieutenant was unmistakably a Bluecoat, only a year removed from the womb of West Point, and as he conceded later on, in safety, he hadn't been jostled or pushed around so much since the Centennial Day jam in Philadelphia.

Bull eyed Tillson with a cold suspicion. Before he could say a word Walsh rasped that the American officer had come to Wood Mountain from Fort Walsh on government business and was being accompanied to the border. The major kept Bull off balance, requesting that six warriors, including One Bull, his relative, be delegated to strengthen the escort to the border.

"I want them to join me and my four men [Corporal George Connor, Constables J. M. Bliss, Ben Daniels, H.R. Parks] and escort this officer to General Miles. I'll wait at the butte [pointing to a hill to the south]."

Sturms wisely confessed he was unable to recognize any of the

Indians he was looking for, not even the Nez Percé who had a white man's name and who was brought before him. He willingly reached the conclusion that inasmuch White Eye was dead nothing further could be done in the case. He wanted to get away – promptly.

The five policemen and the two Americans didn't have to linger at the butte. One Bull and five warriors, including Palopa, the nephew of Spotted Eagle, rode with them. In seven hours they were at Rock Creek, in sight of the improvised boundary markers. Tillson and Sturms carried on impatiently, towards the army picket lines, conveyed almost to Miles's tent by his bitter enemies. "You can trust One Bull with your life," Walsh had assured them.

The Americans were seen first by the general's Indian allies. For a few, fleeting, marvellous moments they had a notion that it was Bull riding in to give himself up. A hundred of them took off with a wild, uncontrollable splurge, risking their necks and their horses on the gopher-hole prairie.

The lieutenant went directly to Miles, presented his report, adding that Walsh was bivouacked at the boundary with an escort of Sioux. The major received an invitation to meet the general.

"Bring everyone with you!"

Not bloody likely! The prospect of an incident, Sioux versus Crow and Cheyenne, was downright certain. Three years ago the Crows had killed six Sioux who were coming into Fort Keogh under a flag of truce. They were shot less than 200 yards from the fort.

With his own men at his side, Walsh rode the mile or so to the border where he was introduced to Miles, the former crockery store clerk. He accepted the general's invitation to visit the next day.

The major set aside his official, regal attire. He showed up at the commander's tent dressed in a serviceable buckskin suit, a wide-brimmed, prairie-dusted, grime-stained slouch hat, and knee-covering Buffalo Bill cavalry boots. This smallish, rugged bush-whacker character with long hair was the superintendent of the Imperial Mounted Police? The Americans couldn't believe it.

Walsh had been flattered by Tillson as able and fearless; Miles would find him pleasant and, disconcertingly, a professed admirer of Sitting Bull and the Sioux. Everybody would agree he was...unorthodox.

"He painted the Sioux character in such glowing colors that were it not for his pleasant Irish accent he might be suspected of consanguinity with the aborigines," one of the general's press corps noted.

Walsh touched an open nerve or two with his assertion the Sioux could outfight their own number of any white troops. The general responded that there were Americans not far off who would not be afraid to put the theory to the test.

Miles changed the subject.

"I have orders to drive all hostiles over the line," he said curtly and dominantly. "They have no business raiding American reservations. They are a menace to the peace and welfare of the citizens of the United States."

Walsh said his orders were to notify U.S. authorities of hostile acts or intentions.

"General, I don't know whether going to hunt buffalo can be called a hostile act or not. These people are hungry."

Miles was not sympathetic.

"Our own Indians need the buffalo. And these hostiles from Canada don't confine themselves to game. I have been told they kill settlers and steal horses, and some of these horses are in Wood Mountain."

"If there are any up there I'll do my utmost to get them identified and returned to the owners," Walsh promised.

The general gave Walsh another broadside.

"There are some Indians in the Sioux village who committed murders on the Yellowstone. I want them. There's a U.S. marshall waiting here to take them into custody."

Hadn't Tillson told the general about White Eye and Sturms's search at close hand among the Tetons? Walsh promised his cooperation again, saying it would be necessary to get in touch with his Government.

"Furthermore," Miles continued, quarrelsomely, "the horses, wagons and cargoes of all Canadians or halfbreeds trading ammunition with the Indians on American soil will be seized."

Walsh replied it was lawful for the traders in Canada to sell ammunition to the Indians for hunting.

The tenseness of the verbal slogging was alleviated when Walsh, in defence of the Indians, remarked that he had seen the best regiments of England and they weren't equal to the Sioux as

178

horsemen or marksmen."That may be so," someone butted in, "because the English have hardly recovered from panic following Braddock's defeat."

The major chuckled. The conversation softened. He confirmed the strength of the hostiles. He said that from what he had heard recently in the lodge of Sitting Bull the Hotchkiss guns had demoralized them.

"General, I tell you honestly, the Sioux don't want to fight the white people any more. Just the other day Spotted Eagle said, 'Tell the white chief I don't want to fight with him, but let him give my young men a chance at those Crows and Cheyennes'!"

For the amusement of all in the tent, the major pantomimed his Sioux friend as the meeting developed pleasantly into reminiscences and yarn-spinning.

When he was leaving with his orderly he promised he would return with two Sioux warriors, one of them the brother of Hump, the leader of the Sioux contingent serving with Miles against their relatives and former friends.

Miles was determined to make life uncomfortable for Canadian halfbreeds caught hunting in his jurisdiction. To him they were a "disturbing element" supplying ammunition to non-treaty Indians. He sent four cavalry companies into the Milk River country to capture all the Métis they could find. The soldiers were glad to get some action; the weather, for late July, was atrociously cold.

The cavalrymen corralled about 400 families of Canadian interlopers. When Walsh was alerted to this latest aggravation, which would knock the bottom out of Wood Mountain trade, he was scouring the Sioux camps, helping two Americans to reclaim stolen horses. They had come hundreds of miles from Fort Custer, at the junction of the Little Big Horn and Big Horn Rivers, to look for their stock. They found seven.

The imprint of the path to the south was by now as familiar to the major as the wagon ruts of the two trails of Fort Walsh. His companions on this latest mission were four Redcoats, the Americans, who were relieved to be leaving with their horses and scalps, a halfbreed scout of Miles's staff, and the two warriors he had promised to produce. One was Long Dog, vicious in war but a lively, humorous addition to any group, especially a weary one on the humdrum prairie. The other was The One Who Kills The

White Man, who wanted to see his brother, the turncoat Hump. Miles had moved twenty miles farther down Rock Creek during the lull.

Walsh interceded successfully for the Canadian halfbreeds, who were released on condition they leave the region. About 130 families later returned to the north.

Walsh was present on July 27 when Miles and Whistler interviewed Long Dog and The One Who Kills The White Man.

"Why don't you surrender and go to an agency?" Miles asked, his imposing, forceful figure hunched over them.

They pointed to Walsh.

"There is our chief. He knows the Sioux heart. His words are our laws."

"Well, major, I know who to deal with. These people appear willing to abide by your decision."

"General, it could be implied by their remarks that I am their dictator, but that would be wrong. I have an influence with the hostiles but not sufficient to persuade them to surrender in their wars."

Walsh said he had detected a tendency to return to the agencies, and had expected that many of the bands would have given up before the winter, but because of the general's campaign it was now unlikely that any significant defections would occur in '79.

"These Indians ask you to allow them to retain their horses and their guns on their own reservation," Walsh stressed on their behalf. "If this could be arranged they will probably give up. If this is not agreed, I can't see them surrendering in a body. Ultimately, though, they will all surrender. This will start with thirty or forty families crossing over and the others waiting to hear of their reception and treatment. Detachment by detachment they will all go; Bull will be the last."

The general suggested that if the Canadian Government would name Walsh to a commission and the United States allocated a qualified person to serve with him, the entire problem could be brought to a close, effectively and satisfactorily.

# ❖❖❖ The Visitor and the Big Guns

We're marching off for Sitting Bull
And this is the way we go–
Forty miles a day on beans and hay
With the regular army, O!

❖❖❖ When General Miles attempted this lyrical melody, with a wobbly bass voice, he was at his headquarters bidding farewell to Walsh and his entourage. The well-used military ditty, reworded, was not especially directed at the Canadians. It was intended for a Chicago newspaper correspondent, John Finerty, who had been dogging Miles's footsteps up to the British line to record his illustrious, adventuresome career with a foamy flourish.

Finerty was intrigued by the legend of the "historic savage known as Sitting Bull." He had asked Miles to sound out Walsh about letting him wander among the hostiles in their Canadian sanctum: "I had not an unnatural desire to represent the American press before the Teton chiefs in their war paint," he later wrote, "especially as the red marauders were making themselves quite at home, and supposedly comfortable, on British soil."

Such was the magnitude of his reportorial urge, and it would be fulfilled, but not without an expression of professional pride and lamentation for the less fortunate. "How much better pleased the dashing soldier would be if he were allowed to advance on the Sioux camp with a force capable of pounding the copper-colored enemy into subjection," Finerty editorialized for his eastern readership, whose latent pioneer spirits thrived on newspaper accounts of the hazards and glory of life on the untamed frontier.

The national appetite for adventure was being aptly aroused and sensationally satisfied by dashing reports in the daily press and illustrated magazines, sometimes written by the principal heroes themselves. The newspapers were publishing hair-raising stories, seized upon by the politicians, of Sitting Bull solemnly swearing an oath of allegiance to the Queen, of an impending invasion by Bull's Canadian army. Editorial writers reacted with armchair observations and valiant solutions: "He should be made to give himself up as a prisoner of war and submit to a trial....A sufficient number of troops should be sent to annihilate him and his bloodthirsty tribe....Sitting Bull not only dislikes Americans, but all whites. He is without doubt a bad Indian....The Sioux are no more under the control of the Mounted Police than they are by American Civil and Military agents."

Without doubt, Finerty, the special correspondent, was on his way to a scoop when he departed under the protection of five Redcoats and two of the infidels. Forty-three miles they rode the first day, a lot of it at the gallop in a vain attempt to thwart the mosquitoes. The heavy rains, and now the humid sun, brought out the insects in plague proportions. The faces, necks and hands of the sweltering riders were covered with red blemishes resembling smallpox. Camp was made at Medicine Lodge Creek, the site where Sitting Bull had staged his sun dance. The holy poles were still standing, the terrain churned up and mangled. The rain had not washed out the thousands of hoof and moccasin marks.

The night was torturous with the heat and insects. Long Dog, who had an aptitude for isolating and retaining the most commonly used profanities of the English language, ran around in his blanket swatting the mosquitoes on his face and neck, each movement prompting a repetitive "Goddamn." He couldn't find any peace; neither could anyone else. Long Dog, in his misery, was also contemplating other miseries, and the memory of them prickled his agitated mind. When he thought no one was listening he would imitate Miles's artillery to himself. "Bang, bang, bang." (The firing.) A pause. "Pop, pop, pop." (The shells coming.) Another pause. "Sonofabitch!"

Those who had been on the trail with Long Dog were accustomed to these goings-on. Finerty had·a sleepless night, but he didn't hold a grudge against the comedian. "He's not so very bad a fellow for an Indian," he concluded.

Breakfast was frugal and quick. Walsh, Finerty and two constables went on ahead and left the others to proceed slowly with the wagon. For twenty miles they filed through the ravines, patched with the yellow and the red of sunflowers and roses; they rode around the gentle slopes of short, green buffalo grass, along the creeks shaded and hidden by tall poplars and maples, and hugged by willows and thorn bushes; then onto the old travois pole route, a legacy of Indians, Hudson's Bay traders, the Montagne des Bois halfbreeds, the freighters and bootleggers. When Finerty first saw the tepees of Bull's camp from afar, little white cones with smoke-browned tops, all aligned in concentric circles, and the thousands of grazing ponies, he realized he had underestimated, as Custer had done, the number of Sioux.

The four of them carried on unnoticed, the policemen in their blend of uniforms and buckskins and Finerty in a blue shirt, military style, and a broad-brimmed white hat. When they reached a rise overlooking the dilapidated police headquarters they were seen from the valley. In less than a minute a bunched blur of mounted Indians and dogs engulfed in a yellow cloud of dust was heading their way. When the riders recognized Walsh they were overjoyed; they shook his hand and slapped him on the back. Finerty, looking very much a representative of the Bluecoats, was eyed with unconcealed hostility.

"They're Long Dog's relatives," Walsh told him. "Some halfbreed scoundrel told them that the old chief, the other Sioux and myself had been murdered in Miles's camp. That's why they're so excited."

The return of the major coincided with a scalp dance in Broad Trail's circle. On display was a Cheyenne scalp, recently removed from one of the turncoat scouts, and the people were celebrating with the usual uproar of drums, singing, stamping and stepping. The enthralled onlookers packed a stretch of elevated flatland a few yards east of the post.

Walsh took Finerty to see the wild display. The major elbowed his way through the armed mob. As the young men, all feathered and painted in dots and streaks, were pushed aside they saw Finerty. He got the impression of not being a welcome guest! The two of them reached the inner ring of observers – the chiefs, headmen, sub-chiefs and the shirt-wearing soldiers, all of them in their ornamental finery – and Walsh led the way to a Red River cart. Finerty was about to get another surprise. There, sitting on the cart, watching the dancers, was a young lady. Fair and pretty and as white as a lily, she had soft brown eyes and cheeks of exquisite bloom. The correspondent was astonished to see "so sweet a female blossom amid such horrible surroundings."

"Who is she?" Finerty asked.

"That's Mrs. Allen, wife of the post trader," Walsh answered. "She's really scared of the Indians, as you can see. She's here to please them."

Nearest to her, with the latest-model Winchester in his lap, was a young, brawny Sioux wearing a gorgeously beaded vest – and a perpetual scowl.

"Who in the hell is that one?"

"That's Big Necklace, a Minneconjou scout; he's one of the biggest villains in the entire Teton camp."

This fellow glared impudently. The major introduced the correspondent to the trader's wife, a courtesy that appeared to please the possessive Big Necklace, her guardian so to speak. He extended his hand to Finerty and forced a grin, *"How!"*

Finerty kept close to Walsh. As the prancing intensified, the crowd pressed in, providing the correspondent with a marvelous box-seat view of Teton faces, a variety of hues of brown, a few bordering on white.

"Who's that one with the zigzag-painted face over there?"

"He's No Neck, a Hunkpapa, one of the most powerful and influential men around here."

No Neck! Finerty had heard of him from the army scouts. Who could forget a name like that? In the councils No Neck was an annoying opponent of Bull, and anyone in this exalted position could be both famous and infamous. His opposition ran deeply, even to the extent of being against Bull's decision to adopt a boy of their enemies, Little Assinibone. When there was fighting to be done, when it was necessary for the Hunkpapa to be unified, No Neck and his dissidents didn't waver, not at the Little Big Horn, not in the confrontation with Bear Coat, not when Bull's father was hacked to death by the Crows. No Neck didn't hesitate that day. He joined in the chase, so furious and prolonged that some of the horses dropped dead from exhaustion.

Walsh pointed out other Hunkpapa notables: One Bull, Old Sit's nephew, young, strong and handsome, a natural resource for power-struck young maidens; Bad Soup, the chief's brother-in-law and a favorite companion; Little Assiniboine, wounded in the thigh in the recent fighting and not bothering to be incapacitated.

Long Dog was there now, and next to him his brother, Pretty Bear, younger, wily, an unlikely friend of any white man; Bear's Cap, old but energetic, not yet fully retired from scalping; Little Knife, the people's choice despite his age and infirmities, honourable and generally considerate; Crow, the speech-maker, a dark-featured, brooding middle-aged thinker who reputedly shouted the war whoop that signalled the Hunkpapa counter-attack at the beginning of the Custer battle; Clouded Horn, in his middle life, sartorially drab, his wisdom in the councils on a par with his dexterity on the battlefield; and contrastingly, White Guts, a war-like dandy, tall and thin, in his prime, tough, an implacable foe of the whites (and the Indians who turned their coats), impiously prone to go as far as killing black robes. He once wanted to finish Father De Smet, who was visiting Sitting Bull on a mission of peace and was receiving Bull's personal guaranteed protection.

Finerty enquired about Sitting Bull. He was not present. Where was the terror? Mrs. Allen interjected that Bull was the nicest man around the trading post; always he treated her with consideration and respect.

"He never hangs around our house at meals as some of the others do."

Walsh assured Finerty he would see Bull before too long.

"You're in luck. The chiefs have called a council outside my quarters and they should all be there."

In the late afternoon the drums stopped, thankfully. The gathering moved on down to the post. Two chairs were placed by the garden fence for Walsh and Finerty. The chiefs, their multi-colored ceremonial blankets wrapped around their waists, sat in a semi-circle, and behind them, lounging in row after irregular row, leaning on their feathered spears, were the warriors, then the horsemen, and on the rim of the crowd the women and children, out of hearing range, unable to see a thing but the backs of the pony riders.

Walsh identified more of the aristocracy for his guest.

With the Oglala chiefs was Broad Trail, well-proportioned and sturdy, a leader with adroit mental and physical resources. When he saw Walsh looking in his direction, a smile came to his manly face. He stood up. He was broad-shouldered, his body daubed with war paint, his eagle-feathered headdress almost touching the ground. He strode out to shake hands with the two white men then returned to the side of The Hero, his brother, a combination orator and priest.

In the crammed semi-circle was the eloquent Oglala philosopher, Bear Killer, who had a broken nose. He was alongside Stone Dog, a young veteran of the wars, at the moment peacefully inclined, highly intelligent and a born motivator who deserved, according to Finerty, a better fate than to be an Indian. Stone Dog was one of Walsh's favourites: "He knows no fear, laughs at death, scorns life's pains. How many times has he said to me, 'Wherever your dead body lies, there mine will also be found'."

Conspicuous in the front row was Low Dog. If looks could kill he would have a thousand scalps. Sullen, sulky, taciturn, he had the unsympathetic eyes of a fanatic and the mouth of uncompromising resolution. One eagle feather protruded from his hair, which was carefully parted in the middle. The braids, wrapped in strands of fur, flopped below his waist. He was clutching an iron-headed tomahawk, made by the whites for trading; the handle was ornamented with beads.

Low Dog had more atrocities to his account than could be remembered. From where Finerty was sitting, which was close enough, he had the appearance of a bad Indian. Real bad. He was, in fact, a volatile troublemaker, a continuing malcontent who could foster dissention; he was an independent and powerful sinew of the free spirits.

What a spree he had at the Little Big Horn. When Low Dog heard the cry, "The chargers are coming!" he couldn't credit his luck. Soldiers, here? It must be a false alarm; it could not be possible they would assault the camp. Never had the Sioux been as strong altogether. He was quick to get his gun and hatchet and wreak havoc in the bunches of retreating Bluecoats. Not until they were all dead did he learn he had helped to put an end to Custer, not that the identity of his enemy would have made any difference. His blood was hot; his heart light and frenzied for killing.

Walsh nodded towards the Sans-Arc contingent. The strikingly tall, gracefully slender figure with the light eyes that contrasted so vividly with his copper-tanned features was Spotted Eagle. The major said he was eloquent, valorous, but never a mischief-maker.

"Gentle when stroked; fierce when provoked," Finerty chipped in.

Iron Horse was an opposite; an ardent hostile, suspicious, arrogant, resolute in his vehemence, a haughty wearer of a long, combat-record headdress.

Prominent allies sitting with the Sioux were two Yanktons: Pretty Hawk, up and coming in the tribal hierarchy, and Strike

The Ree, well qualified for a name connoting violence. Spokesman for the belligerent faction of the Assiniboines was Little Mountain, an incurable hostile.

Absent, but coming from a hunt with more than 300 lodges, were White Eagle, a Teton, and Red Hand, a rebel-type Santee.

"Still no sign of old Bull," Finerty said.

"He probably knows you're here," Walsh replied. "He says he won't speak in council where there are Americans. I think you'll see him before long though."

It was a prediction based on Bull's curiosity, his obligation to power, and his polished histrionics. It was an accurate prediction. Into the conference circle came Bull, bulky on a cream-coloured pony, regally fanning himself with an eagle's wing, helping his soldiers clear a path for him. He stopped behind the seated chiefs to stare pugnaciously at the American. Finerty was uncomfortable. He didn't have to be told he was being analyzed by *the* chief.

Bull was plainly attired, without paint or plumes. Finerty's lasting impressions were of two, fierce, gleaming, half-bloodshot eyes exuding insolent inquisitiveness.

"That's old Bull himself," Walsh confirmed. "He'll hear everything and say nothing until he has something to stir up."

Bull dismounted, and limping slightly led his animal to a shady spot where he sat down, followed by the young men. All was ready. Walsh motioned to the interpreter, Larrivée, and at this the hubbub petered out. Larrivée, a college-educated Montrealer, a squawman (he had two wives), the bane of the black robes, was fluent in Lakota.

"I have come from the camp of the white chief, Bear Coat. He says none of you must go south of the line, which has been shown to you, and which will be your protection as long as you behave yourselves."

Walsh paused until the *"Hows"* and *"Ughs"* died down.

"The white mother cannot protect you if you violate her laws. Your hunting parties must not cross the boundary in search of buffalo and other game. Wait until they come here. They are heading this way now. I saw herds of them near the line as I came in. (This last remark initiated a swelling of more *"Hows"* and *"How kola,"* meaning something akin to "Welcome, friend.")

"Your young men can chase them after they come into the white mother's country. I know your meat is nearly gone, and if the buffalo do not cross the line I don't know what can be done for your relief. One thing is certain, you cannot be allowed to break the law. I am willing to do all I can to help you, within the law...."

As Walsh was speaking he was distracted by a boy warrior who was leaning from his horse, relaying a message to the Hunkpapa chiefs. The interpreter went over to hear for himself. Two young braves who had crossed to the American side to try and direct a herd of buffalo into Canada had been set upon by Miles's Cheyennes. One of them, Pretty Face, was killed and the other wounded.

"Your young men will not hear what I say, therefore they must suffer the consequences. If they had kept here, as I asked, nothing would have happened to them. So long as you remain deaf to my counsel there will be death at your doors and mourning in your tepees."

A succession of *"Ughs"*.

Bad Soup stood up. It could not be expected his intentions would be good.

"Who is that man sitting beside you?"

"This man is a friend of mine. He writes for the white men's newspapers and will tell the straight truth about you."

"Is he not a soldier chief?"

"He is not. It is enough he is a friend of mine. His heart is not bad against the Sioux."

The occasion for speech-making brought The Hero to his feet. With a professional sweep of his arm, southwards, a movement of refined majesty that emphasized his standing as an orator, he adopted a harsh approach to arouse the admiration of his following.

"When my young men go hunting over there, they are met with fire. My women are killed and my children starve. [Grunts of approval from his fellow chiefs.] My grandmother [the Queen] says I must not go to war, and I obey her. I see my people starving. I go to kill the buffalo. The Great Spirit made no lines. The buffalo tastes the same on both sides of the stone heaps. I can find no change. Why then do the Americans meet us with fire when we only wish to feed ourselves and our women and children?

"The Great Spirit has given me a stomach. He has given me the buffalo. I see the buffalo near the stone heaps, and I must not shoot him, even while my children cry for his meat. The Great Spirit never meant to tempt me with the buffalo so near while my children are hungry.

"This strange man hears me. Will he put my words straight before the people of his nation?"

Finerty looked up and nodded.

"The chiefs would like to hear the stranger talk. My brother [Broad Trail], who is chief of the tribe, would speak himself but he is in his paint. I have spoken for him and the Oglalas.

"The Americans ask us to smoke today and shoot us tomorrow." More exclamations of agreement from the throng.

Finerty, understandingly apprehensive, responded to the invitation. His finesse as an observer and recorder of events was being put to an unscheduled test.

"I cannot rival the eloquence of your chiefs. The Sioux are renowned in oratory as well as in war." There was unanimous agreement. When the *"Hows"* faded away Finerty continued.

"I will speak with an honest heart. My business is to write what my people may read. I have not come to fight you or to spy upon you, but to see how you live and to talk with your wise men. [*"How!" "How!"*] All white men do not have bad hearts for the Indian; if I were your enemy I could not sleep in the tepee of the White Sioux [Walsh]. He would cast me out. [*"How!" "How!"*] I can do no more than a simple citizen of the United States – hear what you say and put it before my people. There is no need for me to say more than the Americans do not desire to starve your families or yourselves if you cease to make war upon them. Like yourselves the Americans do not always hear the truth." [*"How!" "How!" "How!"*]

Bad Soup jumped up again.

"Very few Americans speak the truth. I hope this man proves to be different. The Americans have taught the Sioux how to break promises. They took our land, piece by piece, until everything was gone, and we had to take refuge in the country of our white grandmother.

"Are the Americans a people that the Sioux can love? They send Bear Coat and his soldiers to shoot us down; they arm the Crows and Cheyennes, the Bannocks and the Assiniboines to murder our young men. Are the Americans afraid to fight themselves that they hide in a cloud of Indian renegades?"

This remark of ridicule was acclaimed with a chorus of lusty hoots and yells. Bull's smiles signified his agreement.

Bad Soup, buoyed by this reaction of his compatriots, truculently asked Walsh a question: "How long will Bear Coat stay on the Milk River?"

"It's none of your business," Walsh snapped. "He may stay there all summer if your young men keep crossing the line. You don't need to care how long he stays there so long as you obey the laws of the white mother. I have heard that your young men threatened to cut the tents of the halfbreeds if they went to chase the buffalo. The white mother's laws must not be tampered with. The young men who spoke such a thing must have badness in their hearts."

Bear Killer, another Oglala speech-specialist, stepped forward to say the young men did not mean what they threatened.

"We can't always control them, but it is not right they should be shot down because they went across the line to round up the buffalo."

Walsh raised his voice.

"How often have I told them they must not cross the line for any purpose?"

Not a sound from the Indians.

The council ended. Spotted Eagle sauntered up to Walsh to report a hunting party was setting out in the morning as far as the mud huts on the British side.

"Spotted Eagle, see to it my instructions are obeyed."

The chiefs gathered around Walsh, all except Bull. He shook the blanket on which he had been sitting, mounted, and rode off, followed by his retinue of young admirers. Bad Soup was not far behind. Finerty ordered tobacco from the trader and after filling their pipes the notables introduced themselves to the American.

"I would have come up before," Spotted Eagle told Finerty, "but at first I thought you were Bear Coat. I shook his hand once, but his features were hidden by a hat and I could not remember him well." ("I was somewhat flattered at being mistaken for so noted an Indian fighter," Finerty wrote later, "but I felt much more comfortable when the Indians were convinced that my scalp was not quite so valuable after all. Spotted Eagle, who is a chivalric foe, would have treated the general well, but some young buck, thirsting for fame, might have murdered him just for the notoriety

190

of the act, even though [he] himself were killed immediately afterwards.")

The late arrival and early departure of Bull from the council could only mean he had decided to weigh up the American for himself. That evening he called upon the major – the "meejure" was the closest his throaty voice could come to the pronunciation – for the real purpose of talking to Finerty. They discussed the skirmishing with Miles, and when the correspondent mentioned the word retreat, Ol'Sit became upset.

"We did not run away in a panic. I commanded the rearguard until the women and children got over the Milk River, then Little Assiniboine took my place because someone had to make sure the women and children got to safety."

Bull, his dander aroused, dissipated his frustrations during the remaining daylight hours by breaking in young ponies in front of the police quarters. His riding ability was outstanding. Finerty, both his mind and his notebook full of impression of an eventful day, was ready to turn in.

The peace that had enveloped the serenity of the hills and the valley at twilight was transformed into uproar of shouting in the Hunkpapa camp. A woman, the daughter of old chief Black Moon, had walked in from the dead!

Grass Woman, middle aged and showing it, had been mourned as dead, presumably scalped by Miles's scouts when she fell behind in the dash to reach the safety of the Milk River. She had got mixed up in the fighting, cut off from any hope of help. She hid in the sagebrush, frightened to move until dark, while the Crows and Cheyennes, who were looking for trophies, passed nearby many times, their ponies within touching distance.

At night she stumbled northwards towards the Milk River, which she forded in darkness, an extreme act of preservation and perseverance, and from there walked the unmarked way across a hundred, roundabout miles of prairie. After twelve days of hardship and exposure, on a diet of very occasional water, she literally fell into her father's lodge.

Finerty slept well, too exhausted to be disturbed by the continuing wails of the mourners of Pretty Face or the shouts of the celebrants in Black Moon's circle, and too overwhelmed to be contemplating the horrible prospect of being murdered in his slumber by some of "the greatest cutthroats of the plains, demons whose names are written in the shame and blood of the helpless and the innocent, and who deserved to die a thousand deaths for their nameless crimes against decency and humanity."

The next day, the last one of July, 1879, was listlessly hot from the start. The only sound in early morning came from children playing down by the creek behind the police shacks. The older boys were taking their family's horses, frisky and kicking up their heels, to the grass on the hills. A few women were astir at the cooking pots and kettles, preparing whatever they had managed to scrounge. The entire encampment was acutely short of food. At first light Spotted Eagle's hunters had taken the trails to the south with the urgent hope a buffalo herd had conveniently strayed onto the right side of the stone heaps.

Well before the sun reached its full height in the clouless sky the women began to climb the hills for berries. Each day they had to walk farther to bring in a meagre supply to help feed all of the hungry. There was no fresh meat or pemmican. Not an ounce. How much longer could Walsh prevail upon them not to slaughter the horses?

The major, whose responsibility it was to control the famished Sioux while officially rejecting their pleas for the most scanty provisions, rode with Finerty to the top of the highest bluff so that he could fathom the full extent of the Indian assembly. Finerty estimated he could count more than 1,000 lodges, which would indicate a fighting force of about 2,500 with 15,000 ponies. He had already observed there was no shortage of arms and ammunition.

The correspondent was bowled over by this vast spectacle of barbarism. Stretched out before him was the essence of his investigations – the wild, unconquered redskins in an equally uncouth environment. Below were the most powerful war chiefs of the most powerful and dreaded Indian nation.

"It is strange that after centuries of relentless war so large a body, flushed with the memory of more than one gallant victory, should still exist," he recorded in his notebook. "With all my confidence in General Miles as a soldier, and my high opinion of the men of his command, I declare frankly, although I was willing to take whatever chances might have come, I am glad it did not become a part of his duty to charge this nest of human hornets with the 500 available men of his command."

Finerty asked Walsh for permission to stroll around the village, unescorted. The superintendent agreed.

192

The young men observed his hobnobbing with an obvious hostility. Once, when he stopped to watch some lads racing their ponies, a powerful specimen of an aboriginal protester stood before him and thudded the butt of a Winchester close to Finerty's foot. Finerty gave him a look of "Why in the hell did you do that?" The Indian stood his ground with a glare that could only mean, in the most benign interpretation, "Mind your own business and get out of here!"

Finerty recognized the Indian as one of the prisoners taken at Slim Buttes in September '76. (Sioux chief American Horse was mortally wounded by General "Three Star" Crook's column which had attacked his village north of the Black Hills near the Grand River. A few of the soldiers scalped the Indians. The killed included women, children and a tiny papoose. The fight was noted for the inhumanity of the troopers, who were suffering from hunger and exhaustion. Bull, too far away with 600 warriors to help American Horse, harassed Crook's troops and rescued the survivors. "We have been running up and down this country, but they follow us from one place to another," Bull complained in exasperation.)

At that time Finerty was bearded and thinner. He hoped this brute did not have a keen memory. He was lucky. Finerty walked off without a word. As he strolled from one circle to another he saw the women at work. How attractive were the young girls! They were usually well formed, chubby-cheeked, amorously shy without a trace of anxiety or servitude in their features. It appeared they deteriorated, outwardly anyway, when they left the protection of their fathers' lodges for married life. Marriage was an understood contract to love, honour, obey, and do all the work, all of the time. There were no ceremonies, no vows. The girl moved in after the suitor left gifts, usually horses, outside the lodge of her father.

The burden of their responsibilities, willingly accepted, transferred young brides from girlhood to middle-aged womanhood without any lingering transition. Their mode of life on the gaunt, severe prairie could prematurely arch their backs and round their shoulders. It could be almost natural, after years of war, to become coarse or vulgar and sometimes cruel. All these things some of them were. The frail could not survive for long. In a culture that enhanced self-torture, self-denial and yet provided awesome rituals for self-expression, the women could be as hard as the stones they used to pound the meat, yet in their family confines as sensitive as nature with which they shared the earth.

They had many traits in common with their men. They were hero-worshippers. They valued honesty and hospitality. They lavished affection on their children. By and large they had clean habits. They liked to dress colourfully, but their pride of appearance, their dignity, were being subjugated by the poverty that was overwhelming them all.

How many times was Finerty informed by the Sioux that they did not wish to continue the war? Nonetheless, they would rather die fighting, honourably, than by starvation.

The reporter was in Walsh's quarters when White Eagle of the Hunkpapa and Red Hand of the Santees dropped in for a sociable smoke. The major repeated the terms for the American military: surrender horses and armaments.

The mention of these conditions, which were widely known, riled them.

"We have always been horsemen and warriors. We do not want to be slaves or beggars. It is no use, anyway, making treaties with the Americans; they never keep any with the Indians."

It was during this conversation, which touched the open nerve of Sioux resentment and resistance, that an outbreak of wailing stopped them short.

The awful, emotional lamentation grew louder as more people joined in.

Into the room came a pitiful old man, completely distraught, the grief oozing out of him. Between gasps and sobs he recounted to Walsh, via Larrivée, that his son had been carried into camp, shot in the genitals by the Cheyennes. He had been hunting with Pretty Face, who was killed, and managed to escape with his two ponies as far as the Sioux sun dance grounds. There he collapsed and was found by his friends who brought him home.

As he was telling the story a small group of women came in with the news that the young warrior had died. The father broke down, grateful in his agony that his son had not surrendered his scalp to the Cheyennes.

"They didn't know there was an order not to cross the line," White Eagle told Walsh. "Even if he had lived he would have had to be dressed like a woman forever more."

194

While he was being soothed by Walsh, the old man shot some revengeful looks at Finerty. White Eagle later remarked: "You should leave here before too long. The people are upset over the death of Pretty Face and now his companion. They will swear vengeance on Americans."

Finerty decided he would leave at daybreak, the second of August. He spent the rest of the time gathering more impressions. There were war chiefs he had not seen whose reputations for infamy he had heard about time and time again in the tents of the old campaigners who bent the ears of the recruits with the stories of slaughter and heroics from the Yellowstone to the Platte.

Mr. Bull he had seen, and every time they passed each other Ol' Sit glared at him.

"That man is from the other side. I want nothing more to do with the Americans, any of them," Bull told everyone. "They have my country now, let them keep it."

Obviously Bull was in a bad mood; the latest killings had infuriated him. When the chief was in a light-hearted mood, which was quite often, he could laugh his head off. He enjoyed a joke. The hold he had on the people, including some of the notables of the other tribes with whom he was far from popular, bewildered Finerty. What was his mysterious power?

Wrote Finerty: "He was always potent for evil with the wild and restless spirits who believed that war against the whites was, or ought to be the chief object of their existence. He had a strong personal magnetism. His judgment was said to be superior to his courage, and his cunning superior to both. He had not, like Crazy Horse, the reputation for being recklessly brave, but neither was he reputed a dastard. Sitting Bull was simply prudent and would not throw away his life so long as he had any chance of doing injury to the Americans. He was verging on fifty, but hardly looked it. Once seen he can never be forgotten."

The correspondent had a remedy for the likes of Bull and his followers: "When next, if ever, the savages shout their battle cry, civilization must meet them with a stern front and crush them relentlessly."

Finerty's attention was directed to a young, iron-grey horse being led by a not-so-young brave wearing oddments of cavalry uniform. He had a strong, almost Oriental face, around the eyes especially. This was Crow King (meaning Patriarch Crow), one of Bull's leading lieutenants. Highly regarded in the Hunkpapa circles, he was suspicious, irreverent, ill-tempered and not entirely doctrinaire, not devotedly entrenched in all the traditions. He could be prone to the white man's influence. As a young man, when his name was Burns The Medicine Bundle, he had been outstandingly gallant in the wars, and in the hunts he bagged more buffalo than most men. This made him rich with horses, but unlucky in love. Crow King's first wife, his true love, ran off with another man because, she said, he had humiliated her in public.

A confederate of Crow King in the camp was Gall, a big man, both in size and political stature. Gall (Pizi in Lakota) had the appearance of a moody gypsy. Invariably his hair was dishevelled, unbraided, untidily parted. He was probably forty years old, physically powerful, broad-chested, a perennial dominating brooder and warrior. Orphaned in his earliest years, he had missed the normal attentive guidance accorded other children so that he developed in adversity on the inherent quality of his own fortitude. His wife and children were killed in the Custer battle.

The second most notorious celebrity in exile at Wood Mountain had the most benign of names: Rain In The Face. When an infant he had been left outside the lodge during a spring shower. "It's a sign," said his father. "Let him be called Rain In The Face."

The features of this warrior retained a striking aura of youthful comeliness. But behind the disarming smile, underneath the soft, dark skin of his face and the scarred tissue of his body, pulsated a heart that nurtured grudges with an unholy patience.

The inner fury of Rain In The Face was aggravated by a deteriorating wound to his leg. He could hardly drag himself around the lodges. When he was on horseback, which was most of the time, he took a crutch with him. What a fate for a proud man who had once hung by his flesh for six hours at a sun dance; what a privation for the warrior who had sworn revenge to the Custers and had fulfilled it in a legend of infamy.

Elizabeth Custer, widow of the general, wrote of Rain In The Face: "The vengeance of that incarnate fiend was concentrated on the man who effected his capture. It was found on the battlefield that he had cut out the brave heart of that gallant, loyal and lovable man, our brother Tom."

196

Captain Tom Custer, thirty-one, died near his brother, the general. He was found face down, his skull crushed, most of his scalp taken, and several arrows were in his back. The story around the army camps, propagated by writers of frontier sensationalism, was that Rain In The Face had cut out Tom Custer's heart and rode around showing it off, on the tip of his spear. An embellishment to the yarn was that the red savage, savouring his retribution, had eaten the heart, raw. (The police had recovered General Custer's pocket watch and sent it to Mrs. Custer.)

The night before Finerty's departure the hills and the valley reverberated with seemingly earth-level thunder as an impenetrable hailstorm castigated the land and swept on mightily across the unprotected plains. The lightning burst open in the pitch blackness with thick-and-thin criss-crossing streaks that looked like the veins in an old man's legs. The wind tore at the tepee skins, the cracking and shaking putting the fear of an angry Great Spirit in the hearts of the women. At daylight the last of the mass of clouds lifted, the gloom receded, and yellowish patches of clearing skies came up from behind the hills, the outlines rounded with a black definition.

After the uproar over the two men killed by Miles's scouts, Walsh detailed a five-man escort for the American newspaper reporter – four policemen and a halfbreed interpreter. In charge was Sergeant-Major Joe Francis, and as the Fenian sympathizer Finerty commented somewhat sardonically, he was leaving Sitting Bull for an American camp guarded by Queen Victoria's Redcoats: "I hope that none of my green, immortal friends in Chicago or elsewhere will imagine that all of a sudden I have become 'trooly loil' to the British crown."

He admitted his defenders were men whom he would not want to shoot at. They deserved better of their country than to be arresting Indian blackguards. The Sergeant-Major, the whiteness of his hair and moustache contrasted by the vividness of his uniform jacket, wore medals of Crimean and Turkish campaigns. He had been a hussar, one of a regiment that charged with the Six-Hundred into the Valley of Death.

Francis and a constable went as far as Medicine Butte where they turned around for Wood Mountain. They would report to Walsh that the American had left Sioux country without incident. Before parting, Finerty wrung the hand of the sergeant and watched the pair go up the trail, Francis riding in the manner of the hussars, rigid back, seat bumping the saddle, toe in stirrup. What better way to get a rupture!

"I hope the old Balaklava hero doesn't have his head smashed in by an Indian club," Finerty remarked to the others. "I know he doesn't like them."

The four riders – Finerty, Corporal Thomas Burns who was carrying despatches for Miles, Constable James Bliss, and the interpreter who was sweating and swearing in the heat of the high sun – stopped at one of the stone heaps for a meal. There were no signs of life. Smoke from a prairie fire, probably started by Indians to prevent buffalo from migrating into Canada, appeared to be coming from the place where Finerty had last seen Miles. Everywhere there were indications that soldiers had not been long gone. Hungry wolves, for instance. That night the party built up an enormous fire to keep them, and the mosquitoes, at bay. As if by command, the temperature cooled considerably. None could complain it wasn't a good night for sleeping under a full August moon.

Early the next morning the halfbreed, whose prized possession was an old pair of field glasses, detected a bunch of Indians moving towards them. They were a good two miles off.

"Lakota!" he speculated.

"If they're Sioux they'll respect our uniform," said Bliss. "If they're Crows or Cheyennes scouting for Miles, we'd better look out for trouble."

The Indians were closing at a fast pace, shooting their rifles above their heads with one hand and controlling their ponies with the other. The four men cocked their weapons. In the few seconds it took for faces to be recognized, Finerty indentified the Cheyenne Little Wolf. The Indians halted abruptly and Little Wolf leaned down from his pony to grasp the hand of Finerty. "*How!*" He was bony, almost gaunt, his sunken eyes glistening. The other three got some frowns and black looks.

As dashingly as they had arrived the Cheyennes took off for the north. One sweep of the arm by Little Wolf and they were gone.

"If you hadn't been along they would have scalped us for sure," said Burns with relief.

"Don't think so," Finerty replied. They're frightened of Miles's wrath and discipline."

Little Wolf had been persuaded by Miles to become a scout after the chief had fought his way out of exile in the arid and alien Indian Territory in the southland. The inducements of soldier food and paper money were too irresistible.

The two Redcoats, the halfbreed and Finerty found the army camped along the Milk River close to where it joins the White Mud. Miles had received orders to halt his campaign along the Canadian border. His most immediate problem was the disposition of the multitude of Canadian halfbreeds he was rounding up. The Métis, their volatile spirits unimpaired, had transformed their captivity into a massive social event. There were as many cat-gut violins as there were carts, and at night, after supper, when the sky was full of stars, the fiddlers stomped and the men, in their embroidered buckskins, and the women, bedecked in ribbons and trinkets to enliven their black dresses, danced the jig until exhaustion overcame them all.

In less than a week the U.S. Government had confirmed orders to release the halfbreeds. They had to agree never again to hunt where they did not belong. But hunt what? The days of the great buffalo musters were historical.

Sitting Bull, moving about the Canadian plains looking for game, was adamant about his domicile. "As long as there remains a gopher to eat, I will not go back."

There were plenty of gophers at Wood Mountain; catching and eating them was something else. Bull's gopher theme was hardly palatable to Walsh. He was being victimized for his leniency towards Bull (and, allegedly, his penchant for one of his daughters) when the exercise was to get the Sioux out of Canada because the United States had made it clear that the Canadian Government bore all the responsibility for their conduct.

When news of Bear Coat's withdrawal from the border seeped through, it was obvious to Walsh that it would be physically impossible to ensure the good behaviour of his charges. Hunger, with its offshoots of restlessness and rashness, were not subject to artificial international lines and political wrangling.

Small groups of young warriors began leaving Wood Mountain under the pretext of finding buffalo. Whichever way they started out they ultimately trailed south. They travelled lightly, each with a rifle and ammunition and a minimum of clothing (what they were wearing and a blanket). Wrapped around their bodies or over the shoulders were lariats. These youngsters were equipped more for horse theft than carting game. They returned to their camps with good news, as heroes. Many Crow horses were now Sioux horses. There were public exclamations of joy. For a few days, a very few days, the people almost forgot their hunger. There was always the one exception...Bull. He came knocking on Walsh's door with Four Horns and Black Moon, supported by the pick of their warriors. His timing was unfortunate.

Burdened by his problems with the Sioux locally, by the American Government complaining of incursions by these "British" Indians, Walsh was sick, understaffed, ill-housed and very short-tempered.

Bull and the chiefs entered his quarters. Walsh sent for an interpreter, Morin.

"Find out what they want," he barked.

Bull spoke, quietly.

"They want provisions, major, especially tea and tobacco."

This request ignited the short fuse to the gunpowder in Walsh. He jumped up, fists clenched, and exploded. The verbal shrapnel enfiladed the chiefs.

"Have you forgotten you are American Indians? You haven't any right to be in Canada. You've caused us police God knows how much trouble. You've stolen horses; you've been a goddamn, bloody nuisance."

Bull didn't flinch. He was expressionless. Walsh paced the floor, fuming, out of control.

"You seem to think all white men are afraid of you, you bastard. You're wrong. If you want to stay in Canada you'll have to behave yourselves. We've got plenty of our own Indians to look after without being bothered by you. Get your own bloody provisions at the trading posts, and if you keep on making trouble I'll put the whole damn lot of you in jail."

At this Bull butted in. The anger suddenly spilled out of him.

"Be careful," he warned Walsh, "you are speaking to the head of the Sioux nation."

"I know who you are," the major ranted, arms waving. "And another thing, if there's any more horse-stealing I'll put irons on you too, you sonofabitch."

O'l Sit shook with fury; his bloodshot eyes bulged.

"No man can treat me like this!"

Walsh shot back:

"Are you threatening me? Behave yourself or I'll throw you out!"

Bull had passed the limit of his endurance. No one talked to him this way. He went for the revolver he had in his belt. Walsh pounced on him in a furious flash, turned him around by grabbing his arm and breechclout, and hustled him through the doorway where Bull stumbled and fell. Walsh, his Irish blood boiling, couldn't resist the temptation; he booted Bull on the rear end.

Bull's gun was still in his belt. He reached for it again, but this time one of his own men caught him around the waist and wrestled him against the outside of Walsh's rooms. Bull's shoulder and elbow broke the window as he struggled until he had no more strength. He disengaged himself. Panting, sinking to the earth, his back against the building, he sat there, unkempt and perspiring in his dejected humiliation, despondent about all he had lost. When he got up he resolved to rally his adherents at the trading post. Walsh shouted orders to his men.

"Get ready, there may be trouble...Get two long poles from the hay corral and put them across the trail between us and the Indians."

The menacing Sioux, with old Bull front and centre, rode towards the police buildings. When they were well within shouting distance, Walsh turned to the interpreter.

"Tell them not to come past those poles. The first one who does will be sorry."

The Sioux came on to the poles – and there they stopped, looking down at the outnumbered Redcoats (not many more than thirty of them) whose fingers were on the triggers. It was a tense moment of silent decision. The Indians sat motionless on their ponies. In their grip were rifles, clubs, bows and spears. Only the wind, ruffling the manes of the horses, touching the feathers in the warriors' hair, had the nerve to whisper.

Walsh stepped forward.

"Good. You're wise. I don't want you hanging around here. You have five minutes to clear out."

The warriors responded with an incoherent mumbling and muttering. Bull raised an arm, motioning to the south. They wheeled their ponies and left Walsh and his men standing at the poles.

Bull, disgraced in public, returned to the White Mud River where the vast majority of the Sioux were gathered, where the incident with Walsh would be repeated a thousand times.

Technically the Sioux were still in Canada. When the weather changed, when they needed shelter from the wind, and wood for the fires, they moved a couple of miles onto the American side. There was no probability that Miles would attack them; the area was clear of Bluecoats. More than a hundred families of Canadian halfbreeds had the same thoughts. They felt secure enough to build a village of log huts.

Whatever buffalo might be left, the Sioux and the halfbreeds were strategically placed to get them.

Before the snow, Bull had a visitor, the Rt. Rev. Martin Marty, again. His objective was the same as before: to get the Sioux to return to the agencies. The outcome was the same: completely negative. On October 27, 1879, Walsh escorted the bishop to Wolf Point where he could get a boat back to Bismarck before navigation was closed for winter.

Walsh plodded back to his predicament. Above the earth, the crystal-clear skies were already giving way to the ominous accumulation of dark-specked rolls of greyish clouds, confirming predictions of the halfbreeds that winter was going to be early. On the land an equally forbidding prairie fire had decimated the grassland, destroying twenty-five tons of hay. The beef cattle, the policeman's on-the-hoof food supply, had to be moved out. The worries of the job, the advent of cold weather, the everlasting inadequacy of diet and accommodation, were wearing down the physical stamina of the superintendent. He was once more suffering from irritation of the skin.

Aggravation of another kind and dimension was about to come down upon him, a political storm that had been forming for more than three years, an avalanche of words that had Walsh up to his neck in trouble.

The Marquis of Lorne, the Governor General, whose wife, Princess Louise was a daughter of Queen Victoria, had proposed a simple solution to the Sitting Bull business: arrest him. A diligent disciple for the Canadian West, he too modified his views after a few months in office. He suggested to Evarts in a conversation in Toronto during September of '79, that much of the border trouble would be alleviated if both Washington and Ottawa would allow all Indians from both countries to follow their game across each other's boundary. Evarts countered that the Canadian Government should feed the Indians. Lorne replied Canada couldn't afford to.

Ottawa concurred with Lorne; Washington was silent; and Walsh would be soon on the carpet.

He was, unknowingly, contradicting the official line. Macdonald was preoccupied with his national expansion. He wanted the country nice and peaceful so it could be opened up for thousands of immigrants. This man Walsh was interfering with policies that were geared to a white-populated prairie empire.

In a letter to the Indian agent at Fort Buford, written in October, Walsh had stated: "I believe that all the halfbreeds on the Milk River are Canadian and are entitled to take up lands on our side of the line. Our government is anxious to have the people abandon the chase and commence agricultural pursuits, and I am of the opinion that this cannot be accomplished as long as they are allowed to hunt in the Milk River country."

The agent relayed Walsh's letter, the contents of which appeared to be contrary to Ottawa's official stand, to Evarts. In mid-November the U.S. Secretary of State complained to Thornton about the unabated incursion of British Indians and halfbreeds. The incidents were so frequent, Evarts harped, as to be exceedingly embarrassing. He questioned also the contents and status of the Walsh letter that echoed the U.S. viewpoint. Were there two policies?

Officialdom in Ottawa was bowled over. The strongest language was produced to put Walsh in his place. The superintendent's action was "calculated to obstruct the government policy in its relations with the United States regarding the right of Indians and halfbreeds of the plains to follow the buffalo for the purpose of obtaining food, whether in the United States or on Canadian territory."

Commissioner Macleod was informed that Walsh's action called for grave censure: "He should not have taken it upon himself to address an officer of the United States Government on a matter involving government policy without direct authority, and even then without such communication being conducted through the proper channels."

Walsh admitted he had overstepped the mark in his anxiety

to protect the interests of the country. He stated to Macleod his intentions had been misunderstood. He had wanted to advise the agent at Buford that Canada did not wish the halfbreeds to trespass on his reservation. It had been rumoured that Louis Riel was intending to move in with them and that could only mean trouble. Also, the halfbreeds were intercepting the remaining buffalo while Canadian Indians north of the line were starving. And what about Miles, who had ordered the halfbreeds out of the country because they were arming the Sioux?

The reality of winter provided a measure of relief for Walsh. He and his men were cut off by the snow and the temperature. By December it was averaging twenty-five below; occasionally the thermometer dropped to forty. On the inhospitable prairie the natives were in a ghastly state of starvation; at police headquarters the occupants were reasonably comfortable. The staple diet was bacon, pemmican and dried buffalo meat. This dried meat resembled sheets of parchment that had to be saturated with water before they could be boiled or fried. Tea was the most popular drink to warm the bones.

In the comparative warmth of his austere quarters, the major could look back upon the tribulations of fading 1879. His sympathy for the Sioux, which his superiors were regarding as an unforgivable handicap, was being expressed in his reports:

"Considering the agitated state in which these people have been kept by Crow and other Indians stealing their horses and killing their young men while following the chase, and General Miles's expedition driving them from the hunting grounds of the Milk River to the boundary line, their conduct has been extremely good; but this good conduct on the part of a great many is only reached by their fear of being sent back to the United States.... There are some very good people in this tribe, people whose constant cry is for peace and rest, and who will make any sacrifice to maintain it, yet there are others who cannot be trusted."

# ❖❖❖ The Treachery and a Change of Mind

❖❖❖ The deprivation and distress of the exiles in the first month of the new decade were terrible. They were locked in by the snow, isolated from any prospects of hunting fresh meat. They huddled in their lodges crammed in the protective ravines of the White Mud where it flows across the border. Some of the bands had infiltrated thirty miles farther south, along the Big Bend of the Milk River. They were in an equal state of frigid improverishment.

Disease was rampant among the people, and their horses. The women, desperate to save their families, were butchering ponies that had died of scurvy, hacking the flesh off rotting carcasses and putting it into the cooking pots. The children, emaciated, their stomachs bloating, were not strong enough to withstand the infections of winter. There were many deaths; the wails of parental mourning could be heard from the tepees of the chiefs.

The sheer hopelessness could no longer be talked away. Nothing that Bull uttered could submerge reality. He was losing his grip; he was beginning to be a chief without any real followers; his influence was at a low ebb.

This was the opportunity to divide and coerce. There were rations and clothing on the U.S. agencies and Walsh could show them the way! In Canada there would be nothing for them – no food, no clothes, no land, no shelter. Nothing.

Walsh knew that if he could persuade a few families to surrender others would follow. He had selected as his target the chief called The Minneconjou whose band consisted of about fifty lodges, and who had promised to give up arms and horses at the Yankton agency at Poplar Creek, at the Missouri. In the fourth week of January, 1880, The Minneconjou was ready to surrender. He sent a messenger to the major requesting his intercession.

When Walsh got to the camp (he had purposely not alerted

the U.S. authorities of his mission on their territory) he found the chief and his headmen reluctant to take that final step. The spectre of captivity on a reservation was confronting them head-on; they were on the brink of handing over everything. The Minneconjou wanted to call a council. Walsh refused.

"I have said everything to you that I can possibly say. My advice has not changed. Surrender yourselves, your arms and your horses at once."

Walsh stayed with them two hours, repeating his advice. And when he left in his sleigh, The Minneconjou rode with him for four miles. How many more times must the major make his point? The chief turned around despondently, unconvinced, to lead his people into a cordon of Bluecoats. Before long another sixty lodges were in the compound, a total of 110 removed from the destitution of Canada.

Other groups went farther afield to surrender. Twenty or so Brûlé families struck out for the Spotted Tail agency, nearly 500 miles southeast. The adjacent Red Cloud agency was augmented by Waterspout's ragged band. All told, another seventy-five lodges gone.

As deplorable as the living conditions were for the refugees, the principal chiefs could not convince themselves to surrender unconditionally. When the snow eased, when their surviving horses could get their footing, they struggled through the drifts to Wood Mountain.

First came Broad Trail and Little Knife, then Spotted Eagle, Pretty Bear, Long Dog, Stone Dog, Four Horns, Dull Knife, Red Horn and Hairy Chin, the last-named a medicine man who had received all his powers of healing from a dream he once had of a bear.

Hairy Chin was the busiest man among the Sioux. He donned his bear skin, head included, and stalked around on all fours singing the holy chants. Some of his patients were so reduced by starvation they couldn't move. An epidemic of mountain fever was accelerating the death rate and the police were insisting the Indians bury the dead instead of following the usual pagan rites of leaving bodies, wrapped in buffalo skins, to rot on shaky platforms that were put up on the hills, the highest hills reserved for men.

"The conduct of these starving people, their patient endurance, their sympathy and the extent to which they assisted each other, their strict observance of law and order, would reflect credit upon the most civilized community," Walsh would inform his superiors.

The break in the weather encouraged Bull to think of other matters, overwhelmed as he was by the hunger of his camp and his own dwindling prestige. He too journeyed to Wood Mountain in the obscure hope that the police would provide provisions. Also, from there he could encourage the frustrated braves to raid into the United States to regain some of the wealth they had lost in recent weeks – horses. Successful horse-stealing would help re-establish his authority.

In February, one batch of raiders, their presence being hardly anticipated in mid-winter, forded the Missouri and Yellowstone Rivers, raided some settlements, changed direction to the west and were on the way to the Tongue River, a tributary of the Yellowstone, before they were sighted, probably by the Crows. More than 200 miles from any hope of help they were trapped in a ravine by the army. Out of food, almost out of ammunition, and freezing, they gave in without a fight.

U.S. Secretary of State Evarts was again complaining to Canada that the Sioux were armed and ready for war. Canadian reaction was one big shrug. Lord Lorne was inclined to believe the roamers were after buffalo, which most of them were. "Mr. Evarts speaks as though they were bent on hostilities," he wrote Macdonald.

One headstrong band from Canada actually attacked the Fort Custer military reservation and disappeared with a pony herd belonging to the Crow scouts. The raiders got off to a good getaway, aided by the weather, a mixture of snow and rain that helped to obliterate their tracks. They wanted to get to the Powder River, which would lead them to a place where the Yellowstone could be forded. From there they could go almost straight north to Wood Mountain, a total distance of close to 400 miles. Their route passed south of Fort Keogh where Bear Coat Miles was stationed with a considerable force of Bluecoats and Cheyenne scouts, the latter capable of tracking the Sioux by intuition, which they did. When the Sioux and the soldiers collided in combat the raiders were manoeuvred away from the fifty horses they were stampeding to Canada. They fought off the cavalry until dark and vanished, all except five who were captured.

Miles put all his prisoners together at Fort Keogh and sent messengers to Bull's camp that the warriors would be detained until their relatives left Canada to surrender. In due course eight emissaries, displaying the white man's white flag, came down from the Dominion to see what was going on. They were received with consideration and courtesy. Miles had planned an unmiltary campaign to convince all the uncommitted to lay down their arms. A booming settlement had sprouted up around the fort. The general made sure Sitting Bull's investigators saw for themselves some of the innovations of a modern society; telegraph and telephone for example. "The superior advantages that the white man had over the Indian were explained to them."

Everyone had a turn at the telephone. All appeared to tremble during their brief encouter with the Whispering Spirit, their name for the talking machine. Impressed and subdued, the young men returned to Canada with accounts of the white man's latest "medicine" – and with Bear Coat's counsel to forget the past and come back home ready to discard weapons for the tools of agriculture. Miles was by now convinced it would cost less to feed the Indians than fight them.

On the first day of April, 1880, Bull officiated at a council of the chiefs. He affirmed his heart was weak at the sight of despair all around him. He conceded defeat – for others, not for himself.

"I cannot return," he advised them with an air of defiant martyrdom. "If anyone wants to go to an agency I suggest they go at once."

Walsh allayed their fears that the soldiers would be coming north again in the spring to try to force them to the disease-ridden Indian Territory in Oklahoma from where the Northern Cheyenne had escaped. Secretly he was hoping that those who had already trekked back to the agencies would report favourably of their treatment. Nothing that he could say – and he said it all – could influence them more than the reactions of their former neighbours. Truthfully, he reasoned to himself, what was the alternative?

Hunger and illness pervaded the entire encampment as winter maintained a cruel grip. The policemen were doing everything they could to keep the children alive.

"I am pleased to inform you, as no doubt it will give you pleasure to know, that the greatest good feeling and consideration was extended to those poor sufferers by the men at Wood Mountain," Walsh jotted down in his report. "The little that was daily left from their table was carefully preserved and meted out as far as it would go, to the women and children. During these five or six weeks of distress, I do not think that one ounce of food has been wasted. Every man appeared to be interested in saving what little he could, and day after day they divided their rations with those starving people."

Some halfbreeds were helping out too. Apart from humane desires they knew full well, in their isolation, that the Sioux could overcome them at will or whim. One trader, named Cadd, an American accused of dishonest dealing, was attacked by a knife-wielding son of Chief Black Moon. The police come running to save the situation.

The one person whose senses were apparently not touched by the misery that surrounded him, and who had the most to give, was the trader Allen whose wife, forunately for both of them, was admired by the lusty ones. Allen was despised for his repeated short-changing.

One night after the store was shut, a group of starving Indians hammered on his door demanding entry. Allen, his wife and child, and three employees – one of his hired hands was an ex-policeman (temporarily), young Daniel "Peach Pie" Davis who had quit the force to make a fortune as a trader – crouched behind a barricade in the store, armed for the onslaught. It never came, not that night anyhow, but when Allen unlocked his doors in the morning the hungry stormed in.

They considered Allen unworthy of any formal preliminaries. One of the angriest barged past the alarmed trader and thumped open the door to the living room where he grabbed the child from the arms of Mrs. Allen. She came running after him pleading for her baby. Allen, meanwhile, had managed to get a rifle off the rack. With a finger on the trigger he was pointing it at a powder keg. Davis moved near the abductor. He was prepared to shoot him with a revolver.

The Indians were milling around, shouting, calling Allen a liar, a crook, but not prepared to turn their hostility into concerted action. Davis ran for help to Walsh's quarters where the superintendent was wrapped up in bed with a fever.

Walsh immediately ordered a sergeant, Henry Hamilton, and

three constables to rescue the Allens and their employees. The interpreter, "Cajou" Morin, had instructions to warn the Sioux that unless all the whites were unmolested, unless Mrs. Allen and the baby were brought to Walsh, and unless all the Indians were out of the store in fifteen minutes, the major would come over himself to blow them up into the next world.

The policemen swept into the crowded store. Constable Ed "Buffalo" Allen, the biggest and the burliest, an Englishman who once had reclaimed a stolen horse from under Sitting Bull, saw the Indian holding the baby. "Buff" brushed aside the others, got hold of this buck's shoulders with both hands, put a knee into the small of his back and applied pull-and-push until he released the child. The constables, willing to have a real go but restrained by the sergeant, escorted the whites to Walsh who was sitting, covered in blankets, on a box outside his rooms.

The presence of Mrs. Allen toned down the furious invective directed at the bewildered trader. The message was clear; get out and stay out. The Allens packed their belongings, hitched a team, and set off on the trail to Fort Walsh with the major's assurance that he would control the Indians until they were out of the area. The Kendall & Smith Co. store, which had failed to make deliveries to the police when the need was the greatest, which had taken advantage of its native customers, was without a manager. Trader Allen would not be missed; his wife would be. The child died in a few weeks of typhoid fever.

Towards the end of April, as Walsh pleaded compassionately with the chiefs to take their followers to the agencies where they could draw rations, there began a trickle of defectors. A prominent Oglala, The One Who Kills The White Man, was the first independent to break away. He took three lodges to Fort Keogh with the intention of surrendering to Miles. He had a letter from Walsh that he could show to military or government officials if he were stopped en route. It explained the purpose of the Oglala's journey and requested protection and assitance for the family group.

About this time a small group of surveyors from Winnipeg were moving down a long coulee towards the Souris River on their way to investigate coal finds near the U.S. border. In charge was Charles Aeneas Shaw, in his early thirties, from Oak Hill, Toronto. On rounding a bend in the Souris valley they stopped at

210

the sight of about fifty tepees. In an instant they were prisoners of Sitting Bull's own Hunkpapa. Shaw began waving his arms to the north attempting to tell Bull they were not Americans.

"Shaganash, Shaganash," he repeated frantically, trying out his Cree.

The Sioux understood, but they were not convinced they were hearing the truth. They imprisoned the surveyors in a lodge and sent a couple of scouts to trace their trail north or south.

The word was going the rounds that one of the captives had bright red hair. This was Tom Willing, who was too much of an attraction for the women to miss. The more daring of his admirers went behind him, tugged at his flaming mop, and fled with gleeful shrieks.

The surveyors were confined until the scouts returned, after several hours, with confirmation the prisoners must be Canadian. Bull made amends with handshakes and smoking. They all sat around the chief's fire and drew puffs from his pipe. Now they were friends, he proclaimed, eligible for his hospitality.

A circle of warriors, and their white guests squatted within arm's length of a cooking pot that was bubbling, full to the top, with a greasy, all-ingredients stew. Each had a fork stick that he plunged into the pot. For the surveyors it was an unlucky dip. Shaw came up with a muskrat's head, the whiskers and eyes intact. Fortunately it slipped back. With his second try he lanced a duck's foot.

"I can't eat this garbage," Willing whispered to his boss.

"We've got to eat it. If we insult them it will cost us our lives."

Afterwards the whites walked around the camp, amazed by the quantity of equipment taken from Custer's troops. Most of the men were wearing some item of military clothing. Those who had Longknives' trousers were baring their backsides; they had cut holes in the seats for sanitary convenience. U.S. Army branded horses were grazing all around, one of which was claimed to have been ridden by Custer. Soldier scalps were dangling from the entrances to the lodges, and if for no other reason, the surveyors were delighted to say their goodbyes the following morning.

Early in May chief Hairy Chin and twelve lodges were leaving Wood Mountain for the Missouri. He was prepared to ackowledge complete submission to the Americans. Walsh kept plugging away at the others, emphasizing they could not hope for any assistance from the Canadian Government, urging them not to delay in case the U.S. Government stiffened the terms, such as imprisonment in the death-watch Indian Territory.

The major was chafing under growing criticism of his seeming inability to get the Sioux out of Ottawa's hair. He was embittered by the apparent lack of understanding by the higher-ups of his day-to-day problems, by their failure to appreciate his untiring efforts. He contended the wrangling between the U.S. military and the ambitious, corruptible Indian agents was responsible for the continuing alienation of the Sioux. God knows, he consoled himself, he had done everything possible to unload them. If it hadn't been for U.S. policies, or the lack of them, he could have had the Sioux, including Sitting Bull, out of Canada in '79. Ludicrously he had received one letter from an agent down there stipulating no more Indians from Canada could be accepted.

Probably his most vitriolic, in-house detractor was Irvine – not noted as a disciplinarian – who heaped contempt upon Walsh with a vicious pen. He recorded, confidentially of course, that Walsh was not fit to hold a commission being incompetent, untrustworthy and incapable of respect by superiors and subordinates.

The earnestness of Walsh's pleading, the evident truth of his statements of the white mother's deaf ears to the cries of hunger, and reports on the moccasin telegraph of refugees being fed at the agencies, turned a southerly trickle of refugees into a flood. The agencies were unable to handle them all. In rags, gaunt from weariness and hunger, they were shunted on until they could surrender to the army, usually at Fort Keogh.

When Sitting Bull, Spotted Eagle and seven headmen called on Walsh in mid-May, about 1,200 of their once powerful following had deserted them. Bull, fearing for his own life, had not the slightest intention of giving up. The Americans were still insisting on treating the Sioux as prisoners of war and confiscating their most important possessions.

"I want you to know the feeling in our hearts," he pleaded forlornly to Walsh who had by now forgiven him for trying to pull a gun at a previous, stormy encounter. "We have been in the land of the British for three winters, and we have obeyed the laws of the white mother, and the white mother's chiefs have not deceived us. There are now only 150 lodges north of the line. A year ago there were many hundreds. The chiefs who remain desire to stay

212

and have requested that I ask the white mother to give them a home.

"You can tell the white mother and the great father in Washington that Sitting Bull and Spotted Eagle and their followers are prepared to shake hands with the Americans and make a lasting peace.

"These are words never spoken and sentiments never felt by me before. This morning I show you my heart. You can make known my feelings."

The chief, publicly casting aside his animosities to rekindle the fire of hope of becoming a Canadian, indicated he would like to go to Ottawa to meet the white mother's daughter (Princess Louise Caroline Alberta) and to Washington to reassure the great father of his changed heart. Walsh replied he would forward the request to the white mother's great chiefs – and he did, in a report to Ottawa on May 19.

The once powerful and prestigious chieftain, limping and downcast, his influence extending only to his relatives, his close friends and the diehards, withdrew to his tepee with thoughts that perhaps his admission of changed attitudes, and the sparseness of his kingdom, would sensitize sympathetic tendencies in the councils of the Canadian chiefs. He had this haunting suspicion, and fear, that the Americans, if they ever got hold of him, would have him hanged for what had happened to Custer. This too he had heard on the moccasin telegraph.

The Canadian chief of chiefs, Macdonald, as yet unaware of the real situation in Indian country, was bumping softly in the wake of Evarts' persistently censorious onrush against Canada. The Prime Minister, chafing slightly, gave the Americans a going over in a letter to Lord Lorne:

"It ought to have occurred to him [Evarts] that the same uncontrollable circumstances that prevented the U.S. from stopping the Indian invasion of Canada might perhaps prevent Canada from being able to stop the Indians from invading the United States. The American Indians cannot be considered a nation at war with the U.S. They are rather disorderly bands of American subjects which we have a right to expect the American Government would prevent from crossing into Canada and trespassing on our territory."

Macdonald agreed with Lorne it was almost impossible for

either government to control the movements of these wanderers.

"We ought as well try to check the flight of locusts from the south or the rush of buffalo from the north. It seems to me clear that all this simulated indignation of Mr. Evarts is for a purpose. I have seen many Presidential elections in the United States and at every one of them the rival parties tried to excel each other in their patriotism, and that patriotism always consists of attempts to bully England...."

Sitting Bull's immediate problems were far less abstract. His decisions were being questioned; he was getting the treatment from his diminishing subordinates. The challenge came to a head in a stormy council over the arrest by Walsh of one of his warriors. The young man had been giving trader Légaré an undue tirade of insolence. Légaré, who had been appointed magistrate at the village of Wood Mountain, was regarded as an unselfish sympathizer with all the Indians, so that when he complained Walsh recognized this would be Légaré's last resort. The offender was jailed. Bull announced he was going to rescue his compatriot. Internal politics demanded he put up a brave front. He would knock down his detractors with a display of majestic determination.

When the chief, whose last inclination would be to impede his chances of becoming a legitimate citizen of Canada, came up against the major and twenty armed policemen he decided not to press his disadvantage. That night there was speculation he would go on the warpath. The morning came. Not a sign of warlike Sioux. The police kept up the barricades for several days until Bull, humble and subdued, called upon Walsh to ask his forgiveness, which was granted. The major, normally prickly, ill-tempered, tough when harassed, which he was, patted his now docile adversary on the back.

Walsh also became embroiled in a dispute between a Teton and a halfbreed over the ownership of a horse. He came perilously close to losing his life when he went to repossess the animal for the Métis. As he approached he could see several rifle barrels aimed at him through the bushes. It was too late to turn around. He shuddered inside, squared his shoulders, walked on and untied the horse. No one dared to fire the first shot.

Early in July of 1880 four disillusioned Oglala chiefs, men who would not follow old Bull like pack mares, instructed their wives to saddle their horses. They had decided to ask Walsh to determine how the Americans would receive them.

214

Broad Trail, Dull Knife, Stone Dog, and Little Hawk confessed their nostalgic desire to see once again their hunting grounds. They would take their villages out of Canada if the Americans would allow them to settle on Poplar Creek on the Upper Missouri or, better still, on the Tongue River, where Bear Coat was feeding the Indians and promising them land where they could watch the crops grow. They stressed, however, they would never allow themselves to be placed under the jurisdiction of either Spotted Tail or Red Cloud, those two agency loafers who had forsaken the Black Hills.

"I cannot think this would be much of a concession for the U.S. Government to make these poor naked savages and thus end a very disturbed and vexed question along the frontier," Walsh wrote to Macleod.

Broad Trail and his cohorts, who were to get their wish, for the time being, had another reason for turning their backs on Wood Mountain: the messengers had reported in the councils that the "meejure," the White Sioux, the Longlance, was being moved by his chiefs. Like the wind in the trees, the moon between the clouds, the rain on the tepee, he had been taken for granted.

"Now we will have no one here!" The chiefs agreed Walsh's departure would be a bad omen.

It became official. The hierarchy had concluded personnel should be rotated at least once every two years. Walsh was notified of his transfer to Qu'Appelle in the so-called Eastern Division, gateway to the Prime Minister's promised land. His replacement would be Superintendent L.N.F. "Paddy" Crozier from Fort Walsh.

When the news reached Bull he became crestfallen and alarmed. He hurried to the barracks to get the facts. On July 6, nine days before the major departed, he pleaded with Walsh for a home in Canada. "Help me!" he asked.

"It will be wasted labour on my part to try to do any such thing, and a waste of time on your part to await results," Walsh advised. "You should give up all ideas of remaining in Canada."

Bull thought for a moment. "If the white mother is determined to drive me out of her country and force me into the hands of people I know are awaiting like hungry wolves to take my life, will you see the white father in Washington and find out what conditions he would set for me, and whether these conditions would be faithfully and fully carried out?"

Walsh, who had also been granted a leave of absence because of his failing health (the divisional doctor was administering Donovan's Solution of Arsenic to treat his skin disease), replied that with the permission of the Canadian Government he would do what Bull requested, when he reached his home in Brockville.

Not completely bereft of hope, Ol' Sit exchanged farewells with his confidant. It was a sad moment in his hard, restless life. He had discerned in the "meejure" the qualities he steadfastly revered and believed he himself possessed: bravery, stubbornness, loyalty and honesty.

Could he really feel this way about a white man? The chief had brought his war bonnet with him to present to Walsh as a lifelong memento.

"Take it my friend, and keep it. Every feather marks some deed done in war when the Sioux were strong."

On July 8, 1880, Crozier left Fort Walsh for Wood Mountain. Riding alongside was Commissioner Macleod. Upcoming was the irreconcilable Sitting Bull; behind was the fort that Walsh had built, hastily, a hub for thousands of Indians, most of them now without food, their horses so wretchedly reduced they were hardly able to stand up.

"Paddy" Crozier, popular with his superiors, was a determined perfectionist inclined to be impulsively energetic although occassionally subject to deep melancholia. He was born in Newry, Northern Ireland, in 1846, but grew up in the Belleville area of Ontario. He attended Kingston Military School preparatory to a commission in the Argyll Light Infantry and had reached the rank of major before signing on for the NWMP in 1874.

How would he attempt to deal with Bull?

Openly and vehemently critical of Walsh's attitude and approach, the author of castigating, "confidential" anti-Walsh notes to Irvine, Crozier determined to get the better of the vacillating villain from the start. He had the strategy planned: divide and conquer; treat Bull with an obvious lack of deference; isolate him from those he influenced; work on the starving people and concentrate on the plight of their children.

The first to feel the weight of his authority were the Métis. Crozier, who in 1874 had been accorded the distinction of being the first policeman to arrest a whisky trader west of the Red River,

216

hauled in two men, Blondin and Marchand, for trading liquor. He fined them $250 and ordered the whisky – thirty gallons of it – spilled into Wood Mountain soil.

The next to receive his undivided attention was Spotted Eagle. The Sans-Arc notable, probably the most rational and realistic of the chiefs, requested an interview. Crozier got straight to the point: he had received a message from the "Queen's Council House" saying Canada could not grant the Sioux a home, therefore his band should dismantle their lodges and rejoin their comrades already in the United States.

"Now that there is to be no more blood spilt on the American side, I will shake hands with the Americans and live in my own country," Spotted Eagle declared philosophically. He was true to his word. He led sixty-five lodges to Fort Keogh and succumbed to the new world.

Crozier went to the other headmen, bypassing Bull who soon recognized the remaining vestige of his power was being undermined. He was not about to become a nobody. When some of the families ganged together to pack for the journey to the south, Bull and his faithful soldiers forcibly prevented their departure. As a precaution against further persuasions of defection, he took his camp out of Crozier's neighbourly influence to the Burnt Timber hunting range inside the States where an odd buffalo had been sighted.

Farther south, at the agencies, the formidable Rain In The Face had taken over Bull's role. He had a thousand surrendered hostiles virtually under his command at Fort Peck where food was being denied them by the factor. The volunteer captives were on the verge of an uprising.

Crozier, worried by what he had heard of Rain In The Face, by the portents of an early winter (in September the temperature plummeted to zero and snow had already blanketed the plains), dispatched Sergeant Hamilton to check up on Bull. No news was not necessarily good news. In a state of unremitting hopelessnes and reflection, Bull told Hamilton he would soon be returning to his choice natural shelter in Canada, near the Pinto Horse Buttes.

He confided to Hamilton he often thought of Walsh.

"Send him a message that although we are widely separated, my heart is with him. Sometimes I speak to him in my dreams for

I am sorry for many things I have done wrongly. As it always turned out, the 'meejure' was right."

Two thousand miles to the east, Walsh had not forgotten his former "sparring partner." He sat at a desk in the benevolent comfort of his home to fulfill a promise. He overcame his distaste for any kind of paper work and drafted a letter, dated October 7, 1880, to the Hon. Sirs in the cabinet:

"Previous to my departure from Wood Mountain, Sitting Bull requested me to interest myself in his behalf to secure a home for him.

"His first wish is that the Canadian Government would accept him as a subject, and permit him to follow the life of a hunter as long as there are buffalo and other wild game. He asks to enjoy all the privileges extended to Canadian Indians by the U.S. Government, to cross the line for hunting purposes. In the event of the Canadian Government refusing to accept him, having no confidence in anything said to him by agents on the frontiers, his experience being that they are not truthful, he requested me to see the President of the U.S. and ascertain the best terms or conditions under which he would be received by the U.S. Government.

"I think that Bull fears that if he were to return to the U.S. he would receive harsh treatment, but I believe that if he were assured by the President or the Secretary of the Interior that he would not, and if a few concessions were granted him, I could induce him to surrender.

"Bull claims that he should not be blamed for the blood that has been shed within the last few years on the American frontiers, for whatever he did was in defence of the women and children of his tribe."

Walsh went on to explain Bull's religious belief that the Great Spirit provided for both the white man and the red man, but the white man had become so powerful that he defied God and was trying to undo all that He had done. He mentioned Bull's hatred of the acquiescent chiefs Spotted Tail and Red Cloud, one of his predominant fears being that the U.S. authorities would return him to an agency presided over by one of his enemies. This would be too humiliating for him to bear.

"I consider it impolitic to give Bull a reservation in our country. In my opinion he is the shrewdest and most intelligent Indian living. He has the ambition of Napoleon and is brave to a fault.

He is respected as well as feared by every Indian on the plains. In war he has no equals, in council he is superior to all, and every word said by him carries weight and is quoted and passed from camp to camp.

"Up to the present time Bull has had a great many people about him. His pride is being a leader of men. The question is, would he be content in our country without followers, and having been an agitator, would or could he cease to be one if permitted to remain in Canada? Again, as soon as it would be known that he had secured a home in Canada he would be joined by a great number of disaffected Indians at present at U.S. agencies. At least a constant communication would be kept up with him by the Indians south of the line whereby parties would be constantly on the trail, moving to and fro, and would, I fear, prove injurious to our settlers and Indians."

Walsh suggested that Bull's ambition was too excessive to allow him to settle down, to be content with what he would consider an uninteresting life, although at times he had shown a disposition to do so.

"If he were put at the head of an agency, with a large number of people to look after, the government would find him very tractable and useful.

"Bull is a wise man and if properly handled and once induced to accept civilization would and could do more towards the civilizing of the Indian of the plains than any other man living."

Walsh stressed that it was of the greatest importance to both countries that Bull be settled in one or the other.

"While he is wandering about the plains the tranquility of the frontier cannot be considered certain. His unsettled camp keeps up a constant friction amongst the Indians on both sides of the line. The dissatisfied Indians at the American agencies, knowing that they will be welcomed at his camp, and the young warriors attracted by the love of the free life that exists around Bull, cannot become reconciled to living quietly at the agencies.

"While Bull is on the plains the desire will be to join him and his band if only for a short time, because it is known the true and real life of the red man will be found in his camp, where they can, with all the wildness of their nature, take part in the war and scalp dances, where the legends of their fathers will be recounted to them, where war parties can go and return at will, and where the

219

warrior who does not fear the warpath is courted and praised."

In the impatient scrawl of his writing, Walsh pointed out that the tribes of Indians who fought against the U.S. Government either joined Bull in Canada (the Nez Percés) or tried to (the Cheyennes).

"I believe, and Bull's Indian friends believe, that if the U.S. Government would give Bull a reservation at the head of the Tongue River he would accept it. It is a small concession for the U.S. to make in order to end this vexed question, and the people would find that by settling this man on a reservation the Indian problem on the frontier can be more easily solved, and with more satisfaction, than in any other way.

"From Fort Rice on the lower Missouri to Fort Peck on the upper, thousands of Indians are wishing Bull's return and acceptance of an agency, not only because they sympathize with him in his sad position, but because they wish to secure the contentment of their own families, and believe that his wise counsel and truthfulness to them would ensure better treatment from the government – and further, that Bull is the man above all others who is prepared to suffer for them."

Walsh had figured the return of Bull to the U.S. would justify a reduction in NWMP strength of sixty policemen in the southern part of the territories. The money saved, if applied to cultivating the soil, would put Canadian Indians out of the reach of want forever. The method? Open up the land for farmers to feed the natives, and at the same time instruct them in agricultural practices until they could take charge themselves.

"Indians can never be civilized by force of arms.....My experience is that an Indian who gets a sufficient quantity of any kind of food, either meat or vegetable, to sustain himself and family is content and will obey and respect the source from which he derives it. Money expended in cultivating the soil is saved to the public while that expended on soldiers or police is gone forever."

Walsh presented more of his thoughts for top-level scrutiny. He was not averse to claim at least some of the credit for the taming of the universally notorious savage – and indirectly to reply to his critics.

"Neither hunger nor prospective starvation in his camp at any time tended to change this man, as many persons imagine. It was done by patient hard work, days and nights of steady persuasion, argument and illustration to establish in the minds of the Indians a confidence in the people of the United States, and a sense of security in dealing with them.

"I taught them that it was their duty to discipline their hearts to a better feeling towards the people to whom they were naturally allied, and to whom they must return at no distant day, and the necessity of a more friendly and better consideration by them of the conditions of surrender offered by the U.S. Government."

This pronouncement enabled him to broach, in his own defence, accusations that had made the rounds in the Canadian and American press, and had been picked up and spread avidly by his antagonists in the force, that he was inducing Bull to get into show business. (Assuredly Ol' Sit, decked out in feathers and frills and a scowl to match, would be a sure-fire profitable attraction in Toronto and Montreal.) Walsh's enemies could believe he would recruit Bull for public display. They looked down on Walsh as a flamboyant show-off himself, an Indian king, a crude frontier individual, an oddity lax in official duties.

"Idle and absurd as such reports may seem, I feel it my duty to emphatically contradict them, and to say, though I have been asked to assist in securing the engagement of Sitting Bull, I have always declined to do so.

"Another report, as I am informed, has also gained currency, that Bull would have surrendered during the last summer had it not been for the encouragement which I held out to him of possibly being able to return to his camp with better terms of surrender than the United States had accorded to other Indians. As to this, I beg to say that this report is likewise false for I have never given Sitting Bull any such encouragement....After most urgent requests made by Bull, I told him if the Canadian Government would permit me, I would see the President or Secretary of the Interior for him."

Walsh took Bull's plea directly to Sir John A., outlining the reasons why Bull constantly hesitated to commit his uncertain future to the U.S. Government. He asked permission to visit Washington to obtain from President Hayes his attitude to the placement and rehabilitation of Public Enemy Number One.

Macdonald did not trust Walsh, neither did he like his ideas. He contended that so many of Bull's disciples had seen the light it could not be too long before he too would follow them to a reservation. A mission to Washington would therefore be unnecessary. To make sure of this he penned instructions to Walsh's superiors emphasizing the major had no authority to visit Washington, to return to Fort Walsh, or go anywhere near Sitting Bull. Crozier, it could be assumed, was the official winner.

Meanwhile, the durable renegade and his faithful had crossed the Medicine Line, and were back at Wood Mountain.

The Medicine Line, the Indian definition of the boundary, was a source of consternation to the officious Crozier who regarded it as a flagrant example, as constituted, of omissions and looseness in international law that allowed the unruly ones to flit across, do their unlawful thing, return and escape punishment or extradition.

The chief admitted to Crozier, unconvincingly, that his ultimate desire was to join his friends at the agencies, although certainly not immediately. Despite Crozier's persistent, forcible declarations that Walsh would not again be posted to Wood Mountain, the broad visage of Bull revealed he could not accept such finality. He refused to give up hope. Somehow, somewhere the "meejure" was mediating for him.

One dreaded renegade who was rapidly losing all hope was Low Dog. A more menacing, resilient and dedicated antagonist never walked the plains. When he revealed he was debating with his headmen the prospects and outcome of deserting the outcasts, Crozier could foresee the final blow to Bull's power structure. He concentrated the force of his persuasiveness upon Low Dog. On December 3 they had a long chat.

"It is foolish for you and your people to remain here and starve," Crozier impressed upon him. "If any wish to stay behind let them, but why should one man, or a few men, keep back all the others?"

Low Dog replied: "There are people in the camp who want to go. I want to go and I will go. Send your interpreter with me so that he can be a witness that I am telling the truth when I repeat what you have told me. I will take away so many lodges that the rest will be bound to follow."

Crozier concurred. There would be such dissension in the tribe, and so many people would follow the lead of Low Dog that the few remaining, including Bull, would be compelled to go after them. Eight days later Low Dog broke camp in all haste. He left behind a disconsolate chieftain, shorn of every element that had contributed to his pre-eminence, every element except the most important one – indestructibility. Bull, surrounded now by his relatives and the most trustworthy of a dwindling coterie of colleagues, could not relinquish his freedom.

"A warrior I have been. Now it is all over, a hard time I have."

He was still uncaged; he was still a worry for the Government of Canada. Every device to get rid of him having failed, the time had come to re-apply the pressure from the top – at the commissioner level. And there was a new commissioner of the North-West Mounted Police to carry out Macdonald's orders.

On the first day of November, 1880, Lieutenant-Colonel Acheson Gosford Irvine, five years in the force, a prize-winning cavalry swordsman who had opted for a career in the military at the expense of the professions, was promoted from assistant to a full commissioner replacing Macleod, the second commissioner whose combined duties as chief of police and magistrate for the Bow River judicial district were deemed by the Government to be much too onerous for one man.

That was the front-office version. Behind the scenes, Macdonald the money manager, disturbed as ever over police expenditures and alleged economic lassitude at the top, had dusted off the exit sign.

Eighteen days in his new position, Irvine tackled his foremost and most immediate problem: the ouster of Sitting Bull. Five days after leaving Fort Walsh he was confronting the enigma with his own brand of positive thinking, repeating, with as much verbal force as he could summon, the determination of the Canadian Government not to regard him as a Canadian Indian.

Bull listened, and listened, his burning eyes fixed on the single-minded, precise Irvine, an officer devoted to his career. Irvine's instincts indicated to him that Bull and his current second in command, Gall, could see the end of the trail in Canada. They talked and smoked several times before the patient commissioner felt he had achieved his purpose.

"I trust that at no very distant date Sitting Bull and his followers will have quietly surrendered to the U.S. authorities, thus relieving us from what in the past has been a source of great and perpetual anxiety," Irvine recorded for the Prime Minister. Macdonald was happy. Coincidentally, in London, announcements were being prepared of government-assisted immigration to Canada. The prairie was beckoning.

Irvine turned around for Fort Walsh with his companions, satisfied Canada was close to unloading an agitator. They rode along the irregular cart ruts of the established police trail, here and there passing the grisly symbols of an era nearly over, bleached buffalo bones, arched ribs as white as chalk, and fur-tufted skulls with horns and two dark eye sockets as empty and as ominous as the barren terrain.

In a matter of hours all traces of continuity were obliterated by snow so deep in the shelter of the coulees that horses and conveyances had to be dug out. For six days the policemen plodded the nearly 200 miles to the fort. The temperature averaged thirty below. There was no wood to light fires; the suffering from exposure was critical; everyone was frost-bitten. At a point only seventeen miles from home the entire party became stranded. The mounts were immobile. Each officer and man took the harness off his horse, then dug, pushed, pulled and cajoled the animals out of the snow and rode the rest of the way bareback. Fort Walsh was paralyzed by wind-blasted cold and snow; even the mercury in the thermometer had frozen.

The incessant slogging against the elements had convinced the new commissioner he would have to wage war in Ottawa for a higher calibre of recruits. Too many of his replacements had no previous riding experience, a perplexing shortcoming, and in the coming weeks he could be losing seventy-eight veterans whose terms of enlistment were due to expire.

Irvine considered the best class of Mounted Policemen came from the rural areas, strong men who were used to manual labour, men who could ride and care for horses: "Young Canadian farmers are the material for the best soldiers in the world. They can turn their hands to anything....Men addicted to drink are of the most objectionable class."

Irvine's optimism of Bull's pending, permanent departure was flourishing at a time when the chief was being enticed by a Pied Piper from Fort Buford, a scout named Edwin Allison. (To the Indians he was known as "Fish" because he was a slippery character – allegedly a liar and a thief.)

Allison, a cow-punching glory-seeker, had rolled into Bull's encampment in mid-fall with an enticing cartload of hard bread,

224

sugar, bacon, coffee and tobacco. Bull invited Allison and his companion (a soldier-teamster, Private Day, who was dressed as a civilian) to stay in his lodge, which was already crowded. The two white men, crouching to negotiate the entry slip, almost stumbled into the household's pile of cooking-pots and firewood. Around the tepee was Bull's family.

From the left, and closest to the wood, was his younger wife, Four Times, who was sitting on her bed of robes with the twins, boys nearly five years of age. Next, partitioned off, was Crowfoot, Bull's son, at seven years a quiet lad already too old for games, burdened with the worries of his father. Sleeping alongside each other were two almost-grownup daughters, one fourteen and the other seventeen, both enhanced with the perfume of herbs. The last space, closest to the entrance at the right, was reserved for Bull and his older wife, Seen By Her Nation, who was a sister of Four Times.

"Fish" Allison, whose purpose was recognized, was not trusted enough to participate in the councils that would decide what course the Sioux would take. Bull called the chiefs and headmen about him: Gall, Crow King, No Neck, One Bull, Old Bull, He Dog, Black Bull, Fool Heart, Running Horse, Fool Bull, Turning Bear, and so on.

It was agreed. "Go, if you want to," Bull decided. "I will be coming too. Shortly I am going to visit the Redcoat garrison. I want to go there first. I will come where you are soon."

But the majority stuck to their guns (and their horses) and could not immediately convince themselves to take the surrender road. Allison, unsuccessful, was permitted to return to Buford with about twenty lodges under Strong Hand, a token offering to test the veracity of his promises of humane treatment.

When it became apparent the white mother's police were not relenting, the chiefs had second thoughts and drifted away. Gall, who had remained loyal despite his carping and outspoken complaints in council politics, led more than 400 stragglers to a U.S. post. Allison's nostalgic references to their old hunting grounds helped spur them on to thirty-below Poplar Point from where they refused to budge until their kinsmen reported favourably from Buford.

Allison, with the backing of the military, was not about to give up on Sitting Bull. He had enticed Gall with a secret: the great father had plans to make him head chief of all the Hunkpapa if he could persuade Bull to surrender. Now that Gall was virtually a captive Allison saddled up for "Woody" Mountain to bring back the grand prize by himself.

The appearance of this ambitious, intrepid American didn't enthrall Superintendent Crozier. It was his opinion that the recurring visits of American scouts into the dens of hostiles discouraged their oft-repeated intentions to pack up. On this point the Redcoat and the red man would have agreed. The chief eyed them as mercenaries, which is what they were, who were deviously plotting his capture for the rewards that had been promised them by the Bluecoats. He had seen a drawing of himself in a newspaper that showed him with a ring in his nose and horns on his head. How could anyone come to him and say the Americans would not harm him?

Previously Ol' Sit had taken Allison's gifts of food and had spurned him; now he was so poor he couldn't afford to look the other way.

In mid-December, 1880, without farewells, handshakes or embraces with the police, Sitting Bull, the fading patriarch, placed the safety of his followers and himself in Allison's hands. They left Wood Mountain trudging through the snow, their meagre belongings packed on broken-down horses and colts, the utterly despondent women driving the overburdened animals towards the border. The sorry-looking cavalcade, covering twelve miles a day, survived its first crisis early on when one young brave, incensed at the ignominy of the scene, the starvation in his family, threatened "Fish" Allison with a rifle.

"The young man's heart is bad," Bull explained. "His little sister is crying for food."

In the last days of 1880, along the Milk River where it joins the Missouri, it suddenly appeared the Great Spirit had not forsaken them. Out of the mist through the vapour of the freezing river, came a herd of buffalo. The Tetons pounced on them with the old vigor, and their bodies and their spirits were jubilantly revived. They would not surrender – yet. Who knows, perhaps, just perhaps, the Great Spirit had repopulated the earth with their provider.

Bull dispatched Crow King, tall and athletic, to Buford with Allison to determine the state of their relatives. He told them to bring back an American officer with whom he could negotiate.

Ol' Sit was beginning to feel himself again, a master in his own domain, cocky and belligerent. His men had stolen forty-five horses from the Canadian halfbreeds. What fun! But they needed these sturdy horses for the hunts and for the warriors. They could not live again like men unless they had horses.

One reckless halfbreed demanded his horses back from Bull. The chief took away his gun and sent him home, with his life. When Crozier heard of this incident it seemed to him that such provocation was an assurance the old prophet dared not ever again show his face in Canada. One of the officers, Inspector Alexander Roderick Macdonell, formerly of the militia ("Paper Collar Johnnie" to his subordinates) volunteered to attempt to recapture the horses. With one other policeman and an interpreter, all unaware of recent events in the Sioux enclave, Macdonell pursued the thieves into the United States. He succeeded, amazingly, not because Bull wanted to repent, but because of the demoralizing downfall of Gall, whose submissive camp had been wantonly attacked by soldiers.

"Back to the white mother's country!" Bull ordered when he heard of Gall's set-back from Crow King.

Not everyone had the means or the stamina or the will to obey. Crow King gathered these people, the majority, under his wing, and delivered 300 of them, including eighty warriors, to the troops at Wolf Point. Their total wealth consisted of thirteen ponies and five guns. Bull and his indefatigables, forty-three families, with only the smell of meat in their parfleches, turned around. Anticipating that General Terry would be hot on his heels – a correct assumption – he led his bedraggled, tired band elusively all over the place before recrossing the border during the fourth week of January. He would still rather be a fugitive in a strange land (as Allison had once described his plight) than a dead man in his own.

The escape of Bull, again, into Canada aroused howls of consternation in the United States. Irvine and Crozier, it could be said with surety, were likewise disappointed. The Americans, frustrated once more, were prone to condemn British laxity. "Intern him!" they remonstrated. The New York *Herald,* which grossly over-estimated the number of Sioux at large (an impossible 400 lodges), managed to contrive a case of international intrigue, a mystery man, the secret presence and influence of a Canadian officer in Bull's camp on American soil.

The sinister intruder was none other than the police officer who was after the stolen horses and had caught up with Bull. The chief had asked him for a loan of his interpreter, whom he trusted completely, for his impending conference on the army's terms for his surrender. It was not to be.

Outwardly maintaining a stance of haughtiness, the crestfallen old warrior nestled close to the "fort" at Wood Mountain. His warriors, thin and threadbare, too weak to hunt or fight, helplessly fearful of their persistent Indian enemies, the Crees, had been further reduced by some roving Assiniboines who had crept up on two Sioux lodges in Bull's camp and scalped fifteen people. Two survived, with severe wounds, and were cared for by the Redcoats.

What could be Crozier's next move? Conceivably he could flex the muscles of his detachment to have these so-and-so beggarly invaders hustled to the border. There were probably fewer than 200 left.

The superintendent devised a more agreeable approach. In February (1881) he organized a feast. Who could resist? Not Bull. Crozier used the festivities to impress upon his grateful guests the good things of life they were missing with their self-imposed exile. The abundance of staples mixed with pleasant conviviality lulled Bull into a euphoria of good fellowship.

"If I could get a good letter from the soldier chief at Buford that he would treat us well, I might go," Bull said. "I will see about it."

Encouraged by this response, Crozier had Inspector Macdonell, a popular protégé of Walsh who had been promoted from the ranks, lead a deputation of two constables, the intepreter Morin and three Sioux to Major David Brotherton to secure definite commitments from him. The visitors were treated royally by the American officer and were quickly back in Canada with written assurances.

Bull, ever cautious, had sent his own couriers down there – Four Horns, his uncle; One Bull, his nephew; and Bone Club, an aide. A policeman went with them. They met with an army agent at the border, a man who needed whisky to keep the blood flowing. He and the policeman were blood brothers.

One Bull, who had never tasted the white man's firewater, asked for a sample swig.

"Friends," he said, "we're out here together. I want to see how it tastes. I want to see how it feels to be drunk."

Nothing doing. The whites were afraid of drunken Indians and said so. This amused old Four Horns and Bone Club. One Bull never did, nor could he expect to, hear the end of the story of how he frightened the white men with his thirst.

Bull's observers noted their relatives were without guns and ponies. They also noted they were eating regularly. The chief nodded and shrugged when he was told. He weighed this information with the fate of his beloved Little Assiniboine who had been arrested at Wolf Point for being a "noted warrior and murderer." He was in solitary, secured by shackles, in a room with bars where he came close to freezing to death. Little Assiniboine, tough as nails, didn't discard his allegiance to the man who had let him live and had taken him into his lodge as a brother; he never would. All the Sioux, even the turncoats, described him affectionately as a man's man.

Superintendent Crozier, buoyed by the initial success of his festive tactics, laid on another splendid meal that the famished Indians were delighted to savour. After the old campaigner Bull had eaten his fill (if such a state was possible) the commanding officer brought out the letter from Brotherton and translated the contents. Land had been reserved for the Sioux nation; nobody would go hungry; teams of oxen, mares and colts will be provided to help the Indians settle down.

Crozier sat back with satisfaction. Bull stood up, as erectly as he could on a full stomach.

"I don't believe a word of it." he shouted. "It's not a letter from Brotherton. The police made it up on the way back. You have been drinking. I don't accept your word!"

Knowing that he had overstayed his welcome, he flung his blanket around his shoulders with a determination and resolve befitting his obstinacy, motioned to his associates, and shuffled out.

"I don't want to see you again," Crozier bellowed. "I've had too much trouble with you already. You can all go to hell!"

The superintendent was a man of his stern word. In the slowly retreating days of winter the stoic Tetons were facing the prospects of hunting in the next world; in this one there was nothing to eat, not a crumb. The traders were mostly unsympathetic (the Sioux weren't worth a penny) while Crozier had steeled himself to be insensitive. Animosities were cooled only by the everlasting cold and snow.

The impatience in Ottawa over Bull's implacable attitude was pushing Macdonald into a belated vendetta against Walsh, who had been ordered by the doctors to stay at home. The Prime Minister confided he had grave suspicions that the major was not behaving in a straightforward manner in the Sitting Bull affair.

"Walsh undoubtedly has influence with Bull which he tried to monopolize in order to make himself of importance and is, I fear, primarily responsible for the Indians' unwillingness to leave Canada," Macdonald had written Lorne in late 1880. By the end of the year the Prime Minister – sixty-five years old, ailing and fighting for his Pacific Railway – was contemplating drastic action.

"When all this is over I think we must dispense with Major Walsh's services in the Mounted Police."

Walsh wasn't Macdonald's only culprit. He was complaining about a man called Thompson, whom he described as a deserter from the NWMP who had assumed Indian customs and had become an outlaw. "He may exercise, and probably does exercise, a malign influence on Sitting Bull." (Charles Thompson deserted the force three days before Christmas in 1877, for which he was imprisoned during April and May of '78. Subsequently he continued his police duties at Wood Mountain until his discharge in September of '79.)

Macdonald explained to Lorne he could do nothing in the way of arresting Thompson. "We know of no charge against him. He was tried and punished for desertion from the police and subsequently served out his time. Since then he has become an outcast white, assumed Indian habits, and has one or more Indian wives."

On January 25, 1881, when he was exhaustingly on the verge of the CPR victory, Macdonald sent a further private letter to Lord Lorne: "I greatly fear that Major Walsh is pulling the strings through Thompson the deserter to prevent Bull from surrendering. Walsh is still at Brockville and I have given him two months' more leave to keep him there lest he might return and personally influence Sitting Bull."

Macdonald said he regretted "being obliged to play with this

230

man Walsh as he deserves dismissal" but if he were cashiered he would at once go westwards and cause an imbroglio "for he is a bold, desperate fellow." The Prime Minister indicated that when the time was right he would recommend that Walsh be summarily dismissed.

# ❖❖❖ The Hopes and the Inevitable

❖❖❖ The continuing generosity and compassion of Jean-Louis Légaré were unusual in the harshness of frontier existence. The misery of the Sioux bothered his soul; their poverty emptied his pockets. In the beginning they had been welcome customers, yet not necessarily profitable ones. Now they were sullen beggars – and Jean-Louis could be a soft touch. He realized this. He couldn't go on helping for nothing in return. He was going broke at forty dollars a day, the cost of feeding his wards.

Since '79 the Sioux had had precious little left worth trading, but when Légaré moved forty miles farther to the east to open up shop at Willow Bunch after a disastrous fire had destroyed all the grazing land at Wood Mountain, they had followed him.

When Jean-Louis talked to these Sioux no one needed an interpreter. He had sufficient control of their language, and its idiomatic mannerisms, to be understood. Although not loquacious, he knew the right way to say things; he knew when to pause. When he talked they listened. It was as if they were mesmerized by the dark vigour of his physical presence; his eyes had that unnerving quality of concentrating on each individual in a crowded space. Unflappable, he could usually outlast the inscrutables.

Légaré had reasoned that if the police and the Government couldn't get the exiles out of the country perphaps he could. Besides, there might be some money in it. Back in '78 an American scout had convinced him there would be a reward for the man who brought in Sitting Bull to Fort Buford. Brotherton had suggested that the Americans wouldn't forget such a service. Also he had a letter from Crozier, dated April 20, 1881:

My Dear Mr. Légaré,
We received very encouraging letters from the Missouri. The

Indians are being treated as well as could be wished and the Americans appear to be as nice as possible to them.

In spite of all that has been done for him, Sitting Bull still wants to remain in this country, if possible. Nevertheless, in view of what is happening now, I think he will be obliged to follow the others. If you talk to him it would make him appear like a chief in the eyes of his people and would only increase his influence. Then he will use this influence to keep his friends here.

I would like you to send a message to Poplar Point or to Buford to advise the American officer of the number of Indians you have with you. The Americans will send you provisions and vehicles to bring in your Indians.

I am including herewith the copy of a letter received from Major Brotherton.

DON'T LET THE INDIANS KNOW THAT YOU HAVE RECEIVED A LETTER FROM ME.

You know how suspicious they are. They could imagine that we have something in mind. I am writing this to you because Sitting Bull could trick you. You can't believe a single word from him. To be sure I will recompense you for the trouble which you are taking in this business and I will not neglect to inform the government of the great assistance which you have given us.

The trader conferred with the local priest, a fellow Québecois, Father Pierre St. Germain, who encouraged him.

"If the British Government and the Americans can't do a thing with Sitting Bull, I will surrender him," Légaré confided. "If they pay me, that is alright, but anyhow I will have the credit for it."

Légaré set to work immediately. He got word to the lodges he was putting on a feast to which everyone was invited. The incentive was magnetic. Every man, woman and child who could ride, walk or could be moved by travois attended. The sight of all these pitiable people was distressing. Every morsel, every fragment of what was edible, disappeared. Not until then did Jean-Louis attempt to lecture them.

"It is five years since we were first together," the trader began. "I was the first man to shake hands with you when you crossed the line, and I have always been your adviser. I have never said anything to you much before, but this time I have to talk a little to you."

Légaré came directly to his main point.

"This spring there is nothing good for you anywhere. All the halfbreeds are going away – they don't want to see you – and the Mounted Police don't want to see you any more at the fort. You mistrust everyone; everyone mistrusts you.

"I will try to help you, If you don't all want to starve here, if you want to listen to me, I can see only one thing that is good for you. The American Government will receive you this spring and treat you well. If you like your children, and as you are now very poor, you will accept my words; you will surrender very soon."

Légaré stopped right there. Not one word, not a whisper, came from the throng. The chiefs remained seated, looking at each other, and then they conversed among themselves. Légaré could hear the gist. They believed him, but they could not believe the Americans who, they were convinced, were but waiting to get all the Indians all together in order to kill them.

Légaré interjected. "You know very well I never said much to you except when it was necessary."

"*How!*" they chorused.

"If you do not believe me...[Légaré halted and changed his tack]...I will do more. Come with me, as many as you want, chief or brave, thirty or forty. We will go and see Major Brotherton. I will talk for you. I will furnish you with provisions, horses, guns, ammunition and treat you well going to Fort Buford. If you have no good answer from Major Brotherton I will bring you back, every one of you."

"*How!*" they chorused again. One chief shouted: "If he keeps us there what will you do?"

"If he keeps you I will stay with you."

"*How! How! Washtay!* [It is good.]"

Bull, sullen and silent, glanced with contempt at all the weak-hearts. Légaré said that in five days (April 26) he would be leaving for Buford.

"If anyone wants to go with me, be ready on that day."

When departure day came around Jean-Louis was ready with twelve cartloads of provisions and equipment. He led his caravan

234

to the Sioux camp and picked up thirty travellers who were willing to risk the anger of *the* chief. By the end of the day they were twelve miles away from his influence, so they thought, erroneously.

With Légaré out of the way, Bull called a council. Two important decisions were made. One, that the trader should not be allowed to think he had overthrown Sitting Bull. Two, that the strongest, most mobile members of the band should trek to the police fort in the east, Qu'Appelle, where Walsh was thought to be in command. If Bull could talk to the "meejure" he could impress upon him that now there were only 200 or so Tetons left in Canada, the white mother's chiefs would possibly agree to a reservation for them.

One Bull was delegated to deflate the prestige of Légaré. He and four braves chased after the deserters. They went directly to Légaré's tent, trailing behind them his confused, worried followers. One Bull, whose blood ties to his uncle were as true and treasured as his faith in the Great Spirit, had heard it bandied about the white chiefs would pay 20,000 pieces of pay paper for the chief's scalp, and that the son of Black Moon, who had killed many Americans and who was with Légaré, was worth $200 dead or alive. The young brave grabbed hold of the stocky trader and shook him violently.

"We know what you are up to. We know what you are going to do with the people you are taking to Buford. You want to take all the big ones with you because you want to sell them by the pound."

When the bewildered refugees heard these accusations they argued among themselves, shouting back and forth. Légaré, who was in danger of being murdered, pleaded with them not to believe his accusers.

"I am telling the truth," he bellowed above the din.

Half of them continued with him; the others, frightened, returned with One Bull.

Légaré and seventeen Sioux trundled down into the swampy Missouri valley at Buford after eight days on the green, spring-flowering prairie. The dejected Indians gave up what was left of their wealth, their ponies and guns, and joined 1,300 of their comrades who were under guard at the fort. Légaré stocked up with goods for his store, to which he wanted to return in haste.

All his thoughts were at Willow Bunch. God only knows what would be going on back there!

When he got home Légaré found his apprehensions in full (and unprofitable) development. The Sioux, a ragged left-behind collection of the old and the infirm (among them those who were almost blind from their years in smoke-filled tepees) were devouring his supplies of meat, pemmican, flour and tea. Sitting Bull, and the young and the healthy, fewer than a hundred of them, were miles away in unfamilar surroundings, heading for Qu'Appelle. They skirted the Old Wives Lake, the water so brackish and the smell so nauseous that neither men nor horses dared to drink it, then they filed through the low mounds of the dirt hills to shallow Moose Jaw Creek (Arm Creek they called it because they found human arm bones where they stopped). The water was drinkable. Eastwards the going was heavy because of the arid, clay soil that slowed them down as far as Oscana Creek or Pile of Bones (near Regina-to-be), the place where in the heyday of the buffalo the Crees put up corral-like pounds of trunks and branches to trap their never-ending food supply. In 1865 the pile of bones, strung out along the creek, was six feet high. What a difference in 1881! The Sioux were fortunate to bag some skunks on the river banks; the lucky ones got a wolf or two that the women roasted on willow sticks over the fires.

They were thiry miles from their objective, most of the way northeastwards on a bald, treeless plain devoid of shelter, wood, food or water. Make the best of the wolf meat, the wives reminded their husbands. Forget the taste of cooked buffalo tongue, or raw liver, or kidneys! (Forget! It was not possible, such delicacies were everlastingly delicious in the mind.)

Wearily they pushed on, and on, the harnessed ponies dragging the worn travois poles, the people forced to walk. From the plain they came abruptly to a new world, to the steep, gravel-clay fringes of the Qu'Appelle River valley, to clusters of poplars on the south side, and gradually to the willowed, cedared, brush-covered, sun-shaded, velvety lower slopes of the verdant valley, past lakes and sand to the Hudson's Bay buildings, and past small, patchy fields and potato plots to Fort Qu'Appelle, the white-washed, farmlike barracks of the police. Here Bull expected he would once again meet his old confidant and counsellor Major

Walsh. Instead he was confronted by Inspector Sam Steele, a huge figure of militaristic imperialism who stood head and shoulders above him.

In his thirties, an old hand in the force (he had been recruited by Walsh in '73 with the agreed rank of a chief constable, a senior non-commissioned officer), a man of action, for which he had a penchant, an excellent administrator and equestrian, Sam Steele towered before this uninvited visitor with the unshakeable solidity of a dictatorial sergeant-major.

He was a straight-to-the-core man. He delivered the bad news to Bull in one verbal package: Walsh was beyond reach in the east; the Sioux could not hope for any relief from the Government; and their claim for a reservation was out of the question. To make it more official the inspector sent a message to Indian Commissioner Edgar Dewdney who was at Shoal Lake, 160 miles to the east, about halfway to Winnipeg.

Dewdney, Ottawa's mobile pacifier and persuader, came in a hurry and met Bull during the last week in May with his own brand of reassurances of American forgiveness. The chief was not impressed.

"I shake hands with the white man on this side and I feel safe. I shake hands with the Americans and I am afraid of them."

Dewdney, who was a civil engineer from British Columbia, big in stature and railway politics, offered him a police escort, spiced with temptations of provisions, for his return to Willow Bunch. Bull declined. He had not yet explored bustling Qu'Appelle. The locality, the presence of other Indians, the potential of the Hudson's Bay store, and the black robes' mission five miles east, on the north shore of the lake, especially intrigued him. He camped nearby on the high ground.

The Indian commissioner, unwilling to condone violence, convinced that Bull was harmless, had notions of starving these intruders out, not a bizarre inclination considering they were already down to eating roots and gophers.

The presence of Bull's soldiers in the valley shut doors, brought rifles off the racks, and alerted unfriendly Crees and Saulteaux. The Hudson's Bay factor, W. J. McLean, and his wife whose hospitality was normally bountiful, were not about to open the store to these foreigners who had nothing worth trading.

Rebuffed again, Bull did not give up. The black robes at Lebret had a garden full of crops; furthermore, he knew they had recently received a shipment of flour from Fort Ellice.

Father Joseph Hugonard, a young Oblate, was in the mission when he heard the tell-tale sounds of many people and horses coming in his direction. He stepped outside and saw about seventy-five Indians on the grounds. When they got to the gate the horsemen tied their mounts to his fence, all except one who was in the lead. He rode through the gate as far and the mission door before dismounting. He grabbed the hand of Father Hugonard. The priest, who couldn't speak a sentence of Lakota, realized he was being forcibly greeted by Sitting Bull.

The Indians trooped into his house, each one shaking his hand. Those who couldn't squeeze in sat outside. Hugonard distributed tobacco and called for an interpreter. Bull spoke up.

"Black Robe, we meet you as friends. You know there are no buffalo on the plains since the fires last fall. Hunger forced us to leave Wood Mountain and come here. Perhaps we can live by fishing or a little trading. I have never been afraid of an enemy, but I tremble at the sight of our children crying from hunger."

Hugonard sympathized: "I have to send a long way for food, not to trade but for the use of my people over whom I am only a manager, not a factor. We must be good neighbours in this country; we must help one another. I have flour and you have none. You want some and so perphaps you have things which I would be willing to take in exchange."

Bull took off his blanket and gave it to the priest. Others, who were wearing the soldiers' pocket watches (some gold, some minus mechanisms) handed them over. They all went outside and five braves designated their old Custer horses with the well-worn saddles that they would swap for food. All the men produced prized knickknacks from the battle; some swapped their moccasins. The Sioux left with eight bags of flour, dried buffalo meat, bacon, tea, ammunition and clothing – and as many vegetables as Hugonard could spare from his garden.

For a few days – days to relish – the families indulged themselves. Bull, a deliberate, stubborn, pensive, generous autocrat, surrounded by the people he loved and trusted the most, smoked and contemplated. He was sad and reproachful. He had heard that Little Assiniboine was in irons in an army jail, and one of his daughters, Has Many Horses, who went south with her new husband, was in shackles down there. The moccasin telegraph also informed him Légaré had recently persuaded thirty-two of the not-so-faithful hangers-on at Willow Bunch to pack up for Buford where they had been put on a boat and carried down the Missouri to Fort Yates. The river forts must be packed with feeble-hearted Sioux!

How true. One man who saw them there from the deck of the steamer Red Cloud was a Redcoat recruit, Constable R.N. Wilson of Bowmanville, Ontario. This young "pilgrim" (a name accorded all new arrivals from the east) had never before seen any real Indians. At Buford a new universe emerged before him on the river bank, 250 lodges from Canada containing surrendered warriors and their leaders, names coated in infamy by the illustrated press of the day. One of the most notorious was standing alone, near the landing stage, a sulkingly defiant-looking hulk of a man holding a three-knifed tomahawk, the only Indian in sight blatantly displaying a weapon. This was Chief Gall, suffering more and more in his middle age from the wounds of long ago when he was ambushed in his lodge by Long (Tall) Mandan, a Two-Kettle chief, and his soldier friends. He had been bayoneted, kicked and left for dead. Gall's heart was sick with the sight of the whites, yet now he couldn't resist their food and comforts.

Two days up river, at Poplar, young Wilson gazed at another, much bigger encampment of prisioners. There were more at Wolf Point. At the Fort Carroll landing he saw his first Canadian Indians, Bloods. An old-timer told him they were after pinto buffalo. (What he meant, he had to explain, was that the Bloods were on a horse-stealing expedition.)

Fort Carroll was Louis Riel country, and Riel, sallow and dour, actually embarked on the Red Cloud for Benton, but when the Métis rebel found himself in the company of Upper Canadian policemen (the Orangemen in the squad were unsettling him) he got off, after ten miles, at the next wood pile.

While Riel was getting out of the way of the NWMP, Sitting Bull was persisting in getting in their way. Entrenched at Qu'Appelle, near the end of his tether, he was being pressured to give up by Dewdney, Steele and Indian agent Colonel Allan McDonald. Dewdney, aware of the old patriot's phobia of Buford, compassionately offered him a police escort (with plenty of provisions) to

Pembina, south of Winnipeg, from where he could strike out for Fort Totten and on to Standing Rock.

Bull wouldn't budge. He had a pathetic expectation that Walsh would soon appear with the news they so desperately hoped for. As for Walsh, whose enforced tenure in the east had not put him out of touch, he was disturbed over Ol' Sit's deteriorating plight and genuinely sorrowful the chief was hanging on in his misery to talk with him. It could not be. The Prime Minister had forbidden it.

"It would be criminal if something isn't done to relieve Bull from his sad state," he said. So off he went to do something, unofficially, in New York and Chicago, where he had influential, friendly contacts.

His best bet was General William A. Hammond, whom he met in Chicago. He had known Hammond for several years because of his connections in the U.S. Indian Department. Hammond, who was knowledgeable and fair, assured Walsh he could advise Bull that there would be no charges laid against him by the American authorities. For his own peace of mind, Walsh gathered promises from other political acquaintances that they would intercede at cabinet level should it become necessary.

The major returned home with a plan to get in touch with Bull. He contacted an ex-policeman with whom he had served, and could trust, and who was known to Sitting Bull. This was Louis Daniels, currently at the western limits of the Canadian Pacific Railway, in Brandon and, fortunately, about to forsake the real estate boom for the empty land. Daniels made sure Sitting Bull got Walsh's message, which was an assurance he could safely yield to the United States without fear that he would be singled out for special punishment.

The moment had come to accept the inevitable. If Walsh said there was no hope in the Queen's land, there was no hope. If Walsh said the Americans would not kill him, perhaps they would not. Bull, self-contained in his depression, walked up to the bluffs and prayed for the relatives and friends who were going to be delivered to their tormentors. It would be heartening, nevertheless, for the old people to again feel the river winds of their homelands on the lower Missouri.

The downtrodden warlord, after farewells to the few of his comrades who were secretly staying on at Qu'Appelle with the Minnesota refugees, the Santees, started on the long road back.

240

Dewdney had authorized rations for the journey to Willow Bunch.

The people dragged themselves along, hopelessly fatigued, weak and without horses. Progress was slow. Food stocks ran out. On July 2, starving and haggard and straggling up the long valley, they flopped down under the trees near Légaré's store. That same day the chief led them to Légaré's house. Walking with him was the venerable Four Horns, old Moccasin Top, in his eighties, the elder brother of his father, kindly, serious-minded, his blood loyalties not diluted by all the adversity.

Bull stood humbly before Légaré. He recounted the details of privation.

"We will do anything you want if you will feed these people and give us ten sacks of flour."

Légaré laid out a meal and everyone tucked in. When the Indians were full to the brim Ol' Sit stood up.

"These five years I have known you; you never said anything much to me in your life, but I heard many times what you were saying to the others." Bull paused, deliberately, not taking his eyes off Légaré. "I heard in Qu'Appelle that you were carrying my camp to Buford. I started from Qu'Appelle with the same intention, to surrender myself if you give me time for it.

"The Queen's chief (Dewdney) offered to feed us all the way if we surrendered to the Americans. I said, 'No! If I surrender, with nobody else but Jean-Louis will I go.'

"If you wait until we are in a little better order, and fatter, we will go to Buford with you."

Légaré wanted to get them out immediately; the halfbreed settlement could not support them any longer. Also Légaré felt there might be violence, as the Crees were on the warpath. He took a tough stance. He didn't ask them; he told them.

"I will start the day after tomorrow."

"No!" an angry Sitting Bull answered back. "We cannot go as soon as that. If you wait ten days we may be ready."

"I refuse to wait so long. Make it seven days."

Bull grunted. He said he was sick and he walked off.

Légaré went ahead with his preparations. He enlisted seven local Métis to help him: Narcisse Lacerte, formerly of St. Norbert, Manitoba, who in '73 had seen the bodies of the Assiniboines after the Cypress Mills Massacre (as the official interpreter he was chosen second in command to Légaré), Jean Chartrand, Antoine

Gosselin, Louison Piché, Ambroise Delorme, Charles Champagne and André Gaudry, a cripple who had been responsible for persuading Légaré to settle at Willow Bunch. Provisions for an eight-day journey and the skins and poles for thirty-eight lodges were packed into thirty-seven wagons and carts.

On July 10, Légaré announced that all Indians intending to go with him to Buford should pitch their tepees at the starting point. Forty families complied at once. The chief demanded ten sacks of flour "to make bread before we start from here." The trader hesitated. If he gave them that much flour they might not go at all! He sent a man to Bull's lodge with nine sacks. When Bull counted them he lost his temper.

"Jean-Louis is cheating us," he shouted so that everyone could hear. "Because I asked him for ten he gives us only nine."

The trader, one move ahead, made a show of loading more food onto the carts, of herding twenty additional ponies for the trip, of distributing cartridges. Next morning he was ready to start. It was thirty-five miles to the border; 150 to Buford.

Bull, procrastinating to the limits of his ingenuity, demanded two more flour sacks. He got them. In Légaré's store he helped himself to a revolver (worth fifteen dollars), which he tucked into his belt, and field glasses, which he hung around his neck. Légaré, hardly able to stifle his exasperation, ordered his men to get the wheels turning.

Of the thirty-seven carts in the column, twenty-five slowly squeaked and sawed up the gradient to the southeast. The remaining twelve stayed put with Sitting Bull and his unyielding supporters, Four Horns, Red Thunder, White Dog and a small group of rebels. Shortly after, in an act of sulky defiance, they turned their carts around and drifted away in the opposite direction.

"I can't return to the Americans when I can feel their bullet in my hip," Four Horns complained.

Légaré sent all his armed halfbreeds on their trail to reclaim his carts and supplies while he carried on with the main column. The recalcitrants didn't resist when they saw the halfbreeds riding them down; they didn't have the strength to. Bull asked time to smoke and council. As a result he and his remaining headmen changed their minds, and their direction, and tagged on to Légaré the next day – in time for dinner.

More drifters joined the motley cavalcade. Left behind, in

Wood Mountain and Willow Bunch, were pockets of Sioux families who were tied by marriage, frontier-style, to policemen and Métis.

Bull's first night in Légaré's camp could not pass without an incident. At about midnight the trader heard one of the warriors proclaiming, at the top of his voice, that presents were being distributed from the supply carts. Légaré, in anguish and anger, caught the Indians helping themselves to bags of his flour. Eight had already been snatched when he saw one man about to heave a full sack onto his shoulders.

"Put it down," Légaré ordered. "It's not your flour." He put his foot on the sack to emphasize his determination. Frustrated and humiliated, the Indian shot a couple of rifle bullets into the bag. The camp was awakened. Jean-Louis, the benefactor, stood his ground.

"I can't give this man flour. We musn't run out of food before reaching Buford."

Bull, weighing his words, smoothed it over.

"You have a strong heart. You gave us plenty of provisions for the road. The Indian is the same. When he has plenty he gives some to his friends."

The threadbare column traveled in fits and starts across the plain. Bull slowed them down with late starts, stops for smoking, councils and tea-drinking. At this rate Légaré would run out of food – he was distributing 1,000 pounds a day – and his plan, getting closer to a successful conclusion with every turn of a wheel, would simply be dissipated. He would not be able to handle 230 Sioux approaching a doubtful destiny on empty stomachs.

Légaré had to get more provisions, preferably from the American side. Late at night, out of sight and hearing of Bull, he detailed Chartrand, Delorme and a reliable young Indian to slip out of camp with a note for Brotherton at Buford that Sitting Bull, six sub-chiefs and a couple of hundred followers were coming in, but he could not guarantee arrival if their rations ran out. He requested 1,500 pounds of provisions, charged to his account.

The exhausted couriers related the latest Légaré saga to Brotherton. The major, exhilarated over the prospects of having the great American outlaw land right in his lap, sent the messengers to bed while he organized a relief plan that would keep the military out of view. When Légaré's men awoke to the commotion of sixteen mules being hitched to two wagons, they saw soldiers piling on beef, smoked bacon, tobacco and hardtack. There were also small gifts for each of the chiefs. Ready and waiting were Captain Clifford of the 7th Infantry and a Sergeant O'Donnell who were to inconspicuously accompany the relief column.

Clifford had been carefully briefed. Nothing must go wrong. If he had a memory lapse, he could read Brotherton's written orders, dated July 16, 1881... "Sitting Bull and other Sioux chiefs are en route to this post to surrender. You will meet him and bring his party into Buford. Captain Clifford will use the utmost discretion in carrying out his delicate and important mission and allow nothing or any person to interfere with him to prevent his success, and in case he meets with troops, he will, by virtue of his commission, assume command of the whole party and give all the necessary orders in the case. He will notify the Post Commander in advance of his arrival at the post."

This mission had been entrusted to Clifford, who had been on the Little Big Horn battlefield the day after the disaster, because he was known and trusted by some Sioux leaders, although he had never set eyes on Sitting Bull.

At mid-afternoon on July 18, when the heavy heat had slowed Légaré's depressing procession to a crawl 95-odd miles south of the border, men and wagons from the south were spotted by Bull's scouts.

"Americans are coming!"

The chief reined his pony. He struck himself on the breast, imitating the muffled anger of a bear. His anxious eyes soon determined there was no need for alarm. Riding ahead of the food wagons were the two halfbreeds and an Indian. The two soldiers were bringing up the rear, out of view.

Légaré, down to fifty pounds of flour, even smaller amounts of bacon and pemmican, supervised the unloading and announced, as the measure of his relief, a feast for that night. For the Sioux it would be their last feast, their last night, as a free people. The two soldiers joined the camp without any trouble.

Before sunrise on July 19 the empty carts were loaded with women and children carrying the remnants of their baggage. The big, wooden wheels grated into motion for the last few miles to Buford. When the sun had passed its highest point, Ol' Sit, astride his favorite pony, stopped at a well on the Missouri bluffs for a reflective pause. Down there were the two entities: the barracks, the soldiers, the dock, the sternwheelers, all the trappings of the white man's way he had fought to keep out of his life. Beyond were the fading elements of his world, the panorama of his ancestors, Mother earth spread out like a vast spiritual blanket comforting all the living things of nature; the cool river valley, the hills of solitude covered with the sacred stones, no longer the Indian's exclusive domain, and the big sky, the home of the sun, where it seemed the storm clouds were gathering to infinity.

He shifted in his saddle as the pony limbered down the steep coulee into the compound where the Bluecoats were waiting for him. Among them, in the red jacket, was Macdonell of the Mounted, from Wood Mountain, who had refused Bull's final request for Government rations when he had returned from Qu'Appelle, who had defied his threats to take by force what was needed.

"I am thrown away!" Bull had reacted despairingly.

"You are not thrown away," Macdonell had replied. "You've been given good advice. If you want food you must go to your reservation in the United States."

Now there were no words. Bull, anything but a proud chief in his torn calico shirt, tattered black leggings and dusty blanket, allowed himself to be led to a camp site south of the fort buildings, near the boat landing and the post cemetery. Everyone came to gawk at him. His broad-cheeked face was pinched with worry and fatigue. The wild spirit was broken.

The next day, July 20, after his camp had settled down, Bull and his headmen surrendered formally. They rode to Brotherton's office where the commander greeted them in friendly tones. Bull did not respond. He sat impassively silent on his pony, his features obscured by a sloppy bandanna. When he dismounted he sat next to Brotherton and relinquished his Winchester by passing it to Crowfoot, now eight years old.

"Give my gun to the major....My son, if you live, you can never be a man in this world because you will never have a gun or pony."

The lad handed the rifle to Brotherton. Sitting Bull, for the first time in his own memory, was defenceless.

One Bull, his beloved nephew, was standing nearby. The chief glanced at his disarmed, bewildered captains. As powerless as they all were, Bull had not been shorn of his oratory. He finally spoke to Brotherton and his officers:

"Today I am home. The land under my feet is mine again. I never sold it; I never gave it to anyone. If I left the Black Hills five years ago it was because I wanted to raise my family quietly. It is the law of the big women [he looked at Macdonell for a moment] to have everything quiet in that place, but I thought all the time to come back to this country, and when Légaré was bringing my friends here – I heard one of my girls was with him – I decided to start from Qu'Appelle and come with him to Buford. Now I want to make a bargain with the grandfather, a solid one. I want to have witnesses on both sides, some Englishmen, some Americans."

Bull was assured his daughter was well and happy. Brotherton said he and his people would be shipped to Fort Yates to join those who had come in before him. Bull, disappointed, had been expecting a reservation along the Little Missouri where he could hunt and trade in Canada and the U.S., but he did not complain. He would be a leader again, so he thought, of all the people at the Standing Rock Reservation.

Telegraph wires were humming with the momentous news all through the rest of the day. Macdonell was able to get one telegraph off to Ottawa, which is what Commissioner Irvine had ordered him to do. Légaré couldn't wait to get out. He stocked up as fast as he could and departed for Willow Bunch with a final promise to the man he had coerced that he would do his best to get the remaining Sioux (probably about fifty families) to pack up for Standing Rock. Légaré, though, had concluded the human cargo business was putting him in the red at an ungovernable rate.

The upper Missouri steamboat stops were being emptied of surrendered Indians from Canada. Most of them were transported downstream to Standing Rock. Two thousand warriors and families had congregated at Fort Keough where they were peaceful and industrious and were displaying an inclination towards agriculture in the Powder River country they adored, the country where the spirits roamed in contentment.

Their crops were half grown when orders came through for the shipment of the Sioux to the agencies, 300 miles to the east as the crow flies. There were tears, pleading, appeals and prayers, all to no avail. They were herded onto the boats, some of the most

246

famous names of their nation with the bands: Spotted Eagle, Broad Trail, Rain In The Face, Kicking Bear, Short Bull, and so on. Never again would they see their country. Never, not as mortals.

Sitting Bull was put aboard the *General Sherman* on July 29. Three days later the boat docked at Mandan, on the west side of the Missouri near Bismarck. Bull was an instant celebrity, whisked off by carriage for dinner and photographs. The 187 shabby people with him, boxed off on the shore by soldiers, shouted and wailed when the chief was being driven away, convinced he was destined for a rope. Bull stood up in the carriage to quiet them down as he disappeared for a welcome meal in a local hotel.

When the boat continued downstream, the deck packed with Indians, Bull was the focal point of glances and comments from the officers of Fort Lincoln and their ladies. The pretty women, whose good looks, daintiness and preservation of face and figure registered in his manly mind, had no trouble getting his attention. When one of the young things presented this sorry-looking devil with a pear, he courteously returned kindness with kindness. He removed a brass ring from a finger and placed it on one of hers, clasping her hands with his.

As the *General Sherman* was churning a choppy course farther from Canada, the Red River carts carrying Légaré and company were trundling leisurely to Willow Bunch. Jean-Louis was assessing his losses. Unknown to him, others were assessing his contribution to recent events on the Canadian frontier, a frontier now safe for white settlement.

"Much credit here [at Fort Buford] is given to Légaré for his faithful service to the government in finally inducing Sitting Bull to come with him. He has used his own means fully in providing transportation and supplies and should be liberally rewarded." This commendation appeared in the St. Paul *Pioneer Press.*

NWMP Commissioner Irvine heaped praise upon Légaré in letters to Government officials: "At all times [he] used his personal influence with the Sioux in a manner calculated to further the policy of the Government, his honorable course being decidedly marked, more particularly when compared with that of other traders and individuals."

Later in the year of 1881 a petition was received by Prime

Minister Macdonald, who was also the Minister of the Interior and Superintendent General of Indian Affairs, from a group of prominent Westerners requesting monetary compensation for the trader. The Government appropriated $2,000, which was presented to him by Sir Hector Langevin.

Jean-Louis, on record that he alone was responsible for the return of the Sioux, pressed his own claims on the U.S. Government. He asked for $13,412 and eventually received $5,000 (Ninety years after Sitting Bull's departure from Willow Bunch the descendants of the trader would still be claiming $8,000, with interest, from the United States.)

The grateful sigh of police relief over Bull's exit was noted and duplicated in Ottawa. Irvine's year-end report to Macdonald glowed with reminiscences and indulgent, introverted congratulations, and included a repeat appreciation of Crozier.

❖❖❖ The Fame and Misfortune

❖❖❖ Crafty, avaricious, mendacious and ambitious, Sitting Bull possessed all the faults of an Indian and none of the nobler attributes which have gone far to redeem some of his people from their deeds of guilt....

He had no single quality that would serve to draw his people to him, yet he was by far the most influential man of his nation for many years....

I never knew him to display a single trait that might command admiration or respect....

Even his people know him as a physical coward, but the fact did not handicap the man in dealing with his following....

The disastrous retreat to Canada, and the suffering his people underwent while he was leading them, caused him a considerable loss in prestige. Gall and Crow King, his chief lieutenants, found him to be a fraud and a coward, and deserted him....

Rain In The Face and other hereditary chiefs of his people despised him as an incompetent leader and coward....I have contended always that Sitting Bull was a coward....

Sitting Bull, whose medicine was not good for the white man, lurked in the background of all the evil that his people wrought for many a blood-drenched year while the Sioux nation was putting up a merciless and dread protest against the usurpation of their hunting grounds by the white invader....

He was a stocky man, with an evil face and shifty eyes, and he still showed the effect of his desperate experience in the Canadian northwest...

All these opinions, these biographical impressions and descriptions of Bull, came from James "White Hair" McLaughlin, clear-eyed and determined, a former eastern Ontario country boy, a blacksmith's apprentice born in 1842 in Avonmore (of Irish and Scottish ancestry). When he was in his twenties, McLaughlin had turned from the border town of Cornwall to the United States to make his mark, although his Canadian birthright, as he put it, was "an accident of birth the distinction of which I gladly share with some millions of my contemporaries."

Fate, or bad luck, the decisions of others, decreed that Sitting Bull and his Indian agent, McLaughlin – an uneducated immigrant and squawman to his detractors – would first meet on the day McLaughlin arrived at Standing Rock (September 8, 1881) to take charge of the north Dakota agency. Bull, the pride worn out of him, was a prisoner. Nevertheless he surprised McLaughlin with a display of friendliness despite his bitterness at being shipped away, again, down river. As the agent was getting off the boat, Bull was getting on, bound for Fort Randall, an isolated army post on the west bank of the Missouri, near the Niobrara River, supposedly too inaccessible for the chief to receive friendly, commiserating comrades-in-arms to plot the next resistance movement.

After his surrender, when Bull had stepped ashore at Standing Rock, wiping the tears away with the back of his hand, a thousand friends and allies were singing, waving and shouting their greetings from the embankment. The first to reach him was an old pal, Running Antelope. They hugged, cheeked and grasped hands.

The joy of reunions faded; the condemnations of betrayal emerged when it was realized Bull was not going to be accorded the identical treatment of the others who had bowed, under pressure, to the great father in Washington. There was to be no amnesty. He had been right; he knew it all along. He was being thrown away. He was branded a prisoner of war, he and all the last of the faithfuls in Canada, including Four Horns, One Bull and Kills Charging, the son of Four Horns.

Forty or more men and their families were all processed for Fort Randall. Fortunately, the officers and men at Randall, somewhat in awe of the military prowess and reputation of their prisoners, treated them respectfully and humanely. The rations were regular and substantial; the people, particularly the women, re-

250

gained their self-respect, and it enhanced their demeanour and appearance. The chief, a popular figure with his guardians, went out of his way to be unpretentious, to renew his total communion with the Great Spirit.

Gradually, inevitably, he tired of the monotonous daily routine of dependence. He yearned for the hills of his home country, not all that far away to the north, where the clear water flowed, where the buffalo grass blanketed the land, where the trees could shelter and warm his body and soul, where there would be cattle to tend, where all the people would be together with the old lifestyle.

Ironically, his isolation was fostering a legend. By the fall of '82 the volume of his incoming mail necessitated the assignment of an officer to take care of the logistics. Requests for Bull's autograph (which meant his learning to write his name in English) were met for a dollar a time – in advance. The money was used up at the camp store where he liked to window shop. Those admirers in the east who wanted more tangible and durable keepsakes (for example, his pipe, knife or tomahawk) were duly disappointed.

Generally, the feeling of the American public towards the mythical killer of Custer remained antagonistic. The chief was unaware or unconcerned. He was thriving; the robustness of health was showing in his face; his gait was more lively; his mind more relaxed. The camp guards were also relaxed and their inquisitive captive was allowed to visit Indians and halfbreeds in the area. He, in turn, was a frequent host. Gospel grinders were irresistibly drawn to this king of the savages who was overdue to be converted and saved. Bull listened philosophically and patiently to their translations of the Bible and observed, that from his personal experiences, the Indians were more Christian than the Christians.

One or two of the officers, piqued by Bull's kindly references to his custodians in Canada, were telling him that to many Americans (and true Irishmen, of course) the Redcoats were symbols of oppression.

The good behaviour of the captives, Bull's persistent pleading, plus the recommendations of their unwilling jailers, persuaded the authorities to allow the outcasts to be reunited with their relatives on the reservation. On May 10, 1883, they disembarked at Standing Rock (or Sitting Woman Rock, the correct Indian place name). McLaughlin, the reigning white-haired father, met them the next day, whereupon Bull dictated the conditions by which he would allow himself to be governed. McLaughlin rankled with anger at the arrogance of this defeated nomad who was telling the governor how to govern, who was attempting to set himself up as the factor, who was submitting a list of twenty subordinate cohorts who would rule all the Indians, McLaughlin's Indians.

McLaughlin, a strong character, efficient, ambitious and dedicated to the proposition that the greatest need of the red man was the white man's world, rejected Bull's astounding demands. Their second encounter engendered in the agent an obsessive hate and distrust that would endure to the end and beyond.

White Hair's capsule opinions of his adversary were contained in a report in August of 1883:

"He is an Indian of very mediocre ability, rather dull, and much inferior to Gall and others in intelligence....He is pompous, vain and boastful and considers himself a very important personage, but as he has been lionized and pampered since the Little Big Horn, I do not wonder at his inflated opinion of himself....I cannot understand how he held such sway over or controlled men so eminently his superiors in every respect....I firmly believe Sitting Bull will never cause any trouble, he having been thoroughly subdued; his influence is very limited now...."

The agent was underestimating his opposition. The chieftaincy, a life-long tenure, albeit latent or forcibly subdued, could not belong to a white man, or more specifically, to McLaughlin.

In 1884 the Hunkpapa cabins and lodges were astir with an incredible story that the white mother's Redcoats were preparing a campaign to liberate the Black Hills. A stranger in civilian clothes, a mysterious oracle, had appeared out of nowhere on the reservation and was commiserating with the people about the inadequacy of their food handouts and their miserable living conditions. It was his contention the wards of the U.S. Government were being short-changed. (Coincidentally, Prime Minister Macdonald had a low opinion of U.S. Indian agents and regarded them as unreliable administrators.)

The Indians gratefully agreed with this stranger who was predicting a British invasion and subsequent restoration of land to the Sioux. However, he disappeared just as mysteriously as he had appeared. He had never identified himself, although it was assumed he was a Redcoat in disguise. The speculation, and the hope, took years to die out.

McLaughlin, a tenacious manipulator, in a way fearful and jealous of Bull's pervasive presence, revived an old strategy to break down Bull's influence: competing monarchs. The two selected were Gall, the war hero, and Grass, the thinker-politician, a Blackfoot Sioux. An Indian police force was established to consolidate authority.

Any calamitous confrontation was avoided because of Bull's natural qualities of showmanship, which were being enthusiastically recognized and exploited in the big, populated country a train ride away from the eastern boundaries of the reservation. At first, safely close to Standing Rock, there was a spike-driving ceremony in Bismarck for the Northern Pacific Railroad, followed by an exhibition tour of fifteen American cities, which resulted, during the summer of '85, in an incredible engagement with Buffalo Bill Cody's Wild West Show. This permitted the chief to come to Canada again – in more agreeable and illustrious circumstances – and to get out of McLaughlin's hair for a time.

Bull joined the show, ironically, at Buffalo, New York, for fifty dollars weekly. He was worth it. The show went into the black.

In the States, Sitting Bull ("the slayer of General Custer") got a mixed reception as a performer. He was regarded as the villain, overshadowed by the heroic Indian fighter Buffalo Bill, and subjected to barracking and booing. He sold autographed pictures, put away all the oyster stew his stomach could handle, and endured with a calm, prosperous dignity. In Canada the roles were reversed; Bull, by simply being himself, commanded most of the attention and political handshakes (the parliamentarians overcame their previous antipathy towards him) while the newspapers on the route elevated him to the top of their columns.

The *Globe,* of Toronto, in its edition for Saturday, August 22, 1885, carried an advertisement for Buffalo Bill's Wild West (The Greatest Novelty of the Century...First and Last Time in Canada) with Bull's name printed in the biggest capital letters. In smaller print were some of his co-stars: Annie Oakley, the Great Markswoman; Johnny Baker, the Phenomenal Boy Shot; Set Clover, the Cowboy Kid, shooting at marbles and nickels; and Buck Taylor, King of the Cowboys. Sitting Bull, the ad proclaimed, had a staff of fifty-four: White Eagle and fifty-two braves and the one-legged Sioux spy, Frisking Elk.

In keeping with Cody's theatrical genius, the noon parade he organized through Toronto's streets (which featured the old Deadwood coach "baptized many a time in fire and blood") attracted practically everybody to Woodbine racetrack for the show. Many firms had given their employees a half holiday. The grandstands, the paddocks and the homestretch were jammed with young and old straining to get a whiff of the frontier. Buffalo Bill was overjoyed. After all, this was Cody country, the land of his ancestors. His father, Isaac, had migrated to Kansas from Dixie Village, which was less than a two-hour buggy ride from Toronto.

Despite his destiny to be perennially on the winning side in his popular encounters with these exhibition Indians, "Long Hair" Cody figured that in real life the white man was responsible for ninety per cent of the trouble on the frontier. "When an Indian gives you his word that he will do anything he is sure to keep that word."

A tall figure, ostentatious in decorative, fringed buckskins and black, thigh-length boots, Cody was a father to his performers. To Sitting Bull, he was an especially benevolent father. He had the chief in the best lodge, with the best furnishings, in the most prestigious spot.

The chief, amiably disposed to extend his hand to a select few Torontonians, impressed his visitors with a pleasant intelligence. It was agreed fame and notoriety had not gone to his head. (The one exception was his coveted white sombrero – size eight.)

Bull was talkative, although he could not be induced to discuss Custer's fate or the heavy Longknife losses. ("I have answered to my people for the loss of life on our side; let Custer answer to his own people for the loss on his side.") He said he did not have the most pleasing recollections of his stay in Canada because he and his people were very hard up. He mentioned pridefully his association with Major Walsh. When he discovered one of his guests was a very close friend of the former superintendent (Walsh had retired from the force in 1883) he asked whether Walsh ever mentioned his name. The *Globe* reported he was gratified to hear that Walsh had invariably spoken of him "in terms of the warmest approval."

Complimentary remarks were effusive with the mention of the two Canadian Cree notables: Poundmaker and Big Bear, both of whom were in prison.

Poundmaker, adopted son of Crowfoot, a great hunter and a reluctant and honorable combatant in the Northwest Rebellion earlier in the year, had an exclusive niche in Bull's memory. "When our people were very poor, Poundmaker was always very good and generous to us." He couldn't believe Poundmaker had been a rebel if it were true Crowfoot had been completely loyal.

Big Bear, courageously independent, the Mounted Police prototype of a bad Indian, he had not known so well, although he respected his opposition to the new order.

Crowfoot (Bull called him Isapo-muxico) opened Bull's countenance into a natural smile. "He was a friend. I named one of my sons after him, a son who like Crowfoot cannot be happy on a reservation."

Questioned about Louis Riel (who was likewise a prisoner after the failure of his uprising), Bull replied the Métis rebel had approached him five times to join in a war against the Canadian authorities: "I paid no attention to him and told the police of his actions."

When the exhibition season was over, Bull the celebrity retired to his modest cabin at Standing Rock. His most valued memento of show business was a performing horse, Cody's favourite; his most noticeable gain, a reclamation of self-esteem – and several sacks of candy.

In 1887 the chief was invited to join the Wild West company for a grand tour of Europe. Much to the displeasure of McLaughlin (and his mixed-breed Santee wife, who fancied herself being introduced at the court of Queen Victoria) Bull declined because, as he said, his presence was more necessary at home pending a government plot to take more of their lands. It was his duty to fight for the rights of his children the Sioux. Five years previously they had been bullied and nearly talked out of 14,000 square miles in exchange for cattle.

The U.S. commission did not appear until '88. They wanted more than nine million acres for fifty cents an acre. The Great Sioux Reservation would be broken up into six comparatively small domains, islands surrounded by white homesteaders. Bull marshalled all his influence and oratory to prevent any cession of their west-bank Missouri homelands, riding each evening through the camps actually singing his opposition.

The people heard, the majority refusing to sign away what was theirs. The leaders of the tribes were united against the commissioners, who in their disgust advocated the Government implement their recommendations anyhow. The legislators in Washington, on the other hand, were not prepared to precipitate dangerous quarrels with the lawful occupiers of the land.

A year later the Government tried again with more determination and finesse and with a concessive offer of $1.25 an acre. General "Three Stars" Crook, as bushy-bearded as ever, decked out in civilian clothes topped by a white straw hat, was the commission's spokesman. With guile, patience, scorn, blunt truths, camouflage, feasts, dancing, intimidation, and secret meetings organized by McLaughlin, he outmanoeuvred Bull and bought off a nation.

"There are no Indians left but me!" the chief commented sourly as he packed up for his cabin on the Grand River forty miles southwest of the agency. The majority, the so-called progressives, had signed the treaty.

If Bull's future was bleak, it was revengefully non-existent for Brave Bear, who had fled to the Queen's sanctuary after escaping McLaughlin's custody following the slaying of two settlers near Pembina. Brave Bear had stayed with Bull to the end in Canada. Apprehensively, and not so quietly, he became a resident of Standing Rock, where he ultimately came up against McLaughlin again.

Brave Bear, who boasted he had kept the money taken from a farmer he killed near the Canadian border, bribed a white man to take him across the Missouri to get him away from McLaughlin. It was arranged. Unfortunately for him he had dallied long enough at Standing Rock for the reward for his capture to be common knowledge. When Brave Bear got across the river four men were waiting for him.

Brave Bear's escaping days were over. He was locked up in Yankton, the capital of Dakota Territory, convicted of murder, and hanged.

In 1890, a year of discontent, broken promises, reduced rations and fatal epidemics of measles and whooping cough on the U.S. agencies, a year of drought, withered crops, scarcity of game, and of cattle dying of blackleg, the few Tetons still in Canada

256

picked up rumours of a new religion uniting the widely separated tribes of the deserts, mountains and plains.

There was a prophet called Wovoka, a Christian-educated Paiute sheep-herder from Nevada who had visited the next world and had returned as the Messiah with promises of a regenerated earth populated by Indians.

The flames of a vast, wind-fanned prairie fire could not have spread any quicker than Wovoka's gospel. Wild, trance-like ceremonies, demonstrated by the Messiah himself, were called the Ghost Dance rituals, a throbbing, ceaseless wailing of men, women and children circling hand-in-hand, shuffling and prancing in holy attire until the most emotional (and exhausted) collapsed in a trance or "died" to converse with their relatives in the spirit world.

The Ghost Dance lit up a part of every reservation. One of the first Sioux to accept the faith was Kicking Bear, an Oglala by birth, a Minneconjou through marriage. Fortyish, big and surly, a mystic, a fanatical warrior, Kicking Bear had been deposited on the Cheyenne River Reservation after leaving Canada. The hate of his life was the white man. His absolute adoption of the new cult was equalled by only one man, his brother-in-law Short Bull, a Brûlé from the Rosebud Reservation. (Short Bull, a confirmed warrior and medicine man with a rather kindly, confusingly meek disposition, had untapped reserves of influence and leadership. It was Short Bull who had been helped by the police at Wood Mountain back in '78 when he and Stone Dog, who was suffering from an abcess, were sheltered from a winter storm by Walsh.)

When six of Bull's young men witnessed the ceremonials at Cherry Creek they arranged for the principal Ghost Dance disciple, Kicking Bear, to confer with the most formidable living prophet, Sitting Bull, the hardcore non-progressive. The prospects of a religious revival incorporating a new vitality of prophecies and mysticism came as manna from the hereafter land. He attempted to accept it (Christian overtones disregarded) with all the passion of his unconvinced pagan heart and with all the bidding of a high priest. In October McLaughlin sent his Indian police to Bull's neighbourhood to eject Kicking Bear, which they finally did. However, Bull had been converted. He too wanted to visit the other world. He appointed Bull Ghost, familiarly known to the whites at the agency as One-Eyed Riley, as the participating priest.

The craze swept northwards but virtually died at the Canadian border. It spluttered to a short, inconsequential life among some Crees, and Santee Sioux who had a small reserve near Deloraine, western Manitoba. American settlers south of Manitoba had renewed fears of Indians on the warpath until a NWMP patrol put their minds at rest.

The army and Indian agents in the States, some of whom had not taken the Ghost Dance seriously, became alarmed at the militant fanaticism of its adherents. Bull's most voluble dissenters were two white women: one was a Congregational missionary, Mary Collins, and the other a self-appointed adviser, Mrs. Catherine Weldon, a Boston widow, a flag-waver for Indian rights. Her fame spread in the public print as Sitting Bull's white squaw.

The accelerating apprehension of officialdom, which was full of panicky premonitions of a holy war, provided McLaughlin with the opportunity to recommend a remote military prison for his adamant competitor for agency rule. When this advice bombed, he suggested withholding rations.

Miles was suspicious of Indian agents; therefore when Buffalo Bill Cody proposed a plan, featuring himself, for the arrest of Bull the general agreed, fantastically. "Colonel" Cody, who had campaigned with Miles as a scout and who regarded himself as a friend of Ol' Sit, presented himself before McLaughlin in late November with authorization "to secure the person of Sitting Bull and deliver him to the nearest commanding officer of U.S. troops."

The agent was flabbergasted, and angry, and boldly wired Washington while futile attempts were made to drink Cody under the table – and off the trail. Cody's capacity and determination were infinite. (He came from a line of tavern-keepers. His grandfather, Phillip Cody, has been renowned as the host of the Dixie Inn, west of Toronto.) Cody got halfway to Bull's camp, at which point he was tricked into believing the chief had crossed his path in the opposite direction. Back at the agency Cody was confronted with a presidential telegram rescinding Miles's orders.

On December 10, Miles once more ordered the military arrest of Sitting Bull. McLaughlin, with the co-operation of the local garrison commander, had his own plan. Bull, in the meantime, had been asked by the Ghost Dance apostles to join them at Pine Ridge Reservation for the premature appearance of the Indian Christ.

This was it! McLaughlin had set December 20, ration day, for the arrest, a day when most of the Hunkpapa would be away from camp. It would be easy to nab the old devil! When he learned Bull might be gone by then he hurriedly advanced the plot to the fifteenth. Sergeant Red Tomahawk, Indian police, carried the agent's revised orders to his lieutenant, Bull Head, a Grand River neighbour of Bull's. McLaughlin had decided to have his police do the arresting. It was a dictate of pride and politics. Besides, the cavalry would likely start a war. He could keep the soldiers ready in reserve.

That night, a Sunday, the armed police gathered in the cabin of Gray Eagle, Sitting Bull's brother-in-law who could not in his heart forget how the chief had victimized him, how he had been punished to appease the Redcoats for stealing horses during the early days in Canada.

When the darkness began to disappear into the first light of a cold, drizzly Monday morning, about forty policemen surrounded Bull's slumbering village. Everyone was flaked out with the singing, whirling, fasting and fainting, the ritualistic Ghost Dance excitement that had gone on later than usual.

At a signal about a dozen police forded the river, rode around the icy, winter-stark cottonwoods and moved directly towards the rear of Bull's doublesized cabin. They knocked the door open with rifle butts. Bull, naked, was asleep in his low bed with his elder wife. One of the intruders lit a lamp on the wall; the others went over to the bed, lifted him out, informed him of his arrest and warned him not to resist if he wanted to live. His wife gathered his best clothes. He tried to put them on, slowly, with the police impatiently hurrying him up, dressing him, dragging him towards the open door.

The commotion of dogs and horses, the shadowy presence of the blue-uniformed Metal Badges darting about in the half light, and the wailing of the wives, had aroused the village. After Bull had been dragged to the doorway he had to be shoved and kicked outside where a mob of about 150 supporters were taunting the Indian police and pushing them against the cabin. Bull was writhing frantically. "I'm not going," he was shouting in the din. Little Assiniboine was doing his best to soothe him.

Catch The Bear, Bull's foremost Hunkpapa bodyguard, came

bounding around the corner in an uncontrollable fury. When he saw what was happening to Bull, when he realized these Blue Jackets had guns on the chief, he went for them with his rifle, using it as a club, all the time looking for his enemy Bull Head.

Bull was still shouting; now he was urging his soldiers to action with a war cry – *Hopo! Hopo!* (Let's go!). The first shot came from Catch The Bear. He hit Bull Head. As the lieutenant fell he shot at Bull who was twisting and struggling to free himself. The bullet went into his back. Red Tomahawk, who was hanging on to the chief, shot him point-blank from the rear. Bull sagged to the frozen ground, the blood oozing down the front of his clothes. The first bullet had killed him.

The melee intensified; brutal bitterness and vengeance overflowed. Sitting Bull was joined immediately in the Spirit Land by six comrades who had fought to save him or avenge his death: his adopted brother Little Assiniboine, Catch The Bear, Blackbird, Spotted Horn Bull, Brave Thunder and Chase Wounded.

Inside the cabin Bull's seventeen-year-old schoolboy son, Crowfoot, couldn't hide. "Uncles, don't kill me," he pleaded. A policeman gave him a blow to the head which sent him staggering to the door where he fell. He was finished off with Sioux police bullets. Six policemen were dead or dying.

During the turmoil, when guns were firing rapidly and clubs and knives were hacking flesh and bones, Bull's gray circus horse, the one presented to him by Cody, reacted to the familiar show-like confusion of shouts and shots with a trick it used to do for Buffalo Bill. It sat down and raised a hoof. It was as if the spirit of Sitting Bull had entered its body.

There is a legend that all the Tetons, hundreds of miles from the scene, knew of Bull's death when it happened. A ghostly horseman galloped through the snow in the early morning mists onto a high butte, from where he proclaimed, "Sitting Bull is dead."

Walsh was in Winnipeg when he learned of the killing, in the white man's way, in the talking paper as Bull used to refer to the newspaper. After his retirement, he had gone into business with three partners to establish a coal dealership. This venture propelled him into the company of the "coal kings" and the managership of the burgeoning Dominion Coal, Coke & Transportation Co. It had been ten years and five months since he had listened to Bull's parting words at Wood Mountain. Now, one day after the killing of the tough old rebel, Walsh reached for a pen and his company's notepaper to scribble an eulogy:

"I am glad to hear that Bull is relieved of his miseries even if it took the bullet to do it. A man who yields such power as Bull once did, that of a king, and over a wild, spirited people, cannot endure abject poverty, slavery and beggary without suffering great mental pain...and death is a relief. Miles said the Indians were not receiving sufficient food to sustain life. If this be so the cry of the Sioux nation had gone out to Bull, and he heard weeping women and children crying for assistance, and turned no doubt to that power he always looked to for guidance and help, the Spirit Land.

"Bull's confidence and belief in the Great Spirit were stronger than I ever saw it in any other man. He trusted Him implicitly. His sufferings from day to day becoming worse, stronger appeals to the Great Spirit were made until it gave [the white people] an appearance of fanaticism and a craze.

"History does not tell us that a greater Indian than Bull ever lived. He was the Mohammed of his people; the law made him king of the Sioux.

"I regret now that I had not gone to Standing Rock to see him. There were one or two things I would like to have spoken to him about before he died.

"Bull has been misrepresented. He was not the bloodthirsty man reports from the prairies made him out to be. He asked for nothing but justice. He did not want to be a beggar or a slave.... President Harrison thinks it a good thing that Bull is dead, that now the disturbing element is removed the question will be settled without further bloodshed. These are strange words for the president of 60,000,000 of people to express. The Prince of Wales would not speak such words, neither would Generals Grant or Sheridan. Poor Harrison, we will be kind with him and only say that he has never taken the trouble to study the Indian questions and is ignorant of the circumstances that caused poor Bull's death. General Miles told him the Indians were starving. He is glad their leader is dead because his followers will submit easier to starvation.

"Bull, in council and war, was a king of his people. To his superior intelligence in council and his generalship in war every man of his nation bowed. It is a calumny to say he was a coward, or that he ever ran away from a fight. For four years his camp of 1,000 lodges was under my supervision....He had with him the most influential and greatest chiefs of the Sioux nation. Bull ruled this camp with the authority of a king, even at times to an extent that was thought by many to be tyrannical....He was the only (chief) I ever knew who ruled with an authority such as history tell us kings ruled years ago. His word was law and his decrees were obeyed as if supported by a constitutional government. It was often remarked by police force members he was the only real chief on the plains....

"This man, that so many look upon as a bloodthirsty villain, would make many members of the Christian faith ashamed of their doubts and weakness in the faith of their god. If they knew him in his true character – he was not a cruel man, he was kind of heart; he was not dishonest, he was truthful. He loved his people and was glad to give his hand in friendship to any man who believed he was not an enemy and was honest with him. But Bull experienced so much treachery that he did not know who to trust. How or by whom, you say, was he deceived? I would answer by saying everybody....Buffalo Bill was ready to go to his camp on the pretence of friendship but in reality for the purposes of arresting or killing him....

"He is the victim of ambition, soldiers and mercenary men. The army, tiring of routine work, finds a recreation in Indian war. Ambitious officers do not want the nation to forget them. They cannot take the stand as politicians do, but they can take the field against starving Indians.

"One of his prophecies has certainly been fulfilled. While living in Canada he said to me many times, "If I return to the Americans they will kill me.'

"Mr. Johnson of the St. Paul Press makes the last charge against Bull and goes a long way back to find it. He informs the public that at Fort Walsh, during the Terry Commission, Bull insulted General Terry. I was present at that commission and heard every word that passed between Terry and Bull, and I say Bull did not say anything that should have insulted General Terry. He called General Terry's attention to the bad faith of his government....of treaties made and treaties broken, of the disposition of the troops to kill Indians. But nothing more, simply an argument in defence of his people....

"The war between the U.S. and Bull was a strange one. A nation against one man. On the U.S. side there were numbers; on Bull's side there was principle. The one man was murdered by the nation to destroy the principle he advocated – that no man against his will should be forced to be a beggar. Bull was the marked man of his people."

❖❖❖ Epilogue

❖❖❖ The echoes of the Mounties' confrontation with the Sioux can still be heard on the hilltops and in the valleys of southwestern Saskatchewan. They can be heard everywhere in the land by anyone who has an ear for history and the people who fashioned it.

Walsh, in his last months in the force, at Qu'Appelle, on the right of way of the immigrant rush, had a more enjoyable and carefree time than he was used to.

His official zeal was concentrated on maintaining order along the Canadian Pacific Railway line under construction, trying to prevent trading in liquor. William Cornelius Van Horne, the gregarious, steamrolling general manager of the CPR, singled him out for laudatory comments in a letter to Commissioner Irvine on New Year's day, 1883.

Later that year Walsh and Van Horne were seen driving an excursion locomotive west of Moose Jaw – the railway boss on the throttle and the policemen on the brake. (At one stage of his unstable youth, Walsh had been an engine driver with the St. Lawrence and Ottawa Railway.) Once, at the head of a troop of Redcoats, Walsh galloped out of concealment around a moving train, Indian style, to the cheers of the passengers, a party of Ontario editors.

This zest for eyebrow-raising bravado, this tireless craving for histrionics or the unusual, revealed a laxity of concentration with administrative details that resulted in losses of government property in his care. Fortunately, such inattention was not considered serious enough to hinder a retirement gratuity of $1,166.

When he took his leave of the force there were only two men left in his command who had marched with him in '74 from the

264

Red River to the foothills, and only six who could exchange stories of the trials and tribulations of the Sitting Bull era.

After his fling in the coal business, Walsh was appointed by the Liberal Government of Sir Wilfrid Laurier, on August 17, 1897, to the post of chief executive officer (commissioner) of the Yukon, including full command of the NWMP controlling the Klondike Gold Rush.

His year in office was tumultuous, accompanied by charges that political favouritism got him the job. He was privately and publicly accused of a questionable personal and private life, of mismanagement, of graft, of encouraging corruption by government officials, of allowing them to stake claims, of misuse of the Mounted Police. He met these accusations with a brand of casual, self-complacent and self-righteous resoluteness.

"If I were intoxicated in Dawson and that ladies were seen going to or coming from my tent what can you or the government do about it, or what business is it now of yours?...." he would write Clifford Sifton, Minister of the Interior. At his own request, he had left Dawson in August of 1898 to retire to Brockville where he became active in local Liberal politics, and business, and where he fretted, rowed boats, sailed and read until his death in July of 1905.

Crozier resigned from the force on June 30, 1886, into relative obscurity, which was in contrast to the publicity and criticism over his alleged precipitate action and retreat from Duck Lake on March 26, 1885, at the start of the Riel insurrection. Promoted to assistant commissioner in '85, he had been passed over for the top job the following year. After '86 Crozier drifted from fighting Indians in Oklahoma to business. He died, more or less a forgotten man, in 1901, and was buried at Belleville.

Another political victim of the Riel affair was Irvine who likewise rated an entry in Macdonald's black book. The third commissioner (the first Canadian-born), he departed the force in 1886, amid gossip of "looted furs," to become an Indian agent on the Blood Reserve (in "God's Country") and afterwards was a prison warden in Manitoba. A bachelor, he died in 1916.

Jean-Louis Légaré carried on as a storekeeper in Willow Bunch. In 1882 he was robbed and held prisoner by a Cree war party. Luck was on his side when the Indians' guns misfired. He survived to become an active rancher, postmaster, the owner of a cheese factory. He died in 1918, an entrepreneur to the end.

Young Jim Weeks, of Halifax, a hero at the Little Big Horn battle, deserted the U.S. Army in February of 1877 but was soon arrested. The record shows he died on August 26, 1877, at the Crow Agency, Montana, of a pistol shot wound.

Chief White Bird, Nez Percé, never returned to his homeland. He was murdered by an exiled member of Chief Joseph's band in 1882 and was buried near Fort Macleod.

Sitting Bull, in death, remained a controversial figure, a charlatan to his enemies, a patriotic hero to others. The turbulence of his life did not disappear with him into the grave. Initially there were sensational rumours of desecration, that his coffin was empty when buried, his body having been sold to exhibitors or souvernir collectors. The military claimed the body was neither mutilated nor disfigured, that it was sewn up in canvas, put in a rough coffin (the lid secured by screws) and buried eight feet deep in Fort Yates post cemetery.

In this century, in April of '53, in a bizarre dawn raid led by old Gray Eagle, Bull's remains were dug up and reinterred closer to where he was born and where he was killed, overlooking the Missouri River opposite Mobridge, South Dakota. Today he lies under concrete and metal, under a sculptor's carving, a bust chiselled from Black Hills rock, and around the isolated, obscure, vandal-chipped monument is a railing. In death they were able at last to put a cage around him.

The remnants of Sitting Bull's people in Canada, the once dreaded warriors of the plains, became domesticated, and keen to work, cheaply. There were complaints in the summer months of their trespassing on homesteaders' land, of Indian ponies getting at the crops. There were also occasional invitations from American Indians to join forays against the Bluecoats and Montana sodbusters, invitations that were always refused and generally resented.

These lingering Tetons were of much less concern to the Government than the legitimate Canadian Indians who were proclaiming the land had been borrowed from them by the white mother's chiefs, that it had not been bought. A major aggravation was the reluctance of treaty Indians to abandon their hereditary habits for a tedious life of waiting for crops to grow, which rarely did.

266

The police, burdened with an inevitable percentage of unscrupulous adventurers and charlatans in their ranks, the frauds, swindlers and seducers, the Mounted Inebriates, were coming up against bolder opposition and cynicism. "They were sent out here to put down whisky – and that's what they're doing in the most astonishing manner," remarked one virtuous observer.

The Tetons were left alone by the lawmen. They were scattered in the Wood Mountain valleys with the Métis, near where the old, uninhabited police post was tumbling. They hunted what they could, small game that was rapidly decreasing, and in the winter they migrated northwards to a creek close to the Place Where The White Man Mended The Cart With The Jawbone Of A Moose (Moose Jaw). A very few resorted to begging; most were willing to toil for the incoming whites; some hung around the railway selling polished horns and oddments to travelers. They received help from the Indian Department yet demonstrated a strong disposition to be self-supporting. There were about fifty of them all told under the leadership of Black Bull and Whitecap. Prominent among the warriors who had stayed were Big Jim (White Rabbit), Big John (Run With A Thump), Long Dog (he became a local character with a sobriquet of Crazy Jack), Lean Crow, Icigra, Red Bear, The Lung, Brave Heart, Little Eagle, High Back, Big Joe (Kills Two), Old Man Hawk, and Yellow Hawk.

When Riel was recruiting for his revolt, a handful of the Sioux, some in their teens, went along for a taste of the warpath that had been extolled by their fathers the buffalo men (the name given to those who could remember the hunts when the earth trembled with the shuffling herds, so immense that a man might have to wait three days for them to pass by). The rebellion over, their poverty unsurpassed, the rebels walked from Batoche to Moose Jaw to be fed by their kinsmen who had remained loyal to the white mother.

The last survivor of those few exiled Tetons was Julia Lethbridge (Crossed Eagle Quills), a Hunkpapa, who died in 1956 at the age of ninety, at the Standing Buffalo Sisseton Sioux Reservation, Fort Qu'Appelle.

Her presence, and that of all the Teton Sioux in Canada, is perpetuated in the blood lines of Wood Mountain families. The great-grandchildren, fair-haired and black-haired, brown and white, are Canadians.

# ❖❖❖ Bibliography

Allison, E.H. (Scout). *Surrender of Sitting Bull.* The Walker Litho and Printing Co., Dayton, Ohio, 1891.

Andrist, Ralph K. *The Long Death.* The Macmillan Co., New York, 1964.

Baker, Everett. *Trails and Traces.* Modern Press, Saskatoon, 1955.

Berton, Pierre. *The National Dream.* The Great Railway 1871-1881. McClelland and Stewart, Toronto, 1970.

Brown, Dee. *Bury My Heart at Wounded Knee.* Holt, Rinehart & Winston, New York, Chicago, San Francisco, 1970.

Brown, Joseph Epes. *The Sacred Pipe.* University of Oklahoma Press, Norman, 1953.

Creighton, Donald. *John A. Macdonald: The Old Chieftain.* Macmillan, Toronto, 1955.

Custer, Elizabeth. *Boots and Saddles.* Harper & Brothers, New York, 1885.

Dempsey, Hugh A. *Historic Sites of Alberta.* Alberta Government Travel Bureau, Edmonton, 1966.

Finerty, John F. *War-Path and Bivouac.* University of Nebraska Press, Lincoln, 1955. First published in Chicago in 1890.

Frost, Lawrence A. *The Custer Album.* Superior Publishing Company, Seattle.

Haydon A.L. *The Riders of the Plains.* M.G. Hurtig Ltd., Edmonton, 1971. First published in 1910.

Hull, Raymond. *Tales of a Pioneer Surveyor – Charles Aeneas Shaw.* Longman, Toronto, 1970.

Kelly, Nora. *The Men of the Mounted.* J.M. Dent, Toronto, 1949.

Laviolette, Rev. Gontran. *Sioux Indians in Canada.* The Marian Press, Regina, 1944.

MacEwan, J.W. Grant. *Portraits From The Plains.* McGraw-Hill, Toronto, 1971.

McLaughlin, James. *My Friend The Indian.* Superior Publishing Company, Seattle, 1970. Originally published in 1910.

Miller, David Humphreys. *Custer's Fall.* Duell, Sloan and Pearce, New York, 1957.

Mulvancy, C.P. *The North-West Rebellion of 1885.* A.H. Hovey & Co., Toronto, 1886.

Pearl, Stanley. *Louis Riel. A Volatile Legacy.* Maclean-Hunter, Toronto, 1970.

Pennanen, Gary. "Sitting Bull. Indian Without a Country." *Canadian Historical Review,* Vol. 51 no. 2, June 1970, pp. 123-40.

Rachlis, Eugene. *Indians of the Plains.* American Heritage Publishing Co., New York, 1960.

Rasky, Frank. *The Taming of the Canadian West.* McClelland and Stewart, Toronto, 1967.

Rodney, William. *Kootenai Brown, 1839-1916.* Gray's Publishing, Sidney, B.C. 1969.

Rondeau, Rev. Clovis. *La Montagne de Bois.* Canadian Publishers, Winnipeg, 1970.

Sandoz, Mari. *Crazy Horse: The Strange Man of the Oglalas.* Hastings House, New York, 1942.

Sharp, Paul F. *Whoop-Up Country: The Canadian-American West 1865-1885.* University of Minnesota Press, Minneapolis, 1955.

Steele, Col. S.B. *Forty Years in Canada: Reminiscences of the Great North-West.* McClelland, Toronto, 1915.

Turner, John Peter. *The North-West Mounted Police 1873-1893.* King's Printer, Ottawa, 1950.

Utley, Robert M. (ed.) *Personal Recollections of General Nelson A. Miles.* Da Capo Press, New York, 1969.

Utley, Robert M. *The Last Days of the Sioux Nation.* Yale University Press, 1963.

Vestal, Stanley, *Sitting Bull, Champion of the Sioux.* University of Oklahoma Press, Norman. First published in 1932.

Wright, James Frederick Church. *History of the Province of Saskatchewan.* Revised edition, McClelland and Stewart, Toronto, 1955.

## Picture Credits

Order of appearance in the picture section of items listed here is left to right, top to bottom. i: Manitoba Archives; ii: RCMP, RCMP, RCMP; iii: RCMP, Saskatchewan Archives Board; iv: Smithsonian Institution; v: RCMP; vi: RCMP, vii: RCMP; viii: RCMP, Smithsonian, U.S. Signal Corps (U.S. National Archives); ix: Smithsonian, U.S. Signal Corps, U.S. Signal Corps; x: Smithsonian, RCMP, U.S. Signal Corps; xi: RCMP; xii: Smithsonian; xiii: RCMP; xiv: Smithsonian, U.S. Signal Corps, Smithsonian; xv: U.S. Signal Corps; xvi: Glenbow-Alberta Institute.

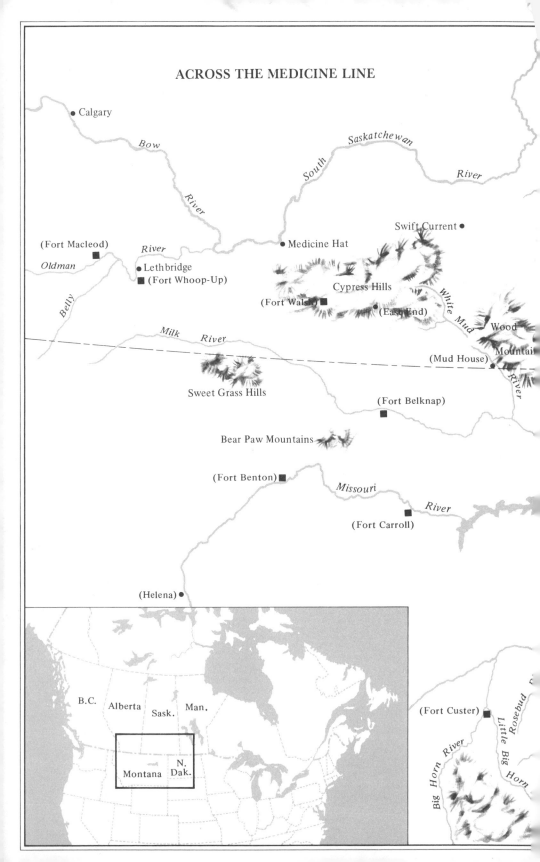

# ACROSS THE MEDICINE LINE

Calgary

Bow
River

Saskatchewan
South
River

(Fort Macleod)

River
Oldman

Medicine Hat

Swift Current

Lethbridge
(Fort Whoop-Up)

Cypress Hills

White Mud

Wood

Belly

(Fort Walsh)

(East End)

Mountain

Milk
River

(Mud House)

River

Sweet Grass Hills

(Fort Belknap)

Bear Paw Mountains

(Fort Benton)

Missouri
River

(Fort Carroll)

(Helena)

B.C.

Alberta

Sask.

Man.

Montana

N.
Dak.

(Fort Custer)

Rosebud

Big Horn River

Little Big Horn